PASSING THE

MARYLAND HIGH SCHOOL ASSESSMENT

IN ENGLISH

DEVELOPED TO THE CURRENT CORE LEARNING GOALS

Zuzana Urbanek
Sara Hinton

Dr. Frank J. Pintozzi, Project Director
Zuzana Urbanek, Project Coordinator

American Book Company
PO Box 2638
Woodstock, GA 30188-1383
Toll Free: 1 (888) 264-5877   Phone: (770) 928-2834
Fax: (770) 928-7483   Toll Free Fax: 1 (866) 827-3240
www.americanbookcompany.com

ACKNOWLEDGEMENTS

The authors would like to acknowledge the dedication and the editorial contributions of Marsha Torrens in the development of this book.

Original graphics are the expertise of Mary Stoddard.

This product/publication includes images from CorelDRAW 9 and 11 which are protected by the copyright laws of the United States, Canada, and elsewhere. Used under license.

Table of Contents

Chapter 3 Analysis of Literature   **73**

Chapter 4 Non-Print Text and Information Resources   **99**

Chapter 5 Extending Meaning   **113**

Chapter 6   Writing Skills: Usage and Conventions   137

Chapter 7   Controlling Language   163

Chapter 10   Writing the Constructed Response   227

Preface

Passing the Maryland High School Assessment in English will help students who are learning or reviewing Core learning goals for the English sections of the **Maryland High School Assessment Test in English**. The tests and chapters in this book support Core learning goals, indicators, and expectations as published by the Maryland Department of Education.

This book contains several sections:

     1) General information about the book itself

     2) A diagnostic test

     3) An evaluation chart

     4) Ten chapters that teach the concepts and skills needed for test readiness

     5) Two practice tests

Goals and expectations are posted at the beginning of each chapter and in the diagnostic and practice tests and a chart correlating all goals, expectations, and indicators to this text is included in the answer manual.

◆

We welcome comments and suggestions about this book. Please contact the project coordinator at

American Book Company
PO Box 2638
Woodstock, GA 30188-1383

Call Toll Free: (888) 264-5877
Phone: (770) 928-2834
Toll Free Fax: 1 (866) 827-3240

Visit us online at
www.americanbookcompany.com

Preface

About the Authors:

Zuzana Urbanek serves as ELA Curriculum Coordinator for American Book Company. She is a professional writer with 25 years of experience in education, business, and publishing. She has taught English abroad as a foreign language, and in the US to native speakers and as a second language. Her master's degree is from Arizona State University.

Sara Hinton has a B.A. from Columbia University and an M.A. in The Teaching of English from Teachers College Columbia University. She taught middle school Language Arts and college courses in writing, grammar, and literature for several years.

About the Project Director:

Dr. Frank J. Pintozzi is a former professor of Education at Kennesaw State University, Kennesaw, Georgia. For over 30 years, he has taught English, Composition, Literature, Reading, and Speech at the high school and college levels. At Kennesaw State University, he also taught upper division and graduate courses to teachers in Language Arts and in the English as a Second Language Endorsement Program. He has written and edited numerous books for college, high school, and middle school students. Currently, he is Executive Vice President and Executive Editor for American Book Company in Woodstock, Georgia.

American Book Company has developed best-selling books on reviewing content standards and passing graduation exams in Alabama, Arizona, California, Florida, Georgia, Indiana, Louisiana, Minnesota, Mississippi, Nevada, New Jersey, North Carolina, Ohio, South Carolina, Tennessee, and Texas.

Maryland High School Assessment in English

Diagnostic Test

The purpose of this diagnostic test is to measure your knowledge in reading comprehension and English Language Arts. This diagnostic test is based on the Maryland Core Learning Goals and Expectations for English Language Arts and adheres to the sample question format provided by the Maryland Department of Education.

General Directions:

1   Read all directions carefully.

2   Read each question or sample. Then choose the best answer.

3   Choose only one answer for each question. If you change an answer, be sure to erase your original answer completely.

4   After taking the test, you or your instructor should score it using the evaluation chart following the test. This will enable you to determine your strengths and weaknesses.

Session 1

Directions

For number 1, read the prompt below. Follow the directions in the prompt for writing your essay.

| 1 | Write a well-organized essay about one interesting aspect of a job or career you might like to have one day. Develop your ideas using details about what the work entails and why you feel your choice is so interesting. Your essay should be developed, logically organized, clear, and descriptive. | 2.1.1 |

Use your own paper to plan your response and to write the final draft of your essay.

Directions

Reynaldo is writing an essay about the daddy longlegs, and his draft requires revisions and edits. Read his draft, and then answer numbers 2 through 6.

Daddy Longlegs—Friends or Foes?

I, when I was little, have many fond memories of playing with daddy longlegs. My own experiences cause me to be totally perplexed by other people's reactions to the little critters. For example, last year, I scared the wits out of a player at football practice simply by dangling one of my long-legged buddies three inches from his nose. The unexpected visitor would have delighted me. However, the quarterback screamed like a starving baby. He even refused to speak to me for the rest of the school year. Why would anyone react that way to a daddy longlegs?

I received the answer this year when my friend started speaking to me again. It seems that my friend, like many others, confused my daddy longlegs with the cellar spider. Many people frequently confuse the two creatures, scientists often refer to the cellar spider as the daddy longlegs spider. Additionally, my friend assumed all spiders had a poisonous bite. Neither of these assumptions is correct.

The real daddy longlegs is not a true spider. It is an arthropod. In the same class with spiders but not the same order. Everyone knows arthropods are much more interesting than spiders. Both the real daddy longlegs and its namesake, the daddy longlegs spider, have eight long legs. However, a close inspection reveals major differences. The daddy longlegs has a single segment body with two tiny eyes. The spider has a body with two segments, eight eyes, and fangs.

Of course, many people might not want to get that up close and personal with a spider. Fortunately, watching the two creatures' behavior from a polite distance may actually tell you more. Daddy longlegs like to hang out under logs or rocks. You might even spot one using its long flexible legs to crawl over a raspberry bush or up a cabin wall. The spider prefers life in a dark corner of a basement. Daddy longlegs dine on plant juices. The spider will catch moths, flies, and any other insects that fly or crawl in your basement. The spider's victims become its dinner. The daddy longlegs cannot produce silk, but its namesake spins sticky, stringy webs with its silk.

Daddy longlegs don't bite and daddy longlegs spiders, unlike many other spiders, can't break skin. Therefore, you have no reason to panic whether it is a real daddy longlegs or a daddy longlegs spider. Remember this the next time you see a daddy longlegs, and don't run for the hills. There is much more to these fascinating creatures than their eight long spindly legs.

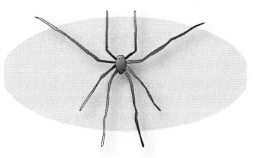

GO ON

2 What is the most effective way to revise the first sentence for clarity?　　2.2.3

F When I was little, I have many fond memories of playing with daddy longlegs.

G I have many fond memories when I was little of playing with daddy longlegs.

H I have many fond memories of playing when I was little with daddy longlegs.

J I have many fond memories of playing with daddy longlegs when I was little.

Read this sentence from the second paragraph.

Many people frequently confuse the two creatures, scientists often refer to the cellar spider as the daddy longlegs spider.

3 What is the correct way to edit this sentence?　　3.3.1

A Many people frequently confuse the two creatures scientists often refer to the cellar spider as the daddy longlegs spider.

B Many people frequently confuse the two creatures; scientists often refer to the cellar spider as the daddy longlegs spider.

C Many people frequently confuse the two creatures: scientists often refer to the cellar spider as the daddy longlegs spider.

D Many people frequently confuse the two creatures — scientists often refer to the cellar spider as the daddy longlegs spider.

4 Which of the answers <u>most effectively</u> combines the ideas in the following three sentences from the fourth paragraph?　　3.1.6

"Daddy longlegs dine on plant juices. The spider will catch moths, flies, and any other insects that fly or crawl in your basement. The spider's victims become its dinner."

F While daddy longlegs dine on plant juices, the spider will catch moths, flies, and any other insects that fly or crawl in your basement and make them its dinner.

G Daddy longlegs dine on plant juices, but the spider will catch moths, flies, and any other insects that fly or crawl in your basement for dinner.

H Daddy longlegs dine on plant juices; the spider will catch moths, flies, and any other insects that fly or crawl in your basement; the spider's victims become its dinner.

J Daddy longlegs dine on plant juices, and the spider will catch moths, flies, and any other insects that fly or crawl in your basement, and the spider's victims become its dinner.

5 Reynaldo read in his language arts textbook that he should avoid using passive voice. According to this advice, which sentence in his essay should be revised?　　2.2.5

A The unexpected visitor would have delighted me.

B However, the quarterback screamed like a starving baby.

C He even refused to speak to me for the rest of the school year.

D Why would anyone react that way to a daddy longlegs?

GO ON

6 Which of these should be revised to correct a sentence fragment? 3.1.4

F The real daddy longlegs is not a true spider.

G It is an arthropod.

H In the same class with spiders but not the same order.

J Everyone knows arthropods are much more interesting than spiders.

Directions

Read the essay "Banding Together." Then answer numbers 7 through 13.

Banding Together

When Sylvia and I decided to start a jazz ensemble in our eighth grade band so we could perform during the Spring Festival, we did not realize what we were getting ourselves into. It seemed like a great idea at first. Sylvia played flute, I played trombone. Within two days, we had recruited Dave to play trumpet and Janet to play saxophone. All we really needed now was a drummer, and we found one in Tobias, a dedicated student who played the sticks on any surface he could find at school.

Next, we talked to the band director, Mr. Greeley, about finding a place to practice. He said, "Our school is a musical school of excellence. You had better be ready to pay the price if you expect me to let you perform in front of the student body and the parents. Look at yourselves! Janet, you have a terrible squeak. Dave, half the time I see you, you are struggling with allergy attacks. Tobias, you break sticks as if they are going out of style. And you, Rick, always have your head tilted to the left when you play the trombone. I have to look at you sideways. I hope this ensemble knows what it's getting into. Not one of you is even first or second chair. But —" he said shaking his finger at all of us. "If you are determined, you can practice after school in the custodial closet. There is no room in the band room since the chorus uses the space then. If you need music, come see me. You have six weeks until the festival."

This talk was a real downer for all of us; then Sylvia said, "We'll show Mr. Greeley what we can really do. But it's not going to be easy."

"Yeah, let's do it!" I said, "We can practice for two hours after school three days a week. Whatever it takes."

Soon we all agreed to start. At first, things worked out great. In the practices, Janet helped Tobias by reinforcing his sticks with tape, Sylvia coached me through to better posture and Tobias brought his air purifier from home to keep Dave's allergies from acting up.

For the first three weeks, we started really getting together as a group. Practicing, playing, having mops fall on our heads and hearing the janitors chuckle as they grabbed their cleaning supplies were just part of our practice experiences.

In the hallways at school, we were constantly ridiculed. We heard comments behind our back, "Those losers? Play jazz? Whatever!" "Have you heard them? Please don't let them out of the (cleaning supply) closet!" "Do yourselves a favor, play for the hearing impaired!"

GO ON

During full band practice at the three-week mark, Mr. Greeley called us aside, "Alright. I want to hear this. Play it for me tomorrow before school, and you had better be primed. See you at 7:30."

We were both very excited and very scared. "What if we mess up?" Tobias asked. "Impossible," I said, "We've been practicing for three weeks!"

I was very wrong. Straggling in at 7:15, we set up and got ready to play our favorite piece from Stevie Ray Vaughan, "Testify." Mr. Greeley walked into the room and calmly sat down, but we were all nervous. We just choked on the song. Dave broke his reinforced stick; I couldn't play right; Janet squeaked from the first note forward; and Dave got so nervous, he was breathing into his asthma respirator instead of his trumpet.

We finished the song because we were determined, and Mr. Greeley noticed. He walked up to us and said, "You all played horribly, but I admire your determination and your courage. From this day forward, I will direct you in your practices, but we will have to practice every day until festival and stay until it's right. Now let's see about moving some more cleaning stuff to outside storage so we have room to practice."

"All right!" we said, and so we went forward.

Practices were intense. Mr. Greeley brought us to a great level of excellence. We had each conquered our own personal fears. We were able to go from mediocre players to the top of our class.

On the day of the performance, we were not nervous. After playing in front of Mr. Greeley, and after practicing every day, we knew we had given this effort our very best. We played great, and the audience gave us a standing ovation. We were victorious because we had fought against the names that we had given ourselves, the names students had also called us and even those our band director initially gave us. We believed that we could be excellent, and that was all that mattered.

---

7 After reading this essay, a reader would most likely conclude that aspiring musicians   1.2.5

   A have to play in large bands first.

   B don't need a director to become good.

   C must practice constantly and stay motivated.

   D should have a variety of instruments in their ensemble.

8 Which word best describes the tone that the narrator uses in this essay?   1.3.3

   F anxious

   G irritated

   H suspicious

   J determined

Read this sentence from paragraph 8.

"Play it for me tomorrow before school, and you had better be primed."

9 In this sentence, *primed* means   1.1.2

   A in position.

   B prepared.

   C on time.

   D started.

10 Write a response that explains the main obstacle to the narrator and his friends becoming good jazz players.   1.2.1
BCR

GO ON

11 What stylistic element used at the beginning of the essay **most** makes the reader curious to read further?

1.2.3

- **A** foreshadowing in the first paragraph
- **B** detailed characterization in the first paragraph
- **C** plot twists revealed in the second paragraph
- **D** the antagonist appearing in the second paragraph

12 Which statement **best** expresses the theme of this essay?

1.3.5

- **F** As long as you plan ahead, you will succeed.
- **G** Never listen to others when determining your future.
- **H** No amount of practice will help if you don't have talent.
- **J** To accomplish big things, it takes hard work and perseverance.

Read these sentences from paragraph 13.

Practices were intense. Mr. Greeley brought us to a great level of excellence. We had each conquered our own personal fears. We were able to go from mediocre players to the top of our class.

13 Which pair of sentences below **best** combines the ideas of the four sentences in this paragraph?

3.1.6

- **A** Because practices were intense, Mr. Greeley brought us to a great level of excellence. We had each conquered our own personal fears; however, we were able to go from mediocre players to the top of our class.
- **B** Practices were intense because Mr. Greeley brought us to a great level of excellence. While we had each conquered our own personal fears, we were able to go from mediocre players to the top of our class.
- **C** Practices were intense, but Mr. Greeley brought us to a great level of excellence. We had each conquered our own personal fears and were able to go from mediocre players to the top of our class.
- **D** Practices were intense — Mr. Greeley brought us to a great level of excellence. We had each conquered our own personal fears: We were able to go from mediocre players to the top of our class.

GO ON

Directions

Read the poem "Loss and Gain." Then answer numbers 14 and 15.

Loss and Gain

When I compare

What I have lost with what I have gained,

What I have missed with what attained,

  Little room do I find for pride.

I am aware

How many days have been idly spent;

How like an arrow the good intent

  Has fallen short or been turned aside.

But who shall dare

To measure loss and gain in this wise?

Defeat may be victory in disguise;

  The lowest ebb is the turn of the tide.

— Henry Wadsworth Longfellow (1807–1882)

---

14 Based on the word choices in this poem, what does the loss mentioned <u>most likely</u> refer to?   1.2.2

  F   losing prized possessions

  G   the loss of a family member

  H   failing to achieve certain goals

  J   not having someone return your love

15 The subject of the last line of this poem is   3.1.3

  A   The.

  B   ebb.

  C   turn.

  D   tide.

GO ON

Directions

Read "A Fishing Trip" below and answer numbers 16 and 17.

A Fishing Trip

The traffic began moving again. Josh was glad to be finished building houses in the Monterey area. Now, he was ready to relax with his son, David, for a couple of weeks at Gunpowder Falls State Park. Josh knew that David would be a little tired since today was the last day of David's tenth grade year; it had been a tough one for him. So, Josh drove slowly in the right-hand lane up Highway 795 on the way home to Manchester, giving David time to unwind before he had to get in the truck. Glancing in his rear view mirror, Josh saw a school bus and thought about his last day of school in the tenth grade. Josh's dad had been in jail again, for the third time. Josh could still see and hear the cell door bars with their mocking clanging: so much like the bells at school and so not like them.

Shaking off his sad memory, Josh looked forward to the vacation ahead. When he got home, he'd pack the tent, sleeping bags, food and cooking gear in the truck. Then he'd pick up David. They would be together for the whole vacation in a secluded wood. They'd fish Loch Raven Reservoir with the new rods they had given each other for Christmas. The cool air and water would refresh their minds and spirits. Josh could already smell the freshly caught trout sizzling over an open fire and could already hear the stories that he and David would share.

16 The <u>most likely</u> reason that Josh wants so much to spend quality time with his son is because   1.2.1

F they both like fishing.

G he has been working too many hours.

H David is having some trouble in school.

J he remembers his own father not being there for him.

17 Which word is <u>most</u> closely related to the theme of this story?   1.3.5

A rejection

B distress

C caring

D worry

Directions

Use the poem "Loss and Gain" and the short essay "A Fishing Trip" to answer numbers 18 and 19.

18 Which statement best expresses a main idea in both texts? 1.1.3

F Remembering the past can be depressing.

G Past losses can help a person turn things around in the future.

H If you don't succeed in one place, try another environment.

J People learn from failures but not from successes.

19 Which purpose would **best** be served by reading these two texts? 1.1.3

A to help in studying about family relationships

B for a research project about attitudes of prison inmates

C when writing an essay about how losses in life can teach lessons

D in striving to understand near-death experiences that people have had

Session 2

Directions

For number 20, read the prompt below. Follow the directions in the prompt for writing your essay.

20 Consider the following quote by philosopher, writer, and publisher Elbert Green Hubbard (1856 –1915):

2.1.4

> *The man who is anybody and who does anything is surely going to be criticized, vilified, and misunderstood. That is part of the penalty for greatness, and every great man understands it; and understands, too, that it is no proof of greatness. The final proof of greatness lies in being able to endure continuously without resentment.*

Write a well-organized essay in which you agree or disagree that those who strive to do great things must endure criticism, scorn and misunderstanding without letting it get to them. Support your position with specific examples from experience, observation and studies. Write a fully developed essay that is logically organized and clearly expresses your ideas.

Use your own paper to plan your essay and to complete your final draft.

Directions

Read the poems "The Sick Rose" and "This world is not conclusion." Then answer numbers 21 through 24.

The Sick Rose

O Rose, thou art sick!

The invisible worm

That flies in the night,

In the howling storm,

Has found out thy bed

Of crimson joy:

And his dark secret love

Does thy life destroy.

—William Blake (1757–1827)

This world is not conclusion

This world is not conclusion;

A sequel stands beyond,

Invisible, as music,

But positive[1], as sound.

It beckons and it baffles;

Philosophies don't know,

And through a riddle, at the last,

Sagacity[2] must go.

To guess it puzzles scholars;

To gain it men have shown

Contempt of generations,

And crucifixion known.

—Emily Dickinson (1830–1886)

[1]certain

[2]level-headedness

21 One interpretation of "The Sick Rose" is that the poet uses allegory to tell about the plight of a woman (Rose) by describing a flower (rose). If the rose in the garden is destroyed by a "worm" (probably a caterpillar), what <u>most likely</u> happens to the woman?   1.2.3

A   She is dying of a terrible disease.

B   Her beauty is destroyed by aging.

C   Her family has found out she is having a secret affair.

D   She loses her mind and imagines things crawling on her.

22 Which word best describes the tone of the poem "The Sick Rose"?   1.3.3

F   eager

G   tragic

H   sinister

J   relieved

23 In "This world is not conclusion," when Emily Dickinson writes, "Philosophies don't know,/And through a riddle, at the last,/Sagacity must go," she is <u>most likely</u> saying that   4.2.1

A   there is a way to figure out the riddle of what happens after death.

B   despite trying, smart people don't know what comes after death.

C   people must let go of earthly reason and accept what comes next.

D   you should not try to be too serious because life is a game.

24 Which statement <u>best</u> captures a significant idea in both poems?   1.1.3

F   Death and whatever comes after it are both great mysteries.

G   Time is fleeting, and people must make the most of it.

H   Life is full of pain, so death is a welcome end for some.

J   No one can control what happens in either life or death.

Directions

Read the paragraph below and notice that it requires revisions and editing. Answer numbers 25 through 27 about changes that will make it a better-written paragraph.

Seahorses Make Great Fathers

From start to finish, a male seahorse does all the parenting. His is indeed a real pregnancy, closely resembling that of mammals, including humans. The seahorse, like a woman with a fetus, provides oxygen, transfers nutrients, and regulates conditions for the babies in his pouch. Remarkably the hormone prolactin which stimulates milk production in women also governs seahorse pregnancy.

Males of the species have fewer than 10 offspring. Then there was James from the Caribbean. Surely the world record holder for "most young in one pouch." His pouch was only half a tablespoon in volume, but in it were packed 1,573 babies. End to end they would have stretched more than 12 yards.

GO ON

25 Which of these is the <u>best</u> way to revise the third sentence for clarity?   2.2.3

  A   A seahorse provides the babies in his pouch with oxygen, transfers nutrients, and regulates conditions, just as a woman would for the fetus in her uterus.

  B   The seahorse does no less for the babies in his pouch than a woman with a fetus in her uterus: provides oxygen, transfers nutrients, and regulates conditions.

  C   The babies in the pouch of the seahorse are provided exygen, nutrients, and regulated conditions, as is a baby in the uterus of a woman.

  D   Just as a woman provides her fetus with oxygen, transfers nutrients, and regulates conditions in the uterus, a seahorse does no less for babies in his pouch.

26 Which is the correct way to punctuate the last sentence in the first paragraph?   3.3.1

  F   Remarkably: the hormone prolactin which stimulates milk production in women also governs seahorse pregnancy.

  G   Remarkably, the hormone prolactin, which stimulates milk production in women, also governs seahorse pregnancy.

  H   Remarkably the hormone prolactin; which stimulates milk production in women; also governs seahorse pregnancy.

  J   Remarkably, the hormone prolactin which, stimulates milk production in women also, governs seahorse pregnancy.

27 Which of these needs to be revised to form a complete sentence?   3.1.4

  A   Surely the world record holder for "most young in one pouch."

  B   Then there was James from the Caribbean.

  C   Males of the species have fewer than 10 offspring.

  D   His pouch was only half a tablespoon in volume, but in it were packed 1,573 babies.

GO ON

Directions

Read the speech below, and then answer numbers 28 through 31.

Remarks by President Clinton During Global Feeding Event

The Roosevelt Room, Dec. 28, 2000, 10:35 a.m. EST

This morning, we gather, just three days after Christmas, the second day of Eid Al-Fitr, a few hours before the last night of Hanukkah; a time sacred to men and women of faith who share a belief in the dignity of every human being; a time to give thanks for the prosperity so many enjoy today, but also a time to remember that much of humanity still lives in astonishing poverty.

Nearly half the human race struggles to survive on less than $2 a day; nearly a billion live in chronic hunger; half the children in the poorest countries are not in school. That is not right, necessary, or sustainable in the 21st century.

The most critical building block any nation needs to reap the benefits of the global era is a healthy population with broad-based literacy. Each additional year spent in school increases wages by 10 to 20 percent in the developing world. Today, however, 120 million children get no schooling at all, 60 percent of them girls. So this year in Dakar, Senegal, 181 nations joined to set a goal of providing basic education to every child in every country by 2015. At the urging of the United States, the G-8 nations later endorsed this goal at our summit in Okinawa.

Experience has shown here at home, and around the world, that one of the best ways to get parents to send their children to school is a healthy meal. That's why today I'm very pleased that we are announcing the grant recipients who are going to help us put in place our $300 million pilot program to provide nutritious meals to school children in developing countries.

The program will provide a free breakfast or a free lunch to some 9 million children in 38 developing nations. Under this pilot program, for example, we will start providing nutritious food to more than 500,000 children in Vietnam. We will start providing high protein bread and milk each day to some 60,000 students in 170 schools in Eritrea. And in Kenya, we will start giving some 1.4 million elementary school children a nutritious meal every single day.

Of course, this initiative by itself is not a solution to the global hunger problem, but it's a down payment and a beginning. Now it's up to Congress, the United Nations, other developed countries, the NGOs (non governmental organizations) represented here, and the next administration to continue this fight. We're going to need the World Bank to implement its pledge to increase lending for education by 50 percent. Developing countries need to make basic education a real priority.

We've worked hard these last few years to put the battle against abject poverty higher on the world's agenda, and America must keep it there. This is not just about our moral obligation to help the needy — although, it is great — it's also part of the answer to what kind of world we want our children to inhabit a generation from now; what do we want to avoid. The world is becoming more and more interdependent and America needs strong and healthy partners. We need to invest in future markets and we need to do it in every part of the world. We want to avoid a world that is hopelessly and violently divided between the rich and the poor; a future in which hundreds of millions of people decide that they have no stake in a peaceful and open global society because there's nothing in it for them and their children.

GO ON

If we can prevent that from happening, it will be good for our economy, for our security and for our souls.

28 Which conclusion about the president's attitude is <u>most</u> supported by information from the speech? 1.1.3

F He believes that providing basic education to all children is of greatest importance.

G He feels that feeding the hungry is higher on the agenda than is sending children to school.

H He wants to limit the amount of money the United States lends to other nations.

J He is asking for all citizens to help fund the global feeding event.

29 In the following sentence from the speech, the underlined phrase means to "pay an installment at purchase." What is the connotative meaning in which it is used here? 3.2.2

Of course, this initiative by itself is not a solution to the global hunger problem, but it's a <u>down payment</u> and a beginning.

A a low amount to pay

B a favor

C a way to get started

D an insult

30 When the president says, "We want to avoid a world that is hopelessly and violently divided between the rich and the poor," he is suggesting that 1.2.2

F developed countries need to stay out of underdeveloped countries.

G hope and peace depend on poverty being brought under control.

H America needs to ensure that its economy stays healthy.

J there will always be poverty, but many nations can avoid it.

Read these sentences related to the speech.

Many people in the world live in desperate poverty.

Education helps people find ways out of poverty.

Once educated, people find creative ways to grow food, start businesses, and trade with others.

31 Which of the following is the <u>most</u> <u>effective</u> way to combine these ideas into one sentence? 3.1.6

A Many people in the world live in desperate poverty; education, which helps people find ways out of poverty, can help them find creative ways to grow food, start businesses and trade with others.

B Education is a way to help the many people in the world who live in desperate poverty to find a way out; once educated, people find creative ways to grow food, start businesses and trade with others.

C People who live in desperate poverty need education because it helps people find ways out of poverty; educated people find creative ways to grow food, start businesses and trade with others.

D The many people in the world who live in desperate poverty need education to help them find creative ways to grow food, start businesses and trade with others.

16

GO ON

Directions

The paragraph below requires revisions and editing. Read it carefully, and then answer numbers 32 and 33.

Komodo Dragons

① Komodo dragons are the largest living reptiles in the world. ② Ten feet long is how big they can grow. ③ They are good and limber climbers and fast runners but not for long distances. ④ These voracious eaters favorite meals are deer and wild boar. ⑤ Even one bite is deadly, as Komodos carry poisonous bacteria in their mouths. ⑥ Long forked tongues help them track fallen prey. ⑦ Like all reptiles, though, they eat much less often than mammals of their size. ⑧ Discovered on the islands of the Indonesian archipelago at the start of the 20th century, Komodos are endangered, with only a few thousand left. ⑨ The islands of Padar and Rinca now serve as nature reserves to protect them.

32 What punctuation is needed in the fourth sentence?   3.3.1

- **F** These voracious eater's favorite meals are deer and wild boar.
- **G** These voracious eaters' favorite meals are deer and wild boar.
- **H** These voracious' eaters favorite meals are deer and wild boar.
- **J** These voracious-eaters favorite meals are deer and wild boar.

Read the following sentence:

The largest monitor lizards, they spend their days sunning and their nights in shallow burrows.

33 Where would be the <u>most</u> logical place in the paragraph to include this information?   2.2.2

- **A** after sentence 1
- **B** after sentence 2
- **C** after sentence 6
- **D** after sentence 7

STOP

17

Session 3

Directions

Read the essay "Shy Shadows: Octopus and Squid." Then answer numbers 34 through 40.

Shy Shadows: Octopus and Squid

As I watch, a shadow glides towards the ocean floor where it disappears into rocks which are pockmarked with holes and craters. I have had a close encounter with the world's first carnivorous predator. No, it is not the shark. My encounter has been with an octopus.

Biologists have identified a class of the Phylum Mollusca (mollusks) as the first active, carnivorous predatory animals. The class is named cephalopoda (Latin for "head-foots"). The class cephalopoda is limited to marine animals and has 600 living species including species of the octopus and the squid.

Luckily for me, the appetites of the two largest mollusks do not usually make them look at humans as dinner. These two prefer to dine on fish and crabs, being in the first active, or hunting, family of animals. Still, it's best to be careful. The predatory animals, the squid and the octopus, display unique behaviors and body systems.

Both of these marine animals are shy and choose to stalk their prey quietly. When threatened, the octopus has been observed actually growing pale. This behavior provides the artifice of greater size and is a defensive action for the octopus. The

octopus can also change colors to blend into the background around it. A different defensive behavior that the octopus and the squid share with cephalopods is the ability to squirt a cloudy fluid which cuts down on the ability of possible attackers to see them.

These strategies, as well as the octopus' tendency to hide in enclosed spaces (rocks, sunken ships or reefs), are necessary for survival. Members of the class of cephalopods may have either an external shell, an internal shell or as in the case of the octopus — no protective shell for the body at all. So the brain, the stomach, the arms and all the other soft tissues are exposed and vulnerable to injury. The squid has an internal shell which gives it the distinctive streamlined shape.

The arms are the most recognizable—and fearsome—features of the octopus and the squid. The octopus' name comes partly from the number of its arms: octo is the Latin word for "eight." Both the octopus and squid use their arms for capturing and eating food. They bring the food to their beaklike jaws to cut it into smaller pieces. The octopus uses its arms also to move along the ocean floor as well

19

GO ON

as using a flow of water through its body to propel it along. It can take water into its body and then squirt the water out, propelling itself at a rapid pace. The squid differs only in that it does not use its arms to move. Instead, the squid stays suspended between the ocean floor and surface and moves only by the method of water propulsion.

The squid is also one of the largest marine animals. Or rather, the giant squid is the largest invertebrate. There are theories that the old stories of sea monsters were spun by sailors who had seen giant squid. These squid can grow up to 70 feet (21.3 meters), and they have the largest eyes of any animal on earth. There are scientists now conducting new research off the coasts of New Zealand and Australia, trying to learn more about this intelligent behemoth of the deep.

Keeping an eye out for the marine creatures which do not turn down humans for lunch, I slowly head towards the rocks where the shadow has hidden. My time is running short, along with the air in my oxygen tanks. I must go back to my own world, away from the hushed, dim world of the cephalopods. Before I go, I catch a last glimpse of the creature, turned a reddish color to match the rocks behind it. We may be afraid of it, but the fragile octopus has every reason to be shy. It has no shell to retreat into . . .

34 In the first paragraph, the author mentions that he is not describing a shark. What is <u>most</u> logically the reason that he refers to the shark?   1.1.1

F He is relying on the readers' prior knowledge of sharks as underwater carnivores to help them understand the octopus.

G He is trying to relate to readers who probably know nothing about mollusks but have a great deal of knowledge about sharks.

H He mentions the shark because he knows that readers will want to know about traits it has in common with the octopus.

J He refers to the shark to imply that the octopus and the squid are like the shark in many important ways.

35 The author's attitude throughout this essay is one of fascination with the often dreaded octopus and the squid. What universal theme does this <u>best</u> fit?   1.3.5

A Tales of monsters are always rooted in something that is real.

B No matter where one looks, humans are the dominant species in nature.

C It is human nature to be afraid of what we don't know very much about.

D Creatures very different from man help us learn a great deal about nature.

36 After reading this passage, the <u>most</u> <u>likely</u> conclusion is that   1.1.3

F the octopus will return to its activities as the diver leaves.

E the octopus will attack the narrator.

H the diver will run out of air before reaching the surface.

J the diver will catch the octopus.

GO ON

Read this sentence from paragraph 4 of the essay.

This behavior provides the artifice of greater size and is a defensive action for the octopus.

37 **The word *artifice* <u>most</u> nearly means** 1.1.2

   A craft.

   B strategy.

   C impression.

   D reproduction.

Read this sentence from the essay.

Luckily for me, the appetites of the two largest mollusks do not usually make them look at humans as dinner.

38 **What is the subject of the verb *make*?** 3.1.3

   F me

   G appetites

   H mollusks

   J them

Read this sentence of the essay.

Keeping an eye out for the marine creatures which do not turn down humans for lunch, I slowly head towards the rocks where the shadow has hidden.

39 **Which of the statements <u>best</u> explains the meaning of this sentence?** 1.2.2

   A The octopus is wary of encountering creatures such as sharks, so it remains in hiding.

   B The narrator is afraid of the octopus and approaches its hiding place cautiously.

   C While the octopus hides in the rocks, the narrator looks around for other sea life.

   D The narrator watches out for creatures like sharks, while trying to get closer to the octopus.

Examine the illustrations.

Octopus

Squid

40 **Write a response that explains how the pictures may support information given in the essay "Shy Shadows: Octopus and Squid." Support your conclusion with appropriate details from both the essay and the illustrations.** 1.1.4

21

Directions

Read the paragraph below. Then answer number 41.

Skiing

(1) In spite of warnings against climbing the snowy mountain, Calvin and his friends made the ascent. (2) They were willing to risk it so they could ski down the pristine powder on the slopes. (3) For nearly three hours, they climbed steadily to the top. (4) Due to an approaching storm, they quickened their pace. (5) On top of the mountain, they saw a beautiful panorama unfold before their eyes. (6) Instead of resting very long, they began their descent along the southern slope. (7) They arrived at the bottom and gathered together. (8) At the foot of the hill, they looked up. (9) They admired the pattern of the tracks their skis had made in the snow. (10) Because of the waning light, they knew they could not make another run. (11) They agreed they would come back soon in order to ski this wonderful mountain again.

41 Which of these is the most effective way to combine sentences 7, 8, and 9?   3.1.6

A They arrived at the bottom and gathered together at the foot of the hill, and then looked up to admire the pattern of the tracks their skis had made in the snow.

B Together, they arrived at the bottom; they gathered together; at the foot of the hill, they looked up, admiring the pattern of the tracks their skis had made in the snow.

C Arriving at the bottom, gathering together, looking up from the foot of the hill, they admired the pattern of the tracks their skis had made in the snow.

D They admired the pattern of the tracks their skis had made in the snow once they arrived at the bottom and gathered together at the foot of the hill and then looked up.

Now answer numbers 42 and 43 about both "Shy Shadows: Octopus and Squid" and "Skiing."

42 These two texts would <u>most likely</u> encourage a reader to   1.2.5

F consider how every season has its appropriate activities.

G enjoy watching extreme sports on television.

H consider taking up an activity allowing experiences with nature.

J analyze a natural phenomenon to make it less mysterious.

22

GO ON

43 Shakira is writing a presentation   2.3.1
about exciting recreation that takes
people into new and different environments,
like scuba diving in the ocean or skiing on
fresh powder. In addition to the two previous
texts, which resource below would **most
likely** add appropriate information for her
presentation?

A   www.magxzine.com
a news item about Tony Hawk and
other skaters raising funds to build
skate parks in urban areas

B   "The Big Bicycle Adventure"
a travel diary of bicycling through the
landscape and towns of Provence,
France

C   *Lonely Planet Vanuatu and New Caledonia*
a book about traveling the islands of
Vanuatu and new Caledonia in the
South Pacific

D   "At Home and in the Garden"
a brochure with tips for home and garden safety and prevention of pollution
by recycling and conserving water and
energy

Directions

For numbers 44 and 45, read the sentence in
bold print. Then choose the clearest and <u>most
effective</u> revision of the sentence.

44 **We read three different poems, each**   2.2.3
one about a different subject, but all of
them with a similar outlook about the
preciousness of life.

F   We read three different poems with a
similar outlook about the preciousness
of life, yet each of them was about a
different subject.

G   Of the three different poems we read,
each one was about a different subject,
but all of them had a similar outlook
about the preciousness of life.

H   Though they had a similar outlook
about the preciousness of life, each
poem we read, of three different ones,
had a different subject.

J   Though each of the three different
poems we read was about a different
subject, all of them had a similar outlook about the preciousness of life.

45 **Because the storm lasted so long,**   2.2.3
several streets were flooded, and the
next morning, no one from the neighborhood
could get to school or to work.

A   The next morning, because the storm
lasted so long and several streets were
flooded, no one from the neighborhood
could get to school or to work.

B   Several streets were flooded because
the storm lasted so long, so no one
from the neighborhood could get to
school or to work the next morning.

C   No one from the neighborhood could
get to school or to work the next morning; the storm lasted so long and several streets were flooded.

D   The next morning, several streets were
flooded because the storm lasted so
long; no one from the neighborhood
could get to school or to work.

GO ON

Directions

Todd is interested in wonders of the world, and he decides to write an essay about the mysterious giant statues on Easter Island. The draft of Todd's essay requires revisions and editing. Read the draft, and then answer numbers 46 through 50.

Easter Island

Easter island is an island in the southern pacific ocean belonging to Chile. The Dutch explorer, Jacob Roggeveen named it Easter Island because he first arrived there on Easter Day, 1722. It is located about 2,200 miles west of Chile, and is one of the most isolated inhabited islands in the world. The island is only about 63 square miles in size, and around 4,000 people live there.

Easter has three active volcanoes but is best known for its numerous *moai*, the impressive and mysterious stone statues that are located along the coastlines. The statues were carved from compressed volcanic ash. They are all monolithic, meaning them are carved in one piece. Some weigh more than twenty tons and are more than twenty feet tall. They were carved during a relatively short and intense period of creative activity on the island a thousand years ago.

The majority of the 887 *moai* statues were still standing when explorer Jacob Roggeveen arrived on the island in 1722. Captain James Cook also saw many standing statues when he landed on Easter Island in 1774. By the mid-19th century, all the statues had been toppled, presumably during wars between rival colonies.

Today, about 50 moai have been re-erected on their ceremonial sites. Easter Island remains one of the most unique places on Earth. It is an open-air museum. The island's inhabitants are among the friendliest people in the world, and the landscape is truly amazing with its volcanic craters, lava formations, beaches, brilliant blue water, and awesome, yet mysterious, stone statues. It would be wonderful to someday see these wonders in person.

46 In which paragraph would the sentence below **best** fit?   2.2.2

No one is quite sure how these statues were built or who built them.

- **F** Paragraph 1
- **G** Paragraph 2
- **H** Paragraph 3
- **J** Paragraph 4

47 What is the correct way to use capitalization in the first sentence of the essay?   3.3.1

- **A** Easter Island is an island in the Southern pacific ocean belonging to Chile.
- **B** Easter island is an island in the Southern Pacific ocean belonging to Chile.
- **C** Easter Island is an island in the southern Pacific Ocean belonging to Chile.
- **D** Easter Island is an island in the southern Pacific ocean belonging to Chile.

GO ON

Read this sentence from the last paragraph of the essay.

It is an open-air museum.

48 Which of these expanded sentences best adds supporting details? 3.1.8

   F   It is an open-air museum showcasing a fascinating but lost culture.

   G   Now that no one is tipping the statues, it is an open-air museum.

   H   Because all the statues are outdoors, it is an open-air museum.

   J   It is an open-air museum full of people all the time.

49 All of these sentences include information that could be documented on a works-cited page EXCEPT 2.3.3

   A   The island is only about 63 square miles in size, and, at last count, its population is around 3,800 people.

   B   Some weigh more than twenty tons and are more than twenty feet tall.

   C   Captain James Cook also saw many standing statues when he landed on Easter in 1774.

   D   It would be wonderful to someday see these wonders in person.

Read this rule from a language handbook.

Pronouns must always agree with their antecedents.

50 What is the correct way to revise this sentence from the essay? 3.3.2

They are all monolithic, meaning them are carved in one piece.

   F   Them are all monolithic, meaning the statues are carved in one piece.

   G   The statues are all monolithic, meaning it is carved in one piece.

   H   The statues are all monolithic, meaning they are carved in one piece.

   J   Best as it is.

EVALUATION CHART FOR MARYLAND HSA ELA DIAGNOSTIC TEST

Directions: On the following chart, circle the question numbers that you answered incorrectly, and evaluate the results. These questions are based on the *Maryland Core Learning Goals and Indicators for English Language Arts and Reading*. Then turn to the appropriate chapters, read the explanations, and complete the exercises. Review other chapters as needed. Finally, complete the Post test(s) to assess your progress and further prepare you for the **Maryland High School Assessment in English**.

Note: Some question numbers will appear under multiple chapters because those questions require demonstration of multiple skills.

Chapter	Diagnostic Test Question(s)
Chapter 1: Meaning and Grammatical Classification of Words	9, 14, 29, 37
Chapter 2: Reading for Understanding	7, 11, 14, 18, 19, 21, 23, 28, 34, 36, 39, 42, 48
Chapter 3: Analysis of Literature	8, 10, 11, 16, 21, 22, 23, 28, 30
Chapter 4: Non-Print and Information Resources	40, 49
Chapter 5: Extending Meaning	7, 12, 17, 18, 24, 35, 36, 42
Chapter 6: Writing Skills: Grammar and Usage	13, 15, 20, 26, 32, 38, 47, 50
Chapter 7: Controlling Language	1, 2, 4, 13, 15, 20, 25, 31, 38, 41, 44, 45
Chapter 8: Conventions in Sentences and Paragraphs	1, 2, 3, 4, 5, 6, 13, 20, 25, 26, 27, 31, 32, 33, 41, 44, 45, 46, 47, 48
Chapter 9: Writing the Essay	1, 4, 11, 13, 20, 31, 43, 49
Chapter 10: Writing a Constructed Response	40

Chapter 1
Meaning and Grammatical Classification of Words

This chapter addresses the following expectation(s) and their related indicators from **Core Learning Goal 1: Reading. Reviewing and Responding to Texts**

Expectation 1.1	The student will use effective strategies before, during and after reading, viewing and listening to self-selected and assigned materials.

This chapter also addresses the following expectation(s) and their related indicators from **Core Learning Goal 3: Controlling Language**

Expectation 3.1	The student will demonstrate understanding of the nature and structure of language, including grammar concepts and skills, to strengthen control of oral and written language.
Expectation 3.2	The student will identify how language choices in writing and speaking affect thoughts and feelings.

WORD MEANING

We give names to ideas, events, objects and, emotions. Often, however, there is no way to tell a word's meaning by the word alone. For example, consider the word "globe." There is nothing about the combination of the letters G-L-O-B-E to suggest the entire Earth, yet everyone knows "the globe" used in any sense refers to a model of all the land, water and sky on the planet.

To learn new words in a language, you need to have skills that allow you to decode what the word means. The most basic skill involves understanding how a word is used within a sentence and detecting the meaning from its use. When we understand the meaning of a sentence, we understand the ideas behind the words used and, as a consequence, the words themselves. The words and ideas in the text surrounding a word are called the **context**. When put together, the context will reveal clues to the meaning of unfamiliar words.

Using **context clues** means looking at the way words are used in combination with other words in their setting. Look at the words *around* an unknown word. Think about the meaning of these words or the idea of the whole sentence. Then, match the meaning of the unknown word to the meaning of the known text.

Meaning and Grammatical Classification of Words

In the following statements, choose the word which best reflects the meaning of the underlined word.

1. Many kinds of green algae remain <u>dormant</u> until rain revives them.
   A. dry   B. dead   C. small   D. inactive

2. Exercise that increases your heart and breathing rates for a sustained period of time is called <u>aerobic</u>.
   A. of short duration   C. requiring oxygen
   B. improving strength   D. silly

By paying attention to context clues, we can determine that algae remain something *until rain revives them.* The opposite of "revive" is "to put to sleep." Therefore, rain does something to bring the algae to life, to wake it up. Of the given choices, only *D* most closely resembles sleep. The other choices simply do not fit within the context, or setting of ideas, contained in the sentence.

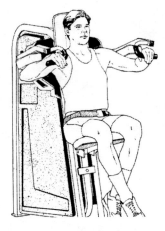

Question 2 is a bit harder to figure out. The meaning of the word "aerobic" is called into question. We can rule out *A* because a sustained period of time would not agree with "of short duration." *B* seems pretty close, except that all exercise does not result in improved strength. Choice *D* is plainly not the answer, because the word "silly" doesn't fit the serious tone of the sentence; it was actually only included to make you laugh and to point out that context is frequently a source of humor. Finally, choice *C* is correct, because the definition "requiring oxygen" satisfies all the requirements of the sentence's context. It most perfectly fits the "setting" of the sentence.

When you encounter an unfamiliar word or phrase in a sentence, consider the function of other words in the sentence. By looking at and analyzing the phrases and **signal words** that come before or after a particular word, you can often figure out an unknown word's meaning.

Study the chart on the following page for examples of context clues and their signal words.

Context Clues	Signal Words
Comparison	*also, like, resembling, too, both, than* Look for clues that indicate an unfamiliar word is similar to a familiar word or phrase. **Example:** The accident *felled* the utility pole like a tree cut for timber. The word *like* provides the clue for the meaning of *felled*, to be cut down.
Contrast	*but, however, while, instead of, yet, unlike* Look for clues that indicate an unfamiliar word is opposite in meaning to a familiar word or phrase. **Example:** Stephanie is usually in a state of *composure* while her sister is mostly boisterous. The signal word *while* is the clue that composure means calm as opposed to boisterous
Definition or Restatement	*is, or, that is, in other words, which* Look for words that define the term or restate it in other words. **Example:** The principal's idea is to *circulate*—or move around—the campus weekly to make sure everything is okay. The signal word *or* points to the restated meaning of circulate.
Example	*for example, for instance, such as* Look for examples used in context that reveal the meaning of an unfamiliar word. **Example:** People use all sorts of *vehicles* such as cars, bicycles, rickshaws, airplanes, boats, and motorcycles. *Such as* signals the meaning of *vehicles*, types of transportation like cars.

Practice 1: Context Practice

Read the following story, and then answer the questions which come after it.

A Thief's Surprise

Andrea and her brother, Dan, arrived early that morning and parked their car near the parade route for the <u>annual</u> Baltimore Christmas Parade. Many shops had closed along the parade route. Dan watched the parade <u>ardently</u>. He wanted to hear his school's band perform the music they had worked on so <u>arduously</u> all semester. Meanwhile, Andrea went window shopping at the glass storefronts nearby. Suddenly she noticed a flash of light off to her left. It came from the reflection of a man's watch. He was looking <u>intensely</u> into the music store window nearby.

Dan was listening <u>intently</u> as the school band marched by. The music was so loud it was deafening. At the same moment, Andrea glanced to the left and <u>discerned</u> the same man just before he used a rock to break through the glass window of the music store. In shock, Andrea ran to get her brother. She screamed, "Dan, come here!" However, he could not hear her above the sounds of the marching band. In <u>desperation</u>, she grabbed Dan from behind and turned him around.

"Dan, there is a man down the street who is robbing a music store!" she exclaimed.

Dan was the star wrestler on his school team and was ready to put his talents to good use. He ran as fast as he could and arrived at the music store just as the thief was coming out of the store. The thief was <u>absconding</u> with an expensive electric guitar. Luckily for Dan, the thief did not have a gun. In an <u>expeditious</u> manner, Dan put the thief into a head-lock and forced him to the sidewalk. By then, Andrea had found a police officer, who arrested the would-be <u>larcenist</u>.

1. Which of the following is closest in meaning to the word <u>annual</u>?

   A. daily   B. monthly   C. weekly   D. yearly

2. In the context of the passage, which of the following is closest in meaning to the word <u>ardently</u>?
   A. with eagerness   C. with integrity
   B. with boredom   D. with anxiety

3. In this passage, which of the following is closest in meaning to the word <u>arduously</u>?
   A. long   B. hard   C. gracefully   D. quickly

4. In this passage, which of the following is closest in meaning to the word <u>intensely</u>?
   A. with great hope   C. with great concentration
   B. with great yearning   D. with great enthusiasm

5. In this passage, which of the following is closest in meaning to the word <u>intently</u>?
   A. indifferently   B. closely   C. impassively   D. unclearly

6. In this passage, which of the following is closest in meaning to the word <u>discerned</u>?
   A. stopped   B. avoided   C. noticed   D. yelled at

7. In this passage, which of the following is closest in meaning to the word <u>desperation</u>?
   A. joy   B. extreme anger   C. annoyance   D. great anxiety

8. In this passage, which of the following is closest in meaning to the word <u>absconding</u>?
   A. caught   B. escaping   C. playing   D. carrying

9. In this passage, which of the following is closest in meaning to the word <u>expeditious</u>?
   A. careful   B. slow   C. quick   D. hesitant

10. In this passage, which of the following is closest in meaning to the word <u>larcenist</u>?
    A. thief   B. mentor   C. musician   D. politician

CONNOTATIONS AND DENOTATIONS

One important part of word choice is knowing the difference between the **connotations** (emotional associations) and the **denotations** (dictionary meanings) of words. For example, the words *delicate* and *fragile* can both mean "easily broken." However, if you told a ballerina that her movements were *delicate*, the ballerina would probably thank you. But, if you told her that her movements were *fragile*, she would probably be offended. While both of these words **denote** "easily broken," the **connotation** of *delicate* is positive while that of *fragile* can be negative.

> **Example:** Both the words *blameless* and *harmless* are **denoted** as **innocent**. However, without understanding their connotation, these words can be misused.

Read the following sentences:

> 1. The nine jurists found the defendant **harmless** in these charges.
>
> 2. The hamster is relatively **blameless** in comparison to the tiger.

In sentence 1, the word *harmless* as it is used in the sentence seems awkward because of its **connotation** as *not dangerous* instead of *not guilty.*

In sentence 2, the word *blameless* seems awkward because of its connotation as *innocent* instead of *not dangerous.*

To understand a story, article or passage, you need to figure out the meanings of words. Sometimes the word has a specific dictionary meaning (denotation), and sometimes the word has a more emotional association (connotation).

Now read the following sentence from O. Henry's short story, "The Last Leaf." Notice how the denotations and connotations of his words and phrases enrich the description of Greenwich Village:

> "In November, a cold, unseen stranger, whom the doctors called Pneumonia, stalked about the colony, touching one here and there with his icy fingers."

O. Henry uses words like "cold," "stranger," "stalked," and "icy fingers" because of their strong connotations. The connotation of the four words together leads to an emotional reaction: they bring up the image or feeling of danger, the grave or the angel of death.

At the same time, we must understand the denotations of words like "doctors" and "Pneumonia" to fully understand that the sentence is referring to a serious illness that medicine could name but sometimes not cure. Today, pneumonia is rarely fatal.

Practice 2: Connotations and Denotations

Use a dictionary or a thesaurus to help you choose the appropriate word for each sentence. On your own paper, write the common denotations and connotations of the word pairs to explain your choice.

Sentence	**Word Choice**
1. You have a very good _____ at getting that job.	A. chance B. opening
2. I understand that there is a(n)_____ for a veterinarian at your clinic.	A. chance B. opening
3. Kyle is very_____ of his right to be at the meeting.	A. forceful B. assertive
4. The victorious nation had a list of _____ demands for the defeated nation.	A. forceful B. assertive
5. The middle-aged people had a(n)_____ appearance.	A. immature B. youthful
6. The sixteen-year old boys acted _____ for their age.	A. immature B. youthful

Practice 3: Analyzing Passages for Connotation and Denotation

Read the description below of Ichabod Crane from "The Legend of Sleepy Hollow" by Washington Irving. In a small group or on your own, list 5–6 words or phrases with connotations that give a more vivid description of Ichabod Crane. Were there any words having only denotations? Share your findings with the class or your teacher.

Ichabod was a suitable figure for such a steed. He rode with short stirrups, which brought his knees nearly up to the pommel of the saddle; his sharp elbows stuck out like grasshoppers'; he carried his whip perpendicularly in his hand, like a scepter, and, as his horse jogged on, the motion of his arms was not unlike the flapping of a pair of wings. A small wool hat rested on the top of his nose, for so his scanty strip of forehead might be called; and the skirts of his black coat fluttered out almost to the horse's tail. Such was the appearance of Ichabod and his steed, as they shambled out of the gate of Hans Van Ripper, and it was altogether such an apparition as seldom to be met with in broad daylight.

Practice 4: Connotations of Words

For each of the following related pairs of words, choose the word that has a positive connotation.

1.	A.	cheap	B.	inexpensive
2.	A.	uninformed	B.	stupid
3.	A.	sparkle	B.	glitzy
4.	A.	shack	B.	cottage
5.	A.	pushy	B.	assertive
6.	A.	police officer	B.	cop
7.	A.	fat	B.	chubby
8.	A.	sip	B.	slurp
9.	A.	old geezer	B.	senior citizen
10.	A.	information	B.	gossip

Practice 5: Connotations and Denotations—A Last Look

A. Comics Connotations

Get a copy of the Sunday paper, read the comics section and think about the jokes. What makes them funny? Go back and write down words or phrases having emotional reactions attached to them. Add what the connotations and denotations are. Think about how connotations make the comics funny. Take your notes to class for a discussion.

B. Ads and Connotations

Look at the ads in your favorite magazine. We all try to ignore the advertisements. They are full of emotional appeals designed to make you want to spend your money on their products. For example, a famous ad reads, "We <u>want</u> to see you <u>smile</u>." For the word "want," the words *wish* or *need* could be used; they mean the same thing. However, *wish* has the connotation of something unlikely to happen, and *need* has the connotation of desperation. For the word "smile," the words *grin* or *smirk* could be used. These last two, while meaning the same facial movement, have negative connotations, and the company wanting you to feel totally comfortable, avoids using them. Look at several ads and note the words that are used to make a reader feel good about the product. Write words that could be used instead but have a negative connotation.

C. News and Connotations

News articles have words which writers carefully choose to persuade readers that their viewpoint is correct. Describing a person as <u>disgruntled</u> has a negative connotation, whereas *unhappy* or *frustrated* are milder words. Read through 3–4 news articles, circling words which do have connotations. Rewrite the sentences with different words and compare the overall effect of the two versions.

Literal and Figurative Meanings

One of the most important things to understand about word meaning is that a word or words can be used in different ways. An author may choose words to tell plain facts, or an author may choose words to give the text a double meaning, or to add **imagery** (pictures in words).

Literal language is words used in their ordinary meaning without exaggeration or inventiveness. Dictionary definitions are written in literal terms. For example, "It is time to feed the <u>cats and dogs</u>." This phrase "cats and dogs" is used in a literal sense for the animals are hungry, and it is time for them to eat.

Figurative language departs from the ordinary meanings of words to emphasize ideas and emotions. Figurative language paints word pictures and allows us to "see" a point. For example: "It is raining <u>cats and dogs</u>!" Cats and dogs do not really fall from the sky like rain as this graphic illustrates. This expression is an **idiom**. An idiom is a common expression or phrase (in a particular language) that has a figurative or imaginative meaning. This sentence really means that the rain is heavy or hard. In this case, it would be difficult or impossible to decide the meaning of an unknown word from the surrounding text.

There are two ways to handle this situation. First, understand the author's purpose for writing a piece of text. If the text is a science book, an employee manual, or a government form, the text's purpose would be to inform. The language in those texts would most likely be literal or factual. Using context clues for these texts would benefit you in finding word meanings. If the text's purpose is to entertain or tell a story, however, context clues may not always work. These kinds of texts often use *idioms, similes, metaphors,* and other *figures of speech* to convey ideas or emotions.

The second way to avoid confusion with the figurative use of words is to become familiar with different idiomatic phrases and with the different types of figurative language: metaphor, simile, personification, hyperbole, and so on.

Read the sentences below, decide the meaning of the **bolded** words or phrases, and, most importantly, think about how you came up with those meanings. On your own paper, write out an explanation of the meaning of each word or phrase and how you decided on this meaning.

1. The Nelsons go swimming once in a **blue moon.**

2. Filing **tax** forms is no one's **cup of tea.**

3. I made a **cup of tea** for lunch.

4. She's a **big cheese** in the Treasury Department, so you should listen to her.

5. Continuing in the **fast lane** of Hollywood society will cost Sloan financially.

Here is an example of how to do a close reading for context clues for the first three sentences. Compare the notes you made on those sentences with the following notes.

READING NOTES:

1. The word "Nelsons" begins with a capital letter, so it must be a family name—"go" is a verb meaning to move or travel—"swimming" is known—"once" is a count of some sort, usually a time—"blue moon" is not known but the moon is often used to figure time.   I think that the swimming is a family activity that this family does not do very often. "Once in a blue moon" sounds close to "once in a while," an idiom

2. "Filing" is a verb meaning putting paperwork in order—"tax" is known to me, what you pay the government—"forms" are documents or paperwork—"no one" is nobody—"cup of tea"—normally means a drinking cup with hot liquid in it. I think that since most of the sentence is about bad stuff, taxes and paperwork, and nobody likes it so a cup of tea must be good. an idiom

3. "I" is the speaker—"made" is a verb meaning to create something—"cup of tea" normally means a drinking cup with hot liquid in it—"lunch" is the midday meal. I think this sentence is just a fact.

Do your notes follow this type of reading? You may go back and change anything you want to in your notes, and discuss with your class the meanings that you decided on for sentences 4 and 5. Then complete the next practice.

Practice 6: Literal and Figurative Meanings

Read each of the following sentences, and then choose the response which is NOT a correct rewording of the sentence.

1. *My parents purchased a new red automobile yesterday.*

    A. My parents bought a new red automobile yesterday.
    B. My parents paid for a new red automobile yesterday.
    C. My parents grasped a new red automobile yesterday.
    D. My parents financed a new red automobile yesterday.

2. *The secret spy set up a red herring for the police.*

    A. The secret spy set up an artful dodge for the police.
    B. The secret spy set up a fish dinner for the police.
    C. ·The secret spy set up a tactic for the police.
    D. The secret spy set up a distraction for the police.

3. *The new guy is making a lot of errors, but his heart is in the right place.*

    A. The new guy is making a lot of errors, but he's healthy.
    B. The new guy is making a lot of errors, but he's sincere.
    C. The new guy is making a lot of errors, but he means well.
    D. The new guy is making a lot of errors, but he has a good attitude.

4. *The extravagant pet food we get for my dog is good for his heart.*

    A. The fabulous pet food we get for my dog is good for his heart.
    B. The superb pet food we get for my dog is good for his heart.
    C. The expensive pet food we get for my dog is good for his heart.
    D. The exaggerated pet food we get for my dog is good for his heart.

5. *Falling off a log can cause grievous harm in treacherous mountain rivers.*

    A. Falling off a log can cause grievous harm in unstable mountain rivers.
    B. Falling off a log can cause grievous harm in false hearted mountain rivers.
    C. Falling off a log can cause grievous harm in unpredictable mountain rivers.
    D. Falling off a log can cause grievous harm in unsafe mountain rivers.

6. *Fly fishing is as easy as falling off a log.*

    A. Fly fishing is as simple as falling off a log.
    B. Fly fishing is as effortless as falling off a log.
    C. Fly fishing is as uncomplicated as falling off a log.
    D. Fly fishing is as instinctive as falling off a log.

IDIOMS

Idioms are phrases or expressions in which the real meaning is different from the literal or stated meaning. For example, the literal meaning of "It's raining cats and dogs" indicates that cats and dogs are falling out of the sky with the rain. However, the real meaning is that the rain is falling heavily from the sky. Another example of an idiom is "The apple does not fall far from the tree." The stated meaning is clear, but the actual meaning is quite different. This expression really says that a child is very similar mentally or physically to a parent.

Practice 7: Idioms

Directions: You can often tell what an idiom means by how it is used in a sentence. In the exercise below, find the best meaning for the underlined idiom in each sentence.

1. Yes, I know everything about her. Her life is <u>an open book</u>.
    A.   written in a book
    B.   boring
    C.   not a secret
    D.   unknown

2. You're constant whining is <u>driving me up the wall</u>.
    A.   making me crazy
    B.   looking at me
    C.   bothering me
    D.   helping me

3. Make an appointment and <u>take up</u> your complaint with Tito.
    A.   get up
    B.   pick up
    C.   go talk about
    D.   drop

4. Do you want your meal for <u>here or to go</u>?
    A.   to eat here or take with you
    B.   to eat here or go without
    C.   today or tomorrow
    D.   to eat here or throw away

5. This teacher is hard on troublemakers, so don't <u>make waves</u> when you're in this class.
    A.   ask questions
    B.   forget your homework
    C.   laugh
    D.   cause a disturbance

6. <u>Knock it off</u>, or I'll tell Dad that you're making a mess!
    A.   quiet down
    B.   open the door
    C.   stop it
    D.   take it out

7. He's bullied us long enough, so today we're going to <u>have it out with</u> Vinny.
    A.   confront
    B.   surprise
    C.   avoid
    D.   meet

8. Mr. Sanchez is so generous that he <u>picked up the tab</u> for our class party.
    A.   got supplies
    B.   ordered the food
    C.   cleaned up
    D.   paid for

9. She <u>caught my eye</u> when she did that amazing dive into the pool.
   A. got my attention
   B. scratched my eye
   C. stared at me
   D. scared me

10. It's hard to decide at the last minute, but <u>off the top of my head,</u> I'd like to go to Six Flags.
    A. in the morning
    B. without thinking
    C. after thinking about it
    D. next week

Practice 8: More Idiom Practice

1. Directions: Make a list of your four favorite idiomatic expressions. Translate them into standard English. Then quiz your classmates on their meaning.

2. Directions: On your own or in a group, write down all the idioms you can make from the following words: ***get, put, take, turn, pick, look, make, dog, cat.*** Examples: get up, get over, etc. Translate them into standard English. Then quiz your classmates on their meaning.

GRAMMATICAL CLASSIFICATION OF WORDS

Once you know the meaning of words, you can use their position and form to determine how they function within a phrase or sentence. For example, look at the functions of words in this sentence.

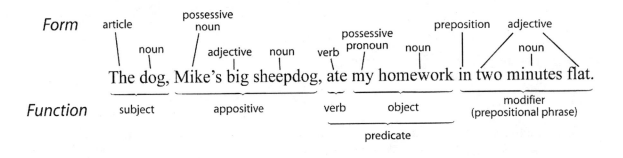

As you know, every complete sentence has a **subject** and a **predicate**. In the simplest sentence, this is a simple subject followed by a verb (example: I am.). Then, other information can be added, such as an **appositive** (a noun or phrase that renames another noun next to it) and an **object** (a noun or phrase that is the recipient of the action in the sentence). An object can be direct, which means it receives the action of a transitive verb.

Example: Dad burnt the toast.

The **direct object**, *the toast*, answers the question of *what* or *when* Dad burnt.

Or, an object can be indirect, meaning it answers the questions *to whom/what* or *for what/whom*. **Indirect objects** are usually placed before direct objects.

> **Example:** Julie gave Paul the letter.

Here, the direct object is *the letter*, as it is receiving the action of the verb (it is being given). The noun *Paul* is the **indirect object**, answering the question, "to whom?"

Practice 9: Grammatical Classification of Words

Read the sentences below and answer the questions that follow each one.

<u>Our yard</u> <u>is filled</u> with a variety <u>of trees and plants.</u> (none of these)
  A   B   C   D

1. In the sentence above, the appositive is _____ .

2. The subject of the sentence is _____ .

3. A prepositional phrase in this sentence is_____ .

4. The simple predicate is _____ .

If I <u>can</u>, I <u>would like</u> to learn <u>the names</u> of all the plants. (none of these)
    A   B   C   D

5. In this sentence, the main verb is_____ .

6. The subject of the sentence is_____ .

7. A direct object in this sentence is_____ .

<u>Learning</u> all the names of these things, <u>the plants</u>, will give <u>me</u> <u>a new hobby</u>!
  A   B   C   D

8. An indirect object in this sentence is_____ .

9. The subject of this sentence is_____ .

10. The appositive in this sentence is_____ .

CHAPTER 1 SUMMARY

Using **context clues** means looking at the way words are used in combination with other words in their setting. Look at the words *around* an unknown word. Context clues can denote:

- comparison
- contrast
- definition or restatement
- example

One important part of word choice is knowing the difference between the **connotations** (emotional associations) and the **denotations** (dictionary meanings) of words.

Literal language is words used in their ordinary meaning without exaggeration or inventiveness. Dictionary definitions are written in literal terms.

Figurative language departs from the ordinary meanings of words to emphasize ideas and emotions. Figurative language paints word pictures and allows us to experience an idea in a concrete way.

Idioms are phrases or expressions in which the real meaning is different from the literal or stated meaning.

Grammatical classification of words can be determined once you know the meaning of the words used and consider their position and function in a sentence.

CHAPTER 1 REVIEW

Read the following article. Then answer the questions that follow.

What Is Ethics, Anyway?

1.   Ethics is a concept we hear about, but few people today stop to think what it really means. However, philosophers and statesmen since the time of Plato have **contemplated** the definition and details of ethics, while others become **tongue-tied** on the topic. Clearly, no one person or even a society invented the concept of ethics, instead, well-founded standards provide a base for ethical concepts.

2.   Some people **equate** ethics with feelings. But being ethical is not simply following one's feelings. A criminal may "feel" robbing a person is okay, when really it is wrong and unethical to steal. Many people may identify ethics with religion, and it is true that most religions include high ethical standards and strong motivation for people to behave morally. But ethics cannot be confined only to religion, or only religious people could be ethical. There are even cases in which religious teaching and ethics clash: for example, some religions **inhibit** the rights of women, which **opposes** the ethical standard of basic justice.

3.   Ethics also is not simply following laws or what is accepted by a society. The laws of civilized nations often embody ethical standards. However, unethical laws can exist. For example, laws have allowed slavery, which is unethical behavior as it takes the freedom of another human being. Therefore, laws and other conventions accepted by a society cannot be the **yardstick** for what is ethical. Doing "whatever society accepts" may be far outside the realm of ethics—Nazi Germany is an example of an ethically **debased** society.

4.   What ethics really refers to is a system of people's moral standards and values. It's **like a road map** of qualities that people want to have to be "decent human beings." It is also the formal study of the standards of human behavior. Ethics relies on well-based standards of "right" (like honesty, compassion, and loyalty) and "wrong" (like stealing, murder, and **fraud**). Ethical standards **encompass** ideas such as respect for others, honesty, justice, doing good, and preventing harm.

1. What is the subject of the first sentence?
   A. Ethics   B. a concept   C. we   D. people

2. In the context of this passage, what does the word **contemplated** mean?
   A. thought about   C. taken apart
   B. looked at   D. examined

3. In this passage, **tongue-tied** is an idiomatic expression that means
   A. excited.   C. speechless.
   B. indifferent.   D. stupid.

4. In the context of this passage, which of the following is closest in meaning to **equate**?
   A. compare   B. multiply   C. make equal   D. flatten

5. In this passage, which of the following is closest in meaning to the word **inhibit**?
   - A. lie about
   - B. live in
   - C. give in to
   - D. hold back

6. In this passage, the word **opposes** comes from the Latin cognate *opponere* which means *put against*. Which of the following English works is derived form *opponere*?
   - A. oppressed
   - B. opposite
   - C. opossum
   - D. opinion

7. In this passage, the word **yardstick** in paragraph 3 is an idiom meaning
   - A. practices.
   - B. view.
   - C. bridge.
   - D. measure.

8. In the fifth sentence of paragraph 3, what is the predicate?
   - A. and other conventions
   - B. accepted by society
   - C. cannot be the yardstick
   - D. for what is ethical

9. Which dictionary definition of the word **debased** best applies to its use in the passage?
   - A. depraved
   - B. enlightened
   - C. impure
   - D. distorted

10. In this passage, **like a road map** is a figurative expression that means
    - A. confusion.
    - B. system.
    - C. book.
    - D. evolution.

11. In this passage, the word **fraud** is from the Latin cognate *fraus* which means *deceit*. Which of the following English words is also derived from *fraus*?
    - A. frog
    - B. draw
    - C. break
    - D. fraudulent

12. In this passage, which of the following is closest in meaning to the word **encompass**?
    - A. steer
    - B. include
    - C. begin
    - D. mean

13. The word *ideas* which follows **encompass** serves what function in this sentence?
    - A. modifier
    - B. predicate
    - C. direct object
    - D. indirect object

Read the following passage, and then answer the questions that follow.

Have you been to the new skateboard park? If not, you've got to go—it is so awesome! It is called Skateboard Survivor Park. The entire complex is arranged so that skateboarders have complete **jurisdiction**. The park's property is a sprawling 27 acres of convenient urban land, close to your neighborhood.

The **empathetic** leader of the venture is J. C. Powell, a compassionate and revered educator. Mr. Powell's idea for this park was that it be a safe but challenging course for fanatical skateboarders. After only a few crises, construction was completed on schedule. The master-of-ceremonies' speech and **subsequent** interviews were made on skateboards; an official showed off the park's unique features. They are **comprised** of grinding rails, half-pipes, ramps, multilevel shelves, and spirals for extreme speed and complicated maneuvers. I **previewed** the park and saw some skateboarders shooting around **like torpedoes** and others bailing out like **falling dominoes**. A **prodigious**, brand-new skateboarding splash fountain has been put in for cooling off and jumping off. The **stupendous** food court, three stories high, can be reached by avenues that are marked "Skateboard Traffic Only." There is a **nominal** entrance fee that gives you the run of the park for as long as you can survive or until closing time. You can also get an **annual** season's pass and come every day for a year. I don't know about you, but I'm voting to grab my board and head over there right now!

The entire complex is arranged so that skateboarders have complete **jurisdiction**.

14. The word *jurisdiction* <u>most nearly</u> means
    - A. protection.
    - B. administration.
    - C. freedom.
    - D. control.

The **empathetic** leader of the venture is J. C. Powell, a compassionate and revered educator.

15. The word *empathetic* <u>most nearly</u> means
    - A. apathetic.
    - B. understanding.
    - C. strict.
    - D. charismatic.

The master-of-ceremonies' speech and **subsequent** interviews were made on skateboards; an official showed off the park's unique features.

16. The word *subsequent* <u>most nearly</u> means
    - A. following.
    - B. previous.
    - C. related.
    - D. startling.

They are **comprised** of grinding rails, half-pipes, ramps, multilevel shelves and spirals for extreme speed and complicated maneuvers.

17. The words *comprised of* <u>most nearly</u> mean
    - A. maximized.
    - B. measured.
    - C. scattered.
    - D. constructed.

I **previewed** the park and saw some skateboarders shooting around like torpedoes and others bailing out like dominoes.

18. The word *previewed* <u>most nearly</u> means
    - A. investigated.
    - B. gave a quick look to.
    - C. looked at ahead of time.
    - D. showed up at.

19. In this passage, the figurative meaning of **like torpedoes** portrays what quality of the skateboarders?
    A. speed
    B. grace
    C. daring
    D. agility

> A **prodigious**, brand-new skateboarding splash fountain has been put in for cooling off and jumping off.

20. What is the predicate in this sentence?
    A. brand-new skateboarding splash fountain
    B. has been put in
    C. has been put in for cooling off
    D. cooling off and jumping off

21. The word *prodigious* <u>most nearly</u> means
    A. wonderful.
    B. very large.
    C. thoughtful.
    D. harmless.

> The **stupendous** food court, three stories high, can be reached by avenues that are marked "Skateboard Traffic Only."

22. The word *stupendous* <u>most nearly</u> means
    A. stupid.
    B. sturdy.
    C. exciting.
    D. exceptional.

> There is a **nominal** entrance fee that gives you the run of the park for as long as you can survive or until closing time.

23. The word *nominal* <u>most nearly</u> means
    A. beginning.
    B. very small.
    C. amount.
    D. reasonable.

> You can also get an **annual** season's pass and come every day for a year.

24. The word *annual* <u>most nearly</u> means
    A. weekly.
    B. quarterly.
    C. monthly.
    D. yearly.

25. Which of the following is classified as an appositive?
    A. *close to your neighborhood* (from sentence 5)
    B. *a compassionate and revered educator* (from sentence 6)
    C. *and complicated maneuvers* (from sentence 10)
    D. *three stories high* (from sentence 13)

Chapter 2
Reading for Understanding

This chapter addresses the following expectation(s) and their related indicators from **Core Learning Goal 1**: **Reading. Reviewing and Responding to Texts**

Expectation 1.1	The student will use effective strategies before, during, and after reading, viewing, and listening to self-selected and assigned materials.
Expectation 1.2	The student will construct, examine, and extend meaning of traditional and contemporary works recognized as having significant literary merit.
Expectation 1.3	The student will explain and give evidence to support perceptions about print and non-print works
Expectation 4.2	The student will assess the effectiveness of choice of details, organizational pattern, word choice, syntax, use of figurative language, and rhetorical devices.

Have you ever considered the fact that reading might be **the single most valuable skill** that a person needs? If you can read well, you can learn about anything. While other talents and abilities are important as you progress through your education, reading is the foundation on which everything is built. Almost anything you want to know or learn about, you can learn by reading.

MAIN IDEAS

The **main idea**, the primary message, or the central point of a passage, will many times be stated directly in the title, the thesis statement, or the conclusion. Sometimes, however, the main idea may only be implied rather than stated directly. Both fiction and nonfiction can contain main ideas.

DIRECTLY STATED OR EXPLICIT MAIN IDEA IN A PASSAGE

At times, you need to locate the **directly stated main idea**. As you review the text, pick out key words and ideas in the title and in the first sentences and last sentences of all the paragraphs. To practice, choose the best statement or restatement of the main idea in the following passage.

East Meets West

(1) It is amazing how the Japanese have retained their cultural heritage while simultaneously integrating many parts of Western culture. One of the most popular adaptations is the style of dress. Many Japanese today wear "Western" style clothing such as business suits, active wear, jeans and T-shirts. Traditional clothing is often reserved for special occasions.

(2) Many Japanese also have adopted Western furnishings into their homes. It is not unusual to have a completely westernized home with only one traditional Japanese room. Western influences can be seen throughout Japanese popular culture, such as fast-food restaurants, music, and the movies.

(3) The Japanese also have more time to devote to leisure. Surveys show that spending time with family, friends, home improvement, shopping, and gardening form the mainstream of leisure, together with sports, and travel. The number of Japanese making overseas trips has increased notably in recent years. Domestic travel, picnics, hiking, and cultural events rank high among favorite activities.

(4) Japan is a land with a vibrant and fascinating history, varied culture, traditions, and customs that are hundreds of years old, yet segments of its society and economy are as new as the microchips in a personal computer.

1. The **best** statement of the main idea is which of the following?

   A. In Japan, you will find evidence of both traditional customs and culture as well as examples of Western-style adaptations.

   B. In Japan, jeans, fast-food, picnics, and personal computers are very popular.

   C. In Japan, people always enjoy traveling overseas, and shopping.

   D. Japanese and American culture are so similar that you really cannot tell the difference between them.

As you review this passage, you will look for key words and sentences in each paragraph. Once again, the title, the first sentences of each paragraph, and the last sentence of the passage contain the key words **Japan**, **culture**, **customs**, **traditions**, **Western-style**, and **adaptation**. Since choice *A* contains all of these key ideas, it would be the best restatement of the main idea of the passage.

Choices *B* and *C* focus only on a few details in the passage. Choice *D* is incorrect because the facts in the passage indicate that the Japanese still maintain some of their traditions. Therefore, Japanese and American cultures are not identical.

IMPLIED OR IMPLICIT MAIN IDEA

First, let's look at the meaning of the word "implied." Consider the following sentence.

Outside, the wind was bitterly cold, and the snow was falling fast.

What season of the year is it? It is winter, of course. Does the sentence state that it is winter? The answer is no, but you can tell it is winter because of the description. If the word "winter" were in the sentence, the season would be **directly stated**. Because the season is described without using the word "winter," the season of the year is **implied** or **implicit**. You may read a paragraph where the **main idea is implied** rather than directly stated. Then, you must develop a different set of strategies to identify the main idea. You are still looking for the central point of the paragraph, but the author may include only details and facts in the selection. No one sentence summarizes the entire paragraph, but together these sentences revolve around a main idea that is not directly stated. The reader must infer what that idea is.

A good approach for determining an implied main idea could be learned by reviewing the paragraph below. Read this paragraph, and answer the question that follows.

Putting Energy Back Into Your Life

Are you getting enough water? Think of your houseplants. When they are short on water, they droop. The same thing happens to you! Our bodies are made up of millions of cells; the principal part of these cells is water. If the cells are low on water, you will function at less than full efficiency. Strive to drink six to eight glasses of water each day.

1. What is the main idea of this paragraph?

   A. Houseplants need water to live.
   B. The body's cells are composed of a high percentage of water.
   C. Our bodies are made up of millions of cells.
   D. Drink water because your body needs it to be efficient.

As you reread this paragraph and its question about the main idea, you learn from the title that the topic is **regaining energy**. However, this paragraph does not deal specifically with regaining energy. Only by examining the whole passage is this topic fully discussed. So the main idea of this paragraph is about the importance of water but not about regaining lost energy. Reading each sentence will help you figure out the main idea.

If you combine all of these factual sentences together, you can arrive at a main idea about the paragraph. That statement, of course, is *D* in your choice of answers. Even though *D* is not directly stated, it is a broad enough summary of all the other sentences in the paragraph. Therefore, it is the **main idea**. The other choices (*A, B* or *C*) are specific facts mentioned in the paragraph, but they are not broad enough to be the main point.

Practice 1: Main Ideas

Read the following passages. The passages have stated or implied main ideas. Find the main idea for each passage.

1. **Volunteering**

Nothing can be more satisfying in life than taking the opportunity to volunteer. Taking time out of your play and work schedule to spend with others can be very rewarding. For instance, spending time with cancer patients in the children's wing of the hospital is really special. Playing games and reading books to the children just make you feel tingly inside knowing you brought a smile to a little child.

One volunteer, Dalilah, made a special impression on the children by teaching them to finger paint with their hands and with their feet. She also taught them magic tricks with coins and handkerchiefs. Everyone who volunteers, whether they teach the children something or just listen to them, makes a difference in their lives. That is what volunteering is all about—making a difference!

A. Nothing can be more satisfying in life than taking the opportunity to volunteer.

B. Volunteering is about making a difference!

C. Everyone who volunteers, whether they teach the children something or just listen to them, makes a difference in their lives.

D. Spending time with sick children reading them stories and playing games with them makes you feel tingly inside.

2. **The House is Burning!**

I was so mad when my mom came home from work and announced that we all had to plan and practice a fire escape plan. We had to go outside as quickly as possible from whatever room we were in when Mom rang the bell. My job was to grab my little brother Josh. We had to meet under the maple tree outside our house. Since there were five of us, Mom assigned us numbers in case she forgot our names in all of the excitement. I hated practicing these fire drills because we had to do them in school, too.

One day after two years of these monthly drills, my sister Ashley was playing with logs in the fireplace. Sparks jumped out of the fire and started burning up the living room carpet. Eagerly, the flames licked the furniture and the wallpaper. Smoke filled all of the rooms, setting off our twelve smoke detectors. It was our familiarity with the escape plan that saved our lives, valuables, and even our pets, Sooty  and Foofoo. Unlike our neighbors who lost all of their valuables in a fire, we were able to save many important pictures and other items that had been in our family for decades.

A. I was so mad when my mom came home from work and announced that we all had to plan and practice a fire escape plan.

B. Unlike our neighbors who lost all of their valuables in a fire, we were able to save many important pictures and other items that had been in our family for decades.

C. I hated practicing these fire drills because we had to do them in school, too.

D. Practicing fire drills is worthwhile when lives and property are saved.

3.   **All the World's a Stage**

Stella and her new friend, Max, were in line for lunch in the cafeteria. Max had just finished telling Stella about the self-defense class he was taking after school. Stella asked Max, "Why don't you show me one of the special self-defense moves you learned?"

"Sure," Max said. "Just watch this!" Max, full of concentration, tilted his head forward and slammed it into his cafeteria tray. Stella and the rest of the lunch-room looked up in shock to see that Max had broken the cafeteria tray, and the skin on his forehead was wide open.

"Are you OK?" Stella asked while Max tried to recover from his display of power.

"Of course I am," Max said as he groped for a napkin to cover the bleeding wound.

"What does breaking a cafeteria tray have to do with self-defense?" Stella asked. Max couldn't respond. He could only see stars spinning quickly around his head.

When Max returned from the hospital, he was just fine except for the thin line of stitches he had on his forehead. One day several weeks later, Max was once again in line next to Stella at lunch. He turned to her and said, "That self-defense move turned out badly. Let me show you a new move I learned in gymnastics class!"

"Please," Stella said, "no more special tricks. Just be yourself, and stick to what you do best."

A.   Just be yourself, and stick to what you do best.
B.   Showing risky tricks in the cafeteria can be dangerous.
C.   You should practice self-defense moves frequently before you show them to others.
D.   You can learn new ways to show off in self-defense and gymnastics classes.

READING STRATEGIES

At some time in your life, you have probably watched running or track events. You may even participate in track or be a runner yourself. Runners learn an important skill that they apply to their individual events—they learn to pace themselves. If someone is running a marathon, he or she has to run at a fairly steady speed in order to last for the entire 26 miles! On the other hand, sprinters need to hit their maximum speed as quickly as possible since they are running a short distance. And, like any other sport, track has its own strategies and tactics.

When you read, you need to be aware of your purpose and vary your strategies to suit the situation just as a runner would. There are three main types of reading strategies that are helpful to know: pre-reading, during reading and, after reading strategies.

PRE-READING STRATEGIES

Pre-reading, or **surveying,** is a way to look over written material and get a general idea what it is about without reading the details. This is also the fastest type of reading because in surveying you read **titles** or **headings, subtitles** or **subheadings,** and **topic sentences** as you look over a page. You also note any **words or terms that are bolded,** since they are obviously important. Noticing any **illustrations, charts,** or **graphs** is also helpful. Pre-reading, or surveying, is the type of reading you would want to do if you are glancing over something like a magazine article to see if it has any potential information for a report. If you have some difficult material to read, pre-reading it first will give you an idea of what the material is about. It gives you an overview of the topic which is helpful before you read more carefully.

DURING READING STRATEGIES

During reading strategies are also important for understanding what you are reading. For example, practice **think-alouds** as you read. Think about and verbalize what you are reading. Write down any thoughts or questions about the material in the text margins, in a journal or on a computer. You should also **underline** or **highlight** key ideas and facts. Make annotations or abbreviations next to main ideas, details and new words. For example, *MI* can stand for main idea, *D* could represent detail and you could circle new words.

AFTER-READING STRATEGIES

After-reading strategies occur when you finish your reading assignment. The purpose of after-reading strategies is to better understand what you have read and to help you remember key ideas and details from the selection. For example, you can create a **concept map** of the chapter or article you read. A concept map is a visual aid that shows the key ideas, details and terms you learned. Most likely, your teachers have taught you to make concept maps in your English, Science, or Social Studies classes.

Creating **study cards** is also a useful after reading strategy. Purchase 5 × 8 index cards. Then write one question on each card from your chapter review, and write the answer on the back of the card. You can also use questions from your during reading strategies. Then, either in a small group or on your own, practice answering the questions on the front of each card before confirming the correct answer on the back of each card.

Whenever you have a reading task to do, consider the purpose and importance of the material and what you need to get out of it, and then approach the task in the most effective way. Using pre-reading, during reading, and after reading strategies is an important way to better remember and understand what you read.

PRIOR KNOWLEDGE AND PREDICTING IN READING

Prior knowledge refers to past experiences and ideas that you recall as you are reading new information. For example, let's say that you are reading a story about a neighborhood fire. The author describes the fire trucks racing to the scene with sirens blaring and yellow lights flashing everywhere. As you read, recall our past experiences and use those images and words to picture the **new** story you are reading. The story becomes easier and more exciting to read because you can connect our memories of real fire fighting or even fire fighting seen on the television news with the story you are now reading.

PREDICTING

Predicting is making a guess about what might happen next in a story you are reading. For example, if you are reading a story about fire trucks racing to a neighborhood fire, you think ahead and try to naturally start to figure out what might happen next. Your curious mind will race forward to the next scene even before the fire trucks arrive. This is one way authors hook their readers into the story so they stay with the story to the very last word.

Of course, your predictions may not always be correct. Let's say that you predict that fire trucks will arrive in time to stop the fire and save the residents. However, as you read further, you find out that the building cannot be saved, but the firemen are able to save the people. Then at least part of your prediction was true. More importantly, the excitement of predicting kept you reading until the end of the story.

To illustrate what predicting is, look at the following sign that is often seen along highways and interstate roads.

You know that the sign portrays a deer crossing the road. Therefore, you could predict that you should drive with more caution because you could hit a deer up ahead.

For further practice, read the following paragraph and then answer the questions.

Many people believe that Africa is full of jungles populated by wild beasts and primitive people with strange customs. From books and movies, others imagine hunters in loincloths throwing spears at elephants and zebras. However, Africa is quite different from what people believe. For example, much of Africa is not jungle but mostly desert or grasslands. You would find less wildlife than expected, and most of these animals live on reserves. Besides small villages, Africa contains large modern cities like Lagos, Nigeria, and Nairobi, Kenya. And instead of hunters in loincloths, many Africans dress just like Americans.

1. According to the passage, if you visited Nairobi, Kenya, how would the men **most likely** be dressed?

   A.   in dashikis

   B.   in pants and shirts

   C.   in robes

   D.   in loincloths

2. If cities in Africa grow larger, what will probably happen to the wildlife?

    A. Wildlife will be seen only in zoos.
    C. Wildlife will be seen only in its natural habitat.
    B. Wildlife will become extinct.
    D. Most wildlife will be seen only in reserves.

To answer question 1, you would look for any facts in the passage that will support your prediction. Since the last sentence states that "many Africans dress just like Americans," the best answer would be *B*. Since American men generally wear pants and shirts, many Africans in large cities would probably dress the same way.

The clearest clue for question 2 is sentence 5 in the paragraph. Less African wildlife is now living in jungles and grasslands. Consequently, a logical prediction would be that as cities get bigger, reserves will probably be the only place you will see wildlife like elephants and zebras. Therefore, *D* is the best answer.

You can use your prior knowledge and predicting strategies before, during, and after you read fiction or nonfiction. Your past experiences and education are essential for learning new information. At the same time, your ability to absorb new knowledge from the written page accelerates when you use your prior knowledge and your predicting skills.

FORMULATING QUESTIONS

Another reading strategy is to formulate questions as you begin reading. Asking questions that can be answered by the text will set some goals and allow you to find important information. Formulate questions using terms such as w*ho*, *what*, *where*, *when*, *why*, *how*, *compare*, *contrast*, *describe*, and *explain*.

DRAWING CONCLUSIONS

Drawing a conclusion is a useful reading strategy. When you draw a conclusion, you form a judgment or opinion based on the details in a passage. S.I. Hayakawa once said that conclusions are *statements about the unknown made on the basis of the known*. To draw conclusions, use all the facts and clues present in the passage.

Read the following paragraph and then answer the question.

> At a signal from the captain, the propeller had been disengaged and the fins placed vertically; then the *Nautilus* had shot up at a terrifying speed, like a balloon being carried into the atmosphere. It cut through the water with a loud quivering noise. We could see nothing. In four minutes, we had covered the four leagues between us and the surface, and after leaping into the air like a flying fish, we came hurtling back down onto the water, making it splash up to a prodigious height.
>
> – Jules Verne *20,000 Leagues Under the Sea*

Based on this paragraph, we can conclude that

    A. the Nautilus was descending into the ocean.
    B. the Nautilus was a flying fish named by the captain.
    C. the Nautilus rose out of the ocean with great force.
    D. the Nautilus raced across the ground at amazing speeds.

To choose the best answer for this question, you should first read the paragraph carefully, paying special attention to the facts and details. Secondly, the question requires you to draw the right conclusion, so you need to narrow your choices to responses that contain stated information from the paragraph. You also should eliminate responses that do not contain facts or details from the passage.

Following this process of logic, you will disregard *A*. Rather than descending, the author says the *Nautilus* "shot up" and leapt "into the air like a flying fish." *B* would be eliminated because the passage does not mention the captain naming the *Nautilus* after a flying fish. The *Nautilus* is compared to a flying fish, but this is different from the *B* response. Choice *D* is not appropriate because the *Nautilus* "cut through the water" and made a splash. Therefore, the best answer is *C*. The facts and details about cutting through water and covering "four leagues between us and the surface," lead us to the conclusion: the *Nautilus* "shot up" and rose out of the ocean with great force.

SUMMARIZING A PASSAGE

The **summary** of a passage is a written statement that contains the message in a passage. Being able to write a summary shows that you understand what you are reading.

Read this passage and choose the best summary.

> The youth gave a shriek as he confronted the thing. He was, for moments, turned to stone before it. He remained staring into the liquid-looking eyes. The dead man and the living man exchanged a long look. Then the youth cautiously put one hand behind him and brought it against a tree. Leaning upon this he retreated, step by step, with his face still toward the thing. He feared that if he turned his back the body might spring up and stealthily pursue him.
>
> – Stephen Crane, <u>Red Badge of Courage</u>

Which of the following statements is the **<u>best</u>** summary for the passage?

A. The living and the dead form bonds of love.
B. Death should not be feared.
C. Never speak badly about the dead.
D. Confronting death can be terrifying.

In choosing your answer, you must determine which statement best expresses the message or meaning in the passage. It should be a statement that most appropriately applies to the events described in the selection. Therefore, the correct answer is *D*.

While the other choices contain general truths, they do not apply specifically to this passage. For example, *A* focuses on love between the living and the dead while the details in the passage convey fear and dread. Likewise, *B* ignores the fear so apparent in the description. Finally, *C* is incorrect because the youth never speaks badly about the dead person. His shock is so great that all he can do is shriek in fear.

Practice 2: Reading Strategies

Read the following passages. Then choose the best response.

1. Before your family's annual Fourth of July picnic, you bought a
    horseshoe set at a yard sale. All of the parts are there, except for
    the directions, so you're not sure how to set up the stakes. Which
    of the following would be the best way to get the information you
    need?

    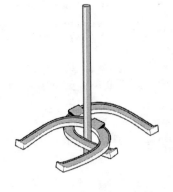

    A. Look up "horseshoes" in the unabridged dictionary.
    B. Go to the library and check out a book on games. Carefully
        read the entire chapter on pitching horseshoes.
    C. Call the manufacturer of the horseshoe set, and ask a cus-
        tomer service representative how to place the stakes.
    D. Look up horseshoes in a general encyclopedia, and pre-read
        the article for information on setting up the stakes.

2. Elijah went to the library to gather information for his history class research paper. He found five
    articles on a database that matched his key words. Elijah printed them out so he could take them
    home. What is the best way for him to make efficient use of his study time?

    A. Elijah should find the key words and phrases in the articles and copy those sentences. He
        should be sure to use those sentences as quotes in his paper.
    B. Elijah should pre-read the articles looking for the key words and phrases. Then he should
        use during reading strategies for those particular sections to determine if they have informa-
        tion that is needed for his paper.
    C. Elijah should practice during reading strategies in each article very carefully and in depth. If
        the database matched them to his key words, they are sure to have very important informa-
        tion in them that will be needed in his paper.
    D. Elijah should pre-read the articles and look for the key words. When he finds them, he
        should use after reading strategies in those sections for information.

3. Michelle was absent from school for a week when she had the flu. She has to make up a biology
    test covering chapters 4 and 5. What is the best approach to prepare for the test?

    A. Michelle should pre-read the chapters to get an overview of what they cover. She then needs
        to apply during reading strategies to each chapter, rereading sections that are unclear. She
        should also answer the chapter questions, study any terms, and do the usual preparation for a
        test.
    B. Michelle should read each chapter one time to get the information. Then she should pre-read
        over the chapter questions to get an idea of the important points and check the definitions of
        any new terms in the chapters.
    C. Michelle should answer all of the chapter questions by reviewing the chapters to find the
        answers. She should just pre-read each chapter to find the definitions of terms. If anything
        seems especially difficult, she should read those sections in depth but not the entire chapter.
    D. Michelle should pre-read each chapter to get an overview, then use during reading strategies
        in the chapters to get a little more information and finally, answer the chapter questions after
        reading the particular sections in depth as necessary to answer the questions.

4. Omar is starting to read *Walden* by Henry David Thoreau. He doesn't understand why this American author would want to live alone away from people near a pond for two years. In his culture, people always live together in large families. Which of the following reading strategies would best help him understand the author's actions?

    A. Study pictures of Thoreau's family and his home to learn more about his personality.

    B. Imagine a world where Omar could live where no one would know or bother him for a long time.

    C. Omar should develop some prior knowledge of the book by researching Thoreau and the Transcendentalist Movement in literature.

    D. Consider that in Thoreau's culture, everyone lived great distances from each other, and people left their families at an early age.

5. Scott just read a newspaper article about the annual Shriners' parade downtown next Friday. Many of the streets along the parade route will be closed to car traffic with no regular parking available. Since he cannot drive to his job downtown on that day, Scott decided to find another way to get to his job, so he checks out the city bus route on the Internet. Which of the following reading strategies is Scott most likely using?

    A. surveying   B. pre-reading   C. summarizing   D. predicting

Hurricanes

Hurricanes are cyclones caused by very low barometric pressure. Their characteristic center, or eye, is an area of relative calm encircled by powerful winds and storms. Once a tropical cyclone reaches winds of 74 mph, it is technically called a hurricane. The National Hurricane Center in Miami, Florida keeps track of storm formation using all types of monitoring devices to determine location and wind velocity. The center then broadcasts information needed by local weather officials to track the progress of the storm and to take the proper steps to warn citizens and visitors of a hurricane's approach.

6. Based on this passage, a valid conclusion would be that

    A. a storm with winds of 80 mph is classified as a hurricane.

    B. hurricanes are caused by rising barometric pressure.

    C. it is impossible to predict a hurricane.

    D. no one knows how fast the winds are in a hurricane.

Flight

When Orville Wright made the first powered airplane flight in 1903 at speeds of 50 kilometers (31 miles) per hour, the significance of his achievement was barely recognized. Yet in little more than half a century following that historic event at Kitty Hawk, astronauts succeeded in orbiting the Earth at speeds measured in thousands of miles per hour and set foot on the Moon.

7. Which is a valid conclusion?
   A. Orville Wright was widely praised for the first powered airplane flight in 1903.
   B. Orville Wright was a pioneer of the Space Age.
   C. Many tourists visit Kitty Hawk each year.
   D. Orville Wright thought he was a failure

Directions: Read each passage. Then select the best summary.

8. We need to remember as well as to celebrate the end of World War I. We need to remember the dead and the wounded, the widows and orphans, the destroyed and broken homes, farms, and businesses. We need to remember these casualties of war. We must prevent another such war from happening.

   – from a newspaper editorial about World War I

   A. Widows and orphans should remember the dead and wounded.
   B. War is part of the human condition.
   C. Remember those who were lost or wounded in the war.
   D. We must prevent war in the future.

9. An old male elephant was dying in the African wilderness. A group of elephants from his herd gathered around this male, trying to get him to stand up. They tried to stroke him with their trunks, raise him with their tusks and put food in his mouth. Nothing seemed to work, so the herd left. However, a mother and her calf remained, standing with their backs to the dead elephant. The mother tried to touch the dead elephant with one foot. Then the herd returned and began circling the dead companion. After a time, they gathered tree branches and grass clumps, scattering these items on or around the body.

   A. Elephants often die alone in the wilderness.
   B. Some animals perform rituals to mourn their dead.
   C. Death is a fact of life in the African wilderness.
   D. The elephant population in Africa is declining because they are hunted and killed.

AUTHOR'S PURPOSE

Now, let's learn more about the concepts and skills that will help you to identify an author's purpose, draw conclusions, make predictions, and summarize text.

As you are reading the text, one thing you want to determine is the author's purpose in writing the selection.

Read the following two passages to determine the author's purpose in writing them.

To the Editor:

Listen up fellow students! As class president, I have a lot of demands on my time, so I'm only going to say this once. Stop drinking those supercharged caffeine sodas! During these last few weeks of exams, I've been seeing people walking around with glazed eyes and jittery hands until they pick up their first morning soda and drink it quickly. Then they show the worst signs of the hyper, ill-tempered caffeine and sugar addicts. The ads on commercials make drinking sodas look so cool. Not true. As students, we need to get smarter and to declare war on the dangers of caffeine and the chemicals in sodas. If you are one of the unfortunate people who can't make it through the day without at least five super-sized colas, take a good look in the mirror and ask yourself how you feel. Then ask yourself "why?" The answer may lie inside your next bottle of soda.

Matt Patel, Class President for 2007

---

excerpt from the Professional Journal of Serious Medical Practitioners' Chronicle

The nation's top research labs are conducting studies into the effects of caffeine and phosphates on the health of teenage students. The Behemoth Chemical Co-op carried out the longest study. It lasted for six months. The study used two groups of college students, a study group that drank soda each day and a control group that drank only sugary mineral water each day.

At the end of the study, the directors found high levels of caffeine, phosphates, blood sugar, and calcium in the study group's blood readings showing that the phosphates were stripping the students' bones of calcium. The tests showed that the students began to develop morning headaches, irritability and mood changes, and feelings of ill health. The control group didn't report the same experience. The blood level readings for the control group had no large differences for the directors to note. The federal government plans to pay for more studies.

Reading for Understanding

Every author writes for a **specific purpose**. You can understand what the author's intent or purpose is from the way an author writes. Look back to the passages about caffeine in soft drinks. Both are written with the viewpoint that sodas or soft drinks can be harmful. Notice the different language used in each one. Which one is written to persuade and which one is written to inform? Matt Patel's editorial to his fellow students is meant to **persuade** them to avoid sodas and colas. On the other hand, the Behemoth Chemical Co-op study is designed to **inform** readers about the dangers of sodas based on a careful research experiment.

An author writing **to inform** will use tone or language that is almost formal. Looking at the professional journal entry about sodas, you can see that the reader is not asked to agree with the findings, the reader is not being directly spoken to with the pronoun "you," there is no strong descriptive language (like best or worst), and there is no appeal for the reader to buy something. (That is one of the most common abuses of persuasive language.) The text is written simply to inform the readers of the results of a research study.

In the following chart, learn the typical purposes authors use in fiction and nonfiction texts.

Purpose	Definition	Reading Selection
to inform	to present facts and details	"Ocean Fishes"
to entertain	to amuse or offer enjoyment	"The Time I Slipped in the Mud"
to persuade	to urge action on an issue	"Raise Penalties for Polluters"
to instruct	to teach concepts and facts	"Tips for Healthy Living"
to create suspense	to convey uncertainty	"Will Tom Win the Race?"
to motivate	to incite	"You can Lose Weight"
to cause doubt	to be skeptical	"Are Adults Responsible?"
to describe an event	to narrate	"9/11/01: America Attacked!"
to teach a lesson	to furnish knowledge	"Mastering Exponents"
to introduce a character	to describe a person's traits	"First Look at Captain Nemo"
to create a mood	to establish atmosphere	"Gloom in the House of Usher"
to relate an adventure	to tell an exciting story	"Lost in a Cave"
to share a personal experience	to tell about an event in your life	"The Time I Learned to Share"
to describe feelings	to communicate emotions through words	"When My Dog Died"

Practice 3: Author's Purpose

Based on the chart of author's purposes, identify the purpose for each of the following reading passages. Then discuss your choices with your class or the instructor.

excerpt from Gen. Robert E. Lee, *Letter to His Son*
Jan. 23, 1861

1.   The South, in my opinion, has been aggrieved by the acts of the North, as you say. I feel the aggression and am willing to take every proper step for redress. It is the principle I fight for, not individual or private benefit. As an American citizen, I take great pride in my country, her prosperity and institutions, and would defend any state if her rights were invaded. But I can anticipate no greater calamity for the country than a dissolution of the Union. It would be an accumulation of all the evils we complain of, and I am willing to sacrifice everything but honor for its preservation. I hope, therefore, that all constitutional means will be exhausted before there is a resort to force.

A.   to inform   C.   to persuade

B.   to describe feelings   D.   to introduce a character

2.   **To the Editor:**

     A nation's shame should never be hidden. A nation's society is so large that to try to hide any wrong would be to grow an even greater evil. To hide a national wrong, every man, woman and child would have to turn a blind eye, would have to wash blood from their hands, would have to deny their fellow citizens and would have to tremble in utter silence so to bury truth. The wrong I want you to consider today is the shameful event of the United States government forcing 110,000 Japanese American citizens into ten military internment camps. Though the cowardice and ruthless cruelty occurred in 1942, sixty years ago, the silence of our nation's people has never been displayed for the evil that it was and still is. It is time for us, as part of a global community, to accept the damnation of the world for one of the most self-righteous displays of human rights violations that has been suffered upon the face of the earth. Join with me in this rewriting of the "glorious" history of the United States government in the era of World War II.

A. to relate an adventure   C. to create suspense

B. to create a mood   D. to persuade

3.   **excerpt from *Tongia's Court of Law Journal***

     The legal brief, prepared for the case before the Federal Appeals Court, included some unclear testimony. The case involves a dispute or a fight between friends on a tennis team. There are three eyewitnesses to the event. All have given their statements to the authorities. One eyewitness says that he only heard the fight as his eyes were temporarily blinded by an overuse of sunscreen. The second eyewitness says that he only saw the argument as he had on his CD Walkman. The third eyewitness says that as an elected government official he cannot say anything for sure about the matter. The case is to be remanded to the state court.

A. to create a mood

C. to teach a lesson

B. to inform

D. to motivate

VOICE

Voice refers to how an author connects with an audience and uses appropriate point of view to convey ideas through writing. It encompasses tone, sense of audience, and sense of originality. This is accomplished through the choice of words and language used to describe an author's ideas and make his point.

AUDIENCE

Authors must consider the **audience**—the person(s) who will read what they write. Unless you are writing in your journal or taking notes in class, you are always writing for a particular audience. It may be your teacher, a friend, your parents, or a manager at work. Knowing your audience gives you important information including the following:

the audience's interest:	what topics or information is of interest to the audience (so you can capture the interest of your readers)
the audience's prior knowledge:	what the audience already knows (so you don't tell the readers something they already know, and you can draw on that prior knowledge)
the audience's vocabulary:	words that the readers understand (so you don't use words that are too easy or too difficult)
what the audience needs to know:	information or explanations that you want the audience to know (so you can choose what information to include)

Read the following two paragraphs written by the same person. Try to develop a picture of the audience that the writer had in mind.

Example 1: Since you're in the market for a new car, I wanted to tell you about mine. My new car is the best one I've owned. It's a 2005 Puma. It's got a 5.0 L overhead cam engine with multi-port fuel injection. It can do 0–60 m.p.h. in 5 seconds. With that much engine, passing cars on the highway is a breeze, but handling corners on back roads is a little trickier than with my old pickup. I love the rush I get when I'm cruising around with my new wheels. You should consider buying one, too.

Example 2: Since you're in the market for a new car, I wanted to tell you about mine. My new car is the best one I've owned. It's a 2005 Puma. This sporty two-door is canary yellow with electric blue racing stripes and silver mag wheels. It has cordovan leather seats and a concert-hall-quality sound system. The sunroof is the perfect finishing touch. You should see the looks I get when I'm cruising around with my new wheels. You should consider buying one, too.

In both paragraphs, the author is telling someone about a new car, but each paragraph includes very different details about the car. Based on these differences, how would you describe the intended audience of each paragraph? What evidence is there for your description?

AUDIENCE INTEREST

How does the writer try to catch the audience's interest in each paragraph? Clearly, the first paragraph is intended for a reader who is interested in a car's power and performance. So, the writer describes the car's engine as well as the car's speed and handling. The second paragraph, on the other hand, mentions nothing about performance. The writer assumes that the audience is concerned with appearance and style, so the description focuses on colors and high-priced options.

AUDIENCE KNOWLEDGE

What does the writer assume that the audience already knows? Since the reader of the first paragraph is interested in performance, the writer assumes that the reader knows what a Puma is and that going 0 – 60 mph in 5 seconds is fast. The reader of the second paragraph may need the author to describe the Puma as a "sporty two-door," but the reader understands well the stunning colors and fine accessories of the new car.

AUDIENCE VOCABULARY

What kinds of words will the audience be familiar with and understand easily? The writer expects the reader of the first paragraph to know technical terms like "5.0 L" and "multi-port fuel injection." While these terms may speak loudly and clearly to the reader of the first paragraph, they may mean nothing to the reader of the second paragraph who appreciates "cordovan leather" and a "concert-hall-quality sound system." Likewise, the reader of the first paragraph may have no use for these terms since they have nothing to do with power or performance.

WHAT THE AUDIENCE SHOULD KNOW

What does the writer want the audience to know? In both paragraphs, the writer wants to share excitement about a new car purchase in order to encourage readers to purchase the same kind of car. The writer shares information that will be of interest to two kinds of audiences and that will encourage readers to purchase a Puma.

Various writing assignments or "real-life" writing situations will require you to address a particular audience, such as parents, teachers, other students, or the editor of a local newspaper. Considering your audience will help you write more effectively.

Practice 4: Audience

For each of the following topics, describe the interest, knowledge, and vocabulary of the given audience as well as what you think the audience should know. The first one is done for you.

1. **Topic:**   Parental Advisory stickers on music CDs

   Audience: parents

   Audience Interest: interested in the welfare of their children

   Audience Knowledge: unfamiliar with specific artists, but aware of rude music

   Audience Vocabulary: some knowledge of teen vocabulary, but mostly not

Audience Should Know: parents, not record companies, need to take responsibility

2. **Topic:**   Parental Advisory stickers on music CDs
    Audience: students
    Audience Interest:
    Audience Knowledge:
    Audience Vocabulary:
    Audience Should Know:

3. **Topic:**   high salaries of professional athletes
    Audience: stadium worker
    Audience Interest:
    Audience Knowledge:
    Audience Vocabulary:
    Audience Should Know:

4. **Topic:**   using lottery to fund public education
    Audience: governor of state
    Audience Interest:
    Audience Knowledge:
    Audience Vocabulary:
    Audience Should Know:

Chapter 2 Summary

The **main idea** or **topic** of each paragraph in a passage is a subordinate idea to the main idea of the **entire passage**.

Using **reading strategies** can help increase your understanding of what you read.

- **Pre-reading** or surveying is a way to look over written material and get a general idea what it is about without reading the details. This is also the fastest type of reading because in pre-reading you read **titles** or **headings**, **subtitles**, or **subheading** and **topic sentences** as you look over a page. **Surveying** is the process of reading very quickly, glancing over the material and picking up key words and ideas.

- **During reading strategies** are also important for understanding what you are reading. You should also **underline** or **highlight** key ideas and facts. **Think alouds** also help you read.

- The purpose of **after-reading strategies** is to better understand what you have read and to help you remember key ideas and details from the selection. For example, you can create a **concept map** of the chapter or article you read. **Study cards** also help you review key ideas.

- **Prior knowledge**, **predicting**, and **formulating questions** are also important reading strategies to use for improving your understanding before, during, and after your reading.

The **main idea**, the primary message or the central point of a passage, will many times be stated directly in the **title**, the **thesis statement**, or the **conclusion**. It may also be implied through the facts stated in the passage.

When you draw a **conclusion**, you form a judgment or opinion based on the details in a passage. To draw conclusions, use *all* the facts and clues present in the passage.

The **summary** of a passage is a sentence that pulls together the **message** in a passage. It is a concise statement gained from reading a selection.

You can understand an **author's purpose** from the way he or she writes. Through voice, an author communicates ideas, keeping **audience** in mind.

CHAPTER 2 REVIEW

A. Answer the following questions about reading strategies.

1. You are preparing to create a poster about the habitat of flamingoes. A friend loaned you a book titled *Exotic Birds of North America*. How can you best determine if the book contains information about flamingoes that would be helpful to you?

    A. Using the table of contents, find the chapter that contains information on flamingoes and read it in depth, looking for facts about flamingoes' habitat.

    B. Pre-read the entire book looking for the word *flamingo*. Copy all of the information on flamingoes.

    C. Read the first and last page of every chapter to see if flamingoes are mentioned.

    D. Check the index to see if flamingoes are listed. Pre-read those pages, and see if there is any information on the habitat of flamingoes.

2. Susannah's English class has just finished reading *Romeo and Juliet*. The class was assigned to write an essay on some aspect of the play. Susannah has written her essay about Juliet's personality, but she needs to add some quotes to it. How should Susannah find appropriate quotes to use in her essay?

    A. Ask her friends what they think was memorable and use those quotes in her essay.

    B. Survey relevant parts of the play, and then read those sections very carefully to find exact quotes that support what she has written in her essay.

    C. Carefully read through the middle of the play, and find some parts of Juliet's dialogue to use as quotes.

    D. Reread the entire play very carefully, and write down every quote that might be useful. From that list, choose the five quotes that are most memorable, and use those in the essay.

B. Read the following passages, and find the main idea.

A friend of mine moved to the United States from Italy when he was fifteen years old. While learning to speak English, he studied the dictionary. Now, three years later, he will blurt out words that those of us who grew up in the United States have never even heard before. Gradually, through many embarrassing arguments when we have been forced to admit our ignorance in our native language, we have learned to keep a dictionary on hand.

Last Halloween, my friends came to my house to watch a Stephen King film about a girl with telepathy. At the climax of the movie, my friend, who had not quite mastered the English language as well as he thought, cried out "Oh, I get it! She has that ESPN thing!"

3. What is the main idea of this passage?

    A. Studying the dictionary pays off.

    B. Americans don't know every word in the dictionary.

    C. Using the wrong word can be embarrassing.

    D. Diligently learning the vocabulary of a new language does not guarantee you won't make mistakes.

Chapter 2

Poaching the Giant Panda

(1) Deeply in debt and desperately seeking a way out, Wu Hui Chen of Shanghai decided to buy, then resell, a giant panda's pelt. His decision will cost him 12 years in a Chinese prison.

(2) Wu went to Sichuan Province, home of the Giant Panda, and paid two men 30,000 yuan—about $5,500—for a panda skin. He returned home, had it photographed, and with the help of his associate Wang Shu, he lured a buyer to Shanghai's Peace Hotel. When the buyer turned over payment of 200,000 yuan, police swooped in and arrested both Wu and Wang. For his help, Wang will spend eight years in prison.

(3) Giant pandas, which number only 1,000 or so in the wild, are at risk of extinction; Chinese poachers and traffickers face the death penalty if they are caught. Still, more than 200 people have been arrested for illegal dealings in panda skins.

(4) Stuart Parkins of the World Wide Fund for Nature says that demand for the exotic pelts is strongest in Taiwan, but exists also in Japan and Hong Kong. The going price is about $10,000.

4. What is the main idea of the passage?
   A. Giant pandas number only 1000 and are in danger of extinction; please help them!
   B. The strongest demand for panda pelts is in Taiwan, but a demand exists in Japan and Hong Kong, also.
   C. Chinese poachers and traffickers face the death penalty.
   D. Poaching pandas is against the law in China and carries severe punishment for those who are caught.

excerpt from *Huckleberry Finn* by Mark Twain

It's lovely to live on a raft. We had the sky, up there, all speckled with stars and we used to lay on our backs and look up at them, and discuss about whether they was made, or only just happened—Jim he allowed they was made, but I allowed they happened; I judged it would have took too long to *make* so many. Jim said the moon could a laid them; well, that looked kind of reasonable, so I didn't say nothing against it, because I've seen a frog lay most as many, so of course it could be done. We use to watch the stars that fell, too, and see them streak down.

5. The main idea of the passage above is
   A. being on a raft is the ultimate time to be alone.
   B. Jim knows more about how things are made than Huck does.
   C. when we see beautiful stars at night, we wonder where they came from.
   D. spend your next vacation looking up at the stars.

Reading for Understanding

Wilma Rudolph

Nothing has been easy for Wilma Rudolph. Born in Clarksville, Tennessee, she was the twentieth of 22 children. Her mother worked as a domestic, and her father was a railroad handyman. As a child she suffered pneumonia, scarlet fever and polio and wore a brace on her leg when she was six years old. It was not an auspicious beginning for an Olympic medal winner, but her mother's determined effort to take her to Meharry Medical College in Nashville for weekly treatment continued until she would walk.

Encouragement of track coach Ed Temple inspired her to run. Wilma ran in America, in Australia, and in the 1960 Rome Olympic games where she won three gold medals, broke two world records, and brought the crowd to its feet in waves of applause. When she joined the Women's Sports Hall of Fame in 1980, she became the first black woman to receive that honor and the first to so honor the Hall of Fame.

Winston Churchill

One of the most famous prime ministers in British history was Sir Winston Churchill. When he attended Harrow public school as a teenager, however, he was known for mischief and poor grades. In fact, this man, who was so admired for his speaking ability, failed his English class at Harrow. If his father had not been so well known, young Winston would probably have been expelled from school.

After finishing at Harrow school, Winston went on to college. Narrowly escaping death, he served very capably in the military in India and Africa. As a British prime minister during World War II, his moving speeches and strong leadership inspired his people to continue fighting against Germany despite the challenges.

In his last years as a prime minister, Winston Churchill was invited back to Harrow to speak at their graduation ceremony. The students looked forward to hearing the wisdom of this man of many accomplishments. After a long introduction by the headmaster, Sir Winston Churchill came to the podium. He gave a short but stirring speech. "Young men, never give up," he said. "Never give up! Never give up. Never, never, never, never."

6. Based on her life, which group would <u>most</u> appreciate Wilma Rudolph's contributions to sports?
   - A. mentally disabled
   - B. gifted athletes
   - C. physically disabled
   - D. former Olympic boxers

7. Winston Churchill was well known for his great speeches. How could you <u>best</u> improve your background knowledge of his speaking abilities?
   - A. listen to some of Churchill's famous speeches on the Internet
   - B. read and study some of Churchill's famous speeches
   - C. review a short biography of Winston Churchill
   - D. interview an older person who heard Churchill speak to a group

Chapter 2

Read the following passages and answer the questions that follow each passage.

The Lost Sea in Sweetwater, Tennessee, is the largest underground lake in the world. The temperature inside the cavern remains at 58° F all year long. Many interesting rooms exist inside the cavern. In one room, you can see rare cave flowers called anthodites. Every second of the tour is a fascinating experience you will never forget.

8. Which of the sentences below provides the <u>best</u> summary of the passage?
   A. In one room, you can see rare cave flowers called anthodites.
   B. The temperature inside the cavern remains at 58° F all year long.
   C. Every second of the tour is a fascinating experience you will never forget.
   D. Touring the Lost Sea in Sweetwater, Tennessee, is a worthwhile experience.

Tomorrow's Jobs

In recent years, the level of educational attainment of the labor force has risen dramatically. Between 1975 and 1990, the proportion of the labor force aged 25 to 64 with at least 1 year of college increased from 33 to 47 percent, while the proportion with four years of college or more increased from 18 to 26 percent. The rates of employment growth for occupations requiring higher levels of education or training are projected to rise faster than the rates of employment for occupations requiring less education or training.

The emphasis on education will continue. Consequently, three of the fastest growing occupational groups will be executive, administrative, and managerial; professional specialty; and technicians and related support occupations. These occupations generally require the highest levels of education and skill and will make up an increasing proportion of new jobs. Office and factory automation, changes in consumer demand, and substitution of imports for domestic products are expected to cause employment to stagnate or decline in many occupations that require little formal education—apparel workers and textile machinery operators, for example. Opportunities for high school dropouts will be increasingly limited, and workers who cannot read and follow directions may not even be considered for most jobs.

Employed high school dropouts are more likely to have low paying jobs with little advancement potential, while workers in occupations requiring higher levels of education have higher incomes. In addition, many of the occupations projected to grow most rapidly between 1990 and 2008 are among those with the highest earnings.

9. Based on this passage, we can predict that:
   A. Sales managers will be in high demand.
   B. Textile workers will be in high demand.
   C. Miners will see more demand for their services.
   D. The janitorial profession will increase dramatically in openings.

10. For what audience is this text <u>most likely</u> written?

    A.   high school dropouts

    B.   unemployed people looking for work

    C.   students planning career goals

    D.   employment agencies needing to know who to hire

11. What is the <u>best</u> summary of this passage?

    A.   Job openings in many manufacturing fields will increase dramatically in the next century.

    B.   Jobs requiring higher levels of education will be in high demand in the next century.

    C.   The United States population as a whole has attained a higher level of education.

    D.   There will be many more jobs available for high school dropouts in the next century.

Blitzkrieg

It was called blitzkrieg—lightning war—and the Germans unveiled it in Poland during September of 1939. It consisted of *stuka* dive bomber attacks, fast tank movements, and mobile infantry deployments, all of which were backed up by heavy bomber attacks. The keys to this whole new tactic were mobility and coordination of a multi-force attack. It was a strategy the Germans developed to avoid the slow, turgid warfare of World War I. It can be reasonably said that this new air-ground, multi-force concept revolutionized modern warfare.

In 1939, the German blitzkrieg overwhelmed Poland. By the end of the first day of the Polish campaign, the Polish Air Force had been largely destroyed; most of it was caught on the ground before it could take off, and thus the Germans had almost immediate air supremacy. Also, German high level bombers attacked Warsaw, reducing most of the Polish rear guard to shambles. On the ground, the German military machine streamed across the Polish border—tanks, the armored cars, and the armored infantry and artillery of the mechanized panzer divisions. All of these were supported by waves of Junkers-87 dive bombers, the deadly *stukas*.

12. Which statement from the passage is a conclusion drawn by the author?

    A.   It can be reasonably said that this new air-ground, multi-force concept revolutionized modern warfare.

    B.   Also, German high-level bombers attacked Warsaw, reducing most of the Polish rear guard to shambles.

    C.   It was called blitzkrieg—lightning war—and the Germans unveiled it in Poland that September of 1939.

    D.   All of these were supported by waves of Junkers-87 dive bombers, the deadly *stukas*.

Powerboating

For many people, the ideal powerboat would have speeds as high as a jet airplane. For others, fuel efficiency is a primary concern. Whatever features people would enjoy in their powerboat, they will always have to make concessions. Each boat cannot possibly fulfill what everyone desires, regardless of how much money a person has. For example, a boat that is big enough to have a living room and an area for catching and cleaning fish will not be fuel efficient and will be too large to bring close to shore. On the other hand, a smaller boat will have much less space and comfort, but its speed and ability to maneuver will be much greater than a larger boat.

Powerboats also serve various functions. For the risk-taker, power boats built for speed and sharp turns can provide hours of amusement. For the more family-oriented person, larger boats provide enough room for all the family members to sit together comfortably. Some boats built with sturdy hulls can be used on the ocean for deep sea fishing or diving. Regardless of the specialization, powerboats will satisfy whatever desire a person wishes to fulfill on the water.

These boats provide a great deal of excitement and amusement. If used properly, they will continue to provide countless enjoyable outings for the millions who have taken up this sport.

13. After reading this passage, one can conclude that powerboating
    A. will become the most popular sport in America.
    B. is an exciting sport for those who are properly trained.
    C. results in millions of dollars of revenue each year.
    D. is an enjoyable water sport for many people.

14. This passage was <u>most likely</u> written for
    A. people considering buying a boat.
    B. fishermen looking for the right boat.
    C. people deciding how to spend their vacation.
    D. tycoons deciding how to spend their money.

A Life Saved or a Life Lost?

Once in India there was a high priest by the name of Devasha who lived in a certain village. His wife, Yajna, was also of high birth. In time, she became pregnant, and the couple had a son whom they named Kanji. This son was a great gift, a precious diamond to be cherished and treasured.

Shortly after the child's birth, Yajna went to the river to bathe. Devasha stayed with the child and cared for him in his mother's absence. Soon, a messenger notified the high priest that presents for performing sacred ceremonies were arriving. In a hurry, Devasha left a pet mongoose to guard the child.

A few minutes later, a poisonous snake slithered toward the child. At the moment that the serpent was about to strike the child, the mongoose saw the snake and quickly killed it out of love for his master.

When the mongoose saw his master return from his duty, he happily ran toward Devasha with the blood of the snake on his fur. Thinking that the mongoose had killed his son, the high priest strangled the mongoose with his bare hands.

When he arrived home, Devasha discovered his son alive and well. Next to his son, he saw the snake that the mongoose killed. He was stricken with grief and wailed loudly. Returning from the river, his wife, Yajna, learned of the incident and denounced her husband for his foolish action.

15. Based on this passage, we can conclude that
   A. Yajna was very upset at the mongoose's actions.
   B. Devasha made a terrible mistake.
   C. the mongoose was trying to befriend the snake.
   D. Devasha does not jump to conclusions.

16. What is Devasha likely to do in the future?
   A. Devasha will learn to trust no one.
   B. Devasha will ask questions before making assumptions.
   C. Devasha will buy a pet serpent.
   D. Devasha will always stay near Kanji.

17. Which of the following best states the author's purpose in writing the story?
   A. to describe
   B. to persuade
   C. to teach a lesson
   D. to relate an adventure

Alcohol

Because alcohol is the most widely promoted drug in our society, it is easily abused. Alcohol is the number one problem among youth. By their senior year in high school, almost all students will have tried alcoholic beverages. Four out of ten will consume five or more drinks in a row every two weeks.

Youth who begin drinking alcohol at an early age will most likely experience alcohol related problems later in life.

Alcohol dependence affects relationships with family and friends. Even low doses can impair coordination while driving a car. Higher doses reduce mental abilities and the capacity to remember information. School grades suffer, and students are more likely to skip classes. Other drugs may also be abused and conflicts with the law are more common.

Girls who drink alcohol are more likely to become pregnant. Babies born to such mothers often develop fetal alcohol syndrome. The effects of this condition on these children lead to mental retardation or physical defects. The offspring of alcoholic parents are also at greater risk for alcoholism themselves.

18. Which of the following is a correct summary of the passage?
   A. Alcohol dependence among youth affects driving, family, and friendships.
   B. Alcohol use by teens in moderation is not a concern.
   C. A nine-year-old drinking alcohol will experience problems in his/her mental and physical health.
   D. Some high school students abuse alcohol by their senior year.

The Experiment

"Before you drink, my respectable old friends," said he, "it would be well that, with the experience of a lifetime to direct you, you should draw up a few general rules for your guidance, in passing a second time through the perils of youth. Think what a sin and shame it would be if, with your peculiar advantages, you should not become patterns of virtue and wisdom to all the young people of the age!"

The doctor's four venerable friends made him no answer, except by a feeble and tremulous laugh; so very ridiculous was the idea that, knowing how closely repentance treads behind the steps of error, they should ever go astray again.

"Drink, then," said the doctor, bowing. "I rejoice that I have so well selected the subjects of my experiment."

With shaking hands, they raised the glasses to their lips. The medicine, if it really possessed such virtues as Dr. Heidegger imputed to it, could not have been bestowed on four human beings who needed it more woefully. They looked as if they had never known what youth or pleasure was, but had been the offspring of nature's old age and always the gray decrepit, sapless, miserable creatures, who now sat stooping around the doctor's table, without life enough in their souls or bodies to be excited even by the prospect of growing young again. They drank off the liquid and replaced their glasses on the table.

– Nathaniel Hawthorne, paraphrase from "Dr. Heidegger's Experiment"

19. Based on the passage, we can conclude that the drinking of the medicine will probably

    A. make the four persons old and gray.
    B. make the four persons drunk.
    C. restore the youth of the four persons.
    D. make the four persons sick.

20. Why did the author write this passage?

    A. to inform
    B. to motivate
    C. to teach a lesson
    D. to create suspense

Population Density

And what about the assertion that as the world population grows, poverty is the inevitable result?

Actually, the amount of poverty in a country has little to do with its population density or even its supply of resources. It does have a lot to do with each country's economic system and how free it is.

Japan, for instance, is one of the most prosperous countries on earth, but it has many more people per square mile than, say India, one of the world's poorest. Likewise, booming Singapore has a population density of more than 10,000 people per square mile. Yet Singapore's per capita income is over 15 times that of Communist-run Cuba, which has 254 people per square mile.

It is no accident that the world's most prosperous countries are those with the freest and least-regulated, least-taxed economies. Thriving Asian economies like those of Japan, Singapore, Hong Kong, Taiwan and South Korea are classic examples of these.

21. Which of the following <u>best</u> states the author's purpose in writing this passage?
    A.   to compare
    B.   to share a personal experience
    C.   to convey uncertainty
    D.   to entertain

22. Which of the following is an accurate summary of the passage above?
    A.   The world's poorest countries are also the most populous.
    B.   Nations with a free economy are the most prosperous.
    C.   Communist countries are the most prosperous.
    D.   The world's most restricted economies are also the most populous countries.

Chapter 3
Analysis of Literature

This chapter addresses the following expectation(s) and their related indicators from **Core Learning Goal 1: Reading. Reviewing, and Responding to Texts.**

Expectation 1.2	The student will construct, examine, and extend meaning of traditional and contemporary works recognized as having significant literary merit.

This chapter also addresses the following expectation(s) and their related indicators from **Core Learning Goal 4: Evaluating the Content, Organization, and Language Use of Text**s

Expectation 4.2	The student will assess the effectiveness of choice of details, organizational pattern, word choice, syntax, use of figurative language, and rhetorical devices

STORY STRUCTURE

Authors use story structure to organize and build stories. For a story, if the structure is not strong, the story will fail to keep the reader's interest.

A story can be told in many different ways. A good writer will use structural tools, or devices, such as **point of view** and **narrator**, **setting**, **plot**, **mood,** and **tone** to build the story in the most satisfying, exciting way or the most thoughtful, conscientious way. Study the following list of structural devices and their features to help you better understand stories. Then you can develop strategies for analyzing literature.

POINT OF VIEW AND NARRATOR

A writer's first step in building story structure is the **point of view** and **narrator**. These two items are related and need to be looked at together. The point of view is the perspective, or outlook, from which a writer tells a story. The narrator is the person who is telling about the dialogue and the action in the story.

The narrator can be a character within the story or an unknown observer looking on and describing the actions and thoughts of characters. For example, Mary Shelley wrote *Frankenstein* from the first person point of view, but she used three different narrators to tell their own stories: Dr. Frankenstein, the creator of the monster; the monster himself; and Walton, the last man to speak to both. The narrators take turns telling their parts of the story.

The point of view and narrator influence the way an author tells a story. Deciding what point of view the author is using to tell a story is a first big step in understanding how that story will work. Once you have identified the point of view, determining the identity of the narrator is the next question that you want to answer.

POSSIBLE POINTS OF VIEW	
First Person	The narrator tells the story from the "I" point of view. In *The House on Mango Street*, Esperanza tells her story as the main character.
Second Person	The speaker is talking directly to the reader and uses the pronoun "you." This is not often used on its own, but the second person point of view is fairly common in poetry, short essays, and songs. The song "You Are My Sunshine" and Jamaica Kincaid's story "Girl" use the second person point of view.
Third Person	The speaker tells a story describing characters as "he," "she," or "they" as in *The Pearl* by John Steinbeck.
• **omniscient**	The narrator is capable of knowing, telling, and seeing all that happens to the characters. In Leo Tolstoy's *Anna Karenina*, the speaker describes all the story action and the inner thoughts of the main characters.
• **limited**	The speaker tells the story knowing only what is seen, heard, and felt through the thoughts and viewpoint of one character, often, but not always, the main character. Ralph Ellison wrote the short story "King of the Bingo Game" using this point of view.

SETTING

The **setting** is the background for the action of a story. Setting includes time, place, and general surroundings. In some cases, the elements of setting are critical to the story. Certain events, like a snow avalanche for example, can't occur just anywhere, so the setting can have an impact on plot by restricting or allowing certain events to occur. The same is true for time period; a writer can't send a Revolutionary War soldier up in an airplane!

The setting can also have an impact on characters. In particular locations or cultures, people are restricted from certain activities by the rules of the society. In Victorian England, the rules of the society would not allow a teenage girl to go out alone with a date. Granted, some characters would break the rules, but that would be an example of the setting affecting the character: one type of character would never do such a thing, but a character who did break the rules would stand out from his or her contemporaries.

Sometimes various aspects of setting are not really important. The particular time, for example, may not have any effect on the story. In fact, a writer may not want to include indicators of the time period so that readers at any time can identify with the story. The same is true for other aspects of setting. A story could take place in an apartment building, but the exact town may not be at all relevant to the story.

- **Time**   When the story occurs, for example, the historical period or season of the year.
- **Place**   Where the story happens, including such things as geographic place, scenery, or arrangement of a house or room.
- **General Surroundings**   Daily habits of characters, including jobs and social activities, as well as the general culture the character lives in.

MOOD AND TONE

Have you ever read a suspenseful, scary story and while you were reading, you started getting a very creepy feeling? That feeling created within the reader is called **mood**. A writer often wants the readers to get a certain emotional feeling while they are reading. At the beginning of a work though, a writer such as Dr. Seuss doesn't give instructions to the reader like "You should feel that you are in a silly mood when you start reading this story." The writer has to create that mood in the reader. This can be done by many different methods. The particular method that a writer uses depends on many factors, including the particular type of writing and the purpose of the writing. Dr. Seuss uses rhyming, silly invented words, outrageous situations, and drawings of ridiculous creatures to set the mood in his books.

The setting and the description of the setting is one of the common methods a writer uses to set the mood. If a story begins with the description of the setting being on a sunny, warm beach, the reader wouldn't expect a hair-raising adventure story to follow. Likewise, if a story begins "It was a dark and stormy night..." the reader doesn't expect a hilarious comedy situation to follow. Certainly, there can be exceptions to this, but writers usually create those exceptions for a specific reason, too.

While mood is the feeling within the reader, **tone** is the writer's attitude toward a topic. Think back to a time when you read something and you could tell that the writer was taking a particular attitude toward the topic. Perhaps the writer was taking the topic too seriously, or not seriously enough. The main way that a writer can convey his or her attitude is through the word choices made while writing. In fiction, a writer can have different tones toward different characters. The choice of words used to describe the character will usually reveal the tone of the writer. One character may be described as chatty and bouncy, while another is described as loud and hyperactive. One of these descriptions has a positive tone, while the other has a negative tone.

Some Words to Describe Mood and Tone			
angry	dramatic	mocking	sad
anxious	fearful	optimistic	satirical
boring	happy	pessimistic	suspenseful
calm	humorous	poetic	sympathetic
cynical	lighthearted	relaxed	tragic
depressed	lofty	threatening	remorseful
hysterical	gloomy	tense	nervous
expectant	lethargic	pensive	tearful
apathetic	disgusting	macabre	silly

Practice 1: Point of View, Narrator, Setting, Mood, and Tone

A. Read the following passage and answer the questions that follow.

excerpt from *20,000 Leagues Under the Sea* by Jules Verne

When I got up, I saw that Captain Nemo and his first mate were on the platform. They were examining the ship's position, exchanging several words in their incomprehensible language.

Here was our situation. Two miles to starboard rose Gueboroar Island, whose coast extended from north to west like an immense arm. Toward the south and east, we could already make out the tops of several coral formations which the ebb tide was beginning to uncover. We had gone aground at high tide, which would make it difficult to refloat the *Nautilus*. Nevertheless the ship had suffered no damage, for her hull was solidly joined. But even though it could never sink or spring a leak, there was a serious danger of its remaining grounded forever on these reefs, and that would be the end of Captain Nemo's submarine.

I was thinking of all this when the captain came over looking as cool and calm as ever. He seemed neither disturbed nor unhappy.

"An accident?" I asked. "No, an incident," he replied.

"But an incident," I retorted, "that will force you once again to live on that land you have been fleeing!"

1. The story is told from the point of view of

    A.   the second person.

    B.   the omniscient third person.

    C.   the first person.

    D.   the limited third person.

2. The narrator of the story is

    A.   Captain Nemo.

    B.   the first mate of the ship.

    C.   an unnamed character within the story.

    D.   an omniscient observer.

3. At the end of the selection, the mood is

    A.   tense.   B.   happy.   C.   relaxed.   D.   boring.

4. The location (setting) of this passage is

    A.   near the sea.

    B.   on a reef.

    C.   under the sea.

    D.   on an island.

5. The time period (setting) of this passage is

    A.   during World War I.

    B.   not revealed in this excerpt.

    C.   in a future time.

    D.   in the present time.

B. Writer's Tone. Make a list of five nouns (people, places, things, ideas). Write a sentence to describe each one. Look at the sentence you wrote and decide if you showed a negative or positive attitude toward that item. Write a new sentence about each one and use the opposite tone of what you used before.

C. Mood. Look through selections you have read in your literature book or some other anthology and find examples of at least four different moods in written works. Make a list of the titles of the four selections. How did the authors establish the mood in their writing? List some specific examples from each piece of literature.

D. Point of View and Narrator. Using the same literary selections that you used for activity C above, write down the point of view and the narrator of each selection as well as the clues that helped you determine them.

PLOT

The events in a story—what happens—is the **plot**. If you are reading a book and a friend asks what the book is about, you would probably begin telling him about the plot. Every story has to have more than setting and characters; something has to happen to the characters!

PARTS OF PLOT

When we discuss plot, it is generally broken down into several parts. The **introduction**, or exposition, brings the reader into the story. Generally, the author gives the setting, introduces the characters (or at least some of them), and begins to tell the reader about the **conflict**, the main struggle of the characters. The conflict usually begins with an **inciting incident**, an occurrence that sets the entire chain of events that put the plot into motion. The inciting incident and all other actions that continue to lead to the story's resolution are part of the **cause and effect relationship** of the action. Conflict is discussed in more detail a little later in this chapter.

The next part of the plot is the **rising action**. During the rising action, the writer will continue to build the conflict and will introduce complications. **Complications** in a plot are just like complications in real life; they are problems that the characters encounter. These events build up to the **climax** or turning point of the plot. The section of the plot after the climax is called the **falling action**. During this part, the loose ends are tied up, various complications may be resolved and the conflict begins to be settled.

The **resolution** is the final section of the plot. Usually, the main conflict is ended in some way—a mystery may be solved, problems are worked out, or some other suitable solution to the conflict occurs.

Since a plot undergoes these many changes, it is important for the author to include appropriate **transitions**. A transition signals, through words, phrases, and shifts in tense, that something new is happening or a turn is being made in the plot.

You can illustrate the parts of plot in a plot diagram to show their relationships.

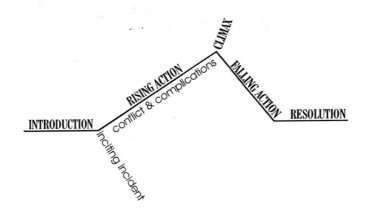

TIME AND SEQUENCE

In a work of literature, **time** may move straight forward from the first event to the last event, such as in the story of "The Three Little Pigs." However, the author of a work of literature may feel that the story will be better remembered or understood by mixing up time. Examples are Homer's *The Iliad* and *The Odyssey*, (in which time moves from the present to the past and back to the present).

Sequence is the order in which events happen in a story. The sequence may not go in a straight time order but may go back and forth in time with the use of **flashbacks**. You are probably very familiar with flashbacks because they are frequently used in movies and television shows. Flashbacks are a useful tool for writers. They allow information about events that are outside of the story's time to be brought into the plot. Without the tool of flashbacks, the writer might have to begin back years and years before the start of the main story. Flashbacks also allow the writer to put in information at various times during the story. Sometimes it may be when the information will be most relevant, and sometimes it might be when the information will have the most impact on the reader or the story.

Foreshadowing is another way that time is changed; however, with foreshadowing, clues are used to hint at future events. Writers often use this technique in mysteries where foreshadowing is a way to let the reader begin figuring out what has happened. With foreshadowing, the reader can try to solve the mystery along with the characters in the book. Foreshadowing is more frequently used just to let the reader have some clue as to what events may be coming within the plot. Often as you read, you may not pick up on the foreshadowing, but after an event occurs, you can think back and see the foreshadowing that the writer gave.

Flashback	A scene or event that happened earlier than the beginning of a story. It is often introduced in the story as a memory, a dream, or a simple retelling of past events by one of the characters. In *Rebecca* by Daphne du Maurier, the narrator tells the story of what happened at Manderley in flashback.
Foreshadowing	Clues about how the plot is going to develop. An author puts these in by various methods and for various reasons. There is a great deal of foreshadowing used by John Steinbeck in *Of Mice and Men*. One example is the way in which Lennie unintentionally destroys things, finally killing a human being, foreshadows the downfall of Lennie and George as well as Lennie's own death.

CONFLICT

In literary plots, the term **conflict** has the same meaning that we use in everyday conversations—a struggle between opposing forces. Some authors and readers consider conflict to be the most important part of the plot. The main conflict affects all other parts of a story; it drives the events and the characters. Conflicts in literature are classified as either internal or external. **Internal conflicts** are those that take place within a single character. These types of conflicts are called **person vs. self.** A character who has to make an important life decision would be an example of someone experiencing an internal conflict. Some examples include Gollum in *The Lord of the Rings,* who must decide whether to help Frodo or thwart his effort to return the ring, and John Nash, who struggles to regain his mental health, in *A Beautiful Mind.*

External conflicts are those caused by forces outside of a character. These conflicts can be **person vs. nature** as in the books *Robinson Crusoe* and *Lord of the Flies* or the movie *Castaway*, or **person vs. person** which is present in countless books, movies, and other literary works. A third type of external conflict is **person vs. society**. In those conflicts, someone, or a group of people, is struggling against some aspect of culture or society. The Disney movie *Mulan* is a good example of such a struggle. Mulan wants her family to be proud of her, so she disguises herself as a young man and goes to war in her father's place. Certainly, she would not have been allowed to do such a thing; Chinese society of her time would not allow a girl to become a warrior. Another conflict that can occur is **person vs. machine**.

In various genres of literature, plot will usually contain more than one type of conflict. The reality TV show *Survivor* would be an example that contains all the types of conflict. Some participants have internal conflicts (person vs. self) over their actions and behaviors. All of the participants are competing against the others (person vs. person) and against the living conditions (person vs. nature). There are often elements of person vs. society conflict when the participants struggle to break free of the rules of society that they are used to living under.

CHARACTERS AND CHARACTERIZATION

Literary works of both fiction and nonfiction contain **characters**, the people who appear in the work. The characters must tell each other and the reader about their ideas and feelings. The way that characters in a story **interact** (behave) with each other is a big part of telling the story. Through their words and actions, the story will come alive for readers.

There are different types of characters in a story. There are the **main characters** who are the most important characters to the story, and there are **minor characters** who may have a connection to the main characters or may be complete strangers to the main character. They are in the story because they have some connection to the plot.

The chart below shows three important character roles.

CHARACTER ROLES

Different types of characters perform different roles or functions in a literary work.

Narrator	The person telling a story. In *Huckleberry Finn*, the narrator is Huck, and he is a main character. Also, in Maya Angelou's *I Know Why the Caged Bird Sings*, the narrator is a young girl who is the main character. Often, the narrator will be a main character. In the case of a third-person narrator, the narrator is NOT a character in the story
Protagonist	The main character(s). Jim and Huck are the main characters in *Huckleberry Finn*. The protagonists are Romeo and Juliet in Shakespeare's famous play of the same name. The protagonist is not always a hero or even a likeable character. For example, Shrek, the ogre in the movie of the same name, is not likeable in the beginning of the movie and certainly does not act like a hero.
Antagonist	An opponent or rival of the hero. The antagonist does not have to be human and can be an idea or belief. The antagonists in Hemingway's *Old Man and the Sea* are the sharks. The Southern laws and culture were the enemy for Huck and Jim in *Huckleberry Finn*.

CHARACTER INTERACTION

In your life's story, *you* are the main character. Think for a moment about how you act with people you know and why you act that way. Characters in literature interact in similar ways. When you are trying to determine the relationships between characters and why characters are interacting in certain ways, you have to examine several aspects of the characters. **Relationships** with other characters and **influences** from various people or events can also have an impact on characters. **Conflicts** with themselves, other characters, and the world can also have a powerful impact. Characters have **motivations** for their actions just as in real life. Sometimes these relationships, motivations, conflicts, and influences are subtle and unstated. As a reader, you have to look carefully and read between the lines to determine what is really happening.

When you try to determine why characters act or react in certain ways, you have to look at the question just as you would in real life. Factors that influence one person may not influence another person. Conflicts can cause one person to fight back and overcome obstacles. The same conflict may overwhelm and defeat another person. Think about characters just as you would real people. Analyze the events that you know about and then make inferences and draw conclusions about how all of the events are working together to create the situations in a story.

Huckleberry Finn by Mark Twain is an example of how authors create a world for characters. Huck and Jim are rafting south on the Mississippi River, **interacting** closely. The following chart shows the main interactions of Huck and Jim.

Relationships	Jim is an escaped slave, running from the law. Huck is a runaway Southern boy. He is fleeing from responsibility and his abusive father. How these two characters will work out a relationship on the raft is an important part of the story.
Motivations	Jim has never known freedom and wants to be free to join his wife and child. Huck has lived without rules for most of his life. He also wants to be free and irresponsible by leaving his home.
Conflicts	Huck has a major internal conflict (a conflict inside his mind). How should he treat Jim, the runaway slave with him on the raft? Huck is not quite ready to free himself of the cultural prejudices of his time between white people and black people but learns he can talk to Jim and depends on him as a friend. Jim also has a conflict, but his is an external conflict (a conflict outside of himself). He's a hunted runaway. How can Jim get home with his freedom and keep Huck safe, so no one can blame him for any harm to Huck?
Influences	Huck is influenced by ideas he's been brought up on: black people should be slaves and treated as beneath white people. The same ideas influence Jim, but on the river, he's able to take new ideas for himself: the ideas of true justice and humanity. Jim is able to influence Huck with pure honesty and friendship.

At the journey's end, Huck has worked out his internal conflict: Jim is his friend. Jim has also worked through his conflict: he has his freedom. Twain creates interest in the plot through conflicts since Huck doesn't turn Jim over to the law as soon as he can; influences give it suspense as the reader can't be sure of Huck's loyalty to Jim; relationships and motivations make both characters likeable because they have good reasons for running away.

CHARACTERIZATION

The main trait of a dog is its loyalty to its master. Likewise, the **traits** or features of characters show what you can expect of their behavior: silly, serious, loyal, kind, rude, educated, street-smart, and so on. To create vivid characters, the author develops them in several ways. **Description** is the most obvious way to develop a character. **Narration** about a character often reveals important information. Certain narrators can often tell information about a character that might not be revealed otherwise. Characters' **actions** tell a great deal about them. You've probably heard the saying "actions speak louder than words." The same is true of literary characters. Sometimes characters reveal more than they intended to by their actions. **Dialogue**, what characters say, and **dialect**, how they say it, are two other important ways that a reader learns about characters.

Character Traits and How They Are Developed

Description   An author can tell how characters look and dress and what their ages are, just as you might describe a friend of yours to someone.

Narration   The telling of the story through a speaker. The speaker could be one of the characters or could be an unknown observer. The speaker will tell how other characters feel or think about another character or will describe how they act towards that character.

Dialogue   Conversation between two or more people. People in literature speak to each other as people in real life do.

Dialect   Used to portray a character's cultural and regional heritage by illustrating his manner of speaking. Mark Twain is famous for his use of the Southern dialect in his novels and short stories.

Actions   The actions of a character can show the character's true self. Just as in real life, you can form your impressions about a character more accurately by what he or she does than by what he or she says.

In talking or writing about literature, one of the qualities of a character that is important to note is whether the character is **round** or **flat**. Another way of describing literary characters is with the terms **static** and **dynamic**. The chart below gives definitions for these terms.

Types of Characters

flat   A one-dimensional character; reader has limited knowledge about the character; often a stereotype and/or a minor character and/or static

round   A multi-dimensional character; reader knows many personality aspects of the character; usually a dynamic and/or a major character

static   A character that does not experience change or growth during the time frame of a literary work; at the end of a work, he is essentially the same as at the beginning of the work; often flat

dynamic   A character that undergoes a significant change or personal growth during the time frame of a literary work; usually round

---

Practice 2: Characters and Characterization

Read the following passage for content, and then answer the questions.

One of the most inspiring "rags to riches" stories is absolutely true. A boy child was born a slave in 1856. As a slave, he wasn't allowed to go to school. After the Civil War, the one dream that the boy had was to get an education. In 1872, Booker Taliafero Washington journeyed to the Hampton Institute in Virginia. The young man had neither money nor references, but he had a clear desire to learn and to help others learn. Luckily, he had come to the right place since the Institute trained black teachers.

Washington was a successful student and was quickly employed as a teacher. When a black college, the Tuskegee Institute, was built in Alabama, Booker T. Washington became its first president. Washington proved to be a true leader and a man of vision. He was a handsome man and kept himself healthy and physically fit. He spoke well to individuals and large groups. He was able to translate his vision for the college into words so that he was able to raise a great deal of money for the Institute's growth. One of the people he convinced to help was Andrew Carnegie. Carnegie was a

Tuskegee Institute

man who had also risen from poverty to become successful. Carnegie visited the college and helped fund many of Washington's ideas for expanding the work of the Institute. Washington was also good at recruiting the leaders in other educational fields. George Washington Carver, a botanist, was one of these people who came to the Institute.

Booker T. Washington

Booker T. Washington was the first black man to dine at the White House. President Teddy Roosevelt invited him to come. The two men shared many views, including the need for healthy physical activity, the value of books and knowledge, and the power of morality.

In his time, Booker T. Washington was a great leader for his people, encouraging them to learn skills to become economically equal with the white race. He did, however, believe in the system or philosophy of the races being kept separate. He was called "The Great Accommodator." Other black leaders grew impatient seeing the slow change within the United States, and they urged stronger measures to gain equality. Washington was on a speaking tour in New York City when he fell ill. He asked to be taken home to the South to be buried. He made it back to Tuskegee where he died.

1. From the passage, what can you infer about the motivations that Booker T. Washington had for achieving all that he did?

    A. He was motivated by the desire to escape poverty, to help others live out their dreams, and by the love of learning for itself.

    B. Booker T. Washington was motivated by the criticism of his peers to excel and change his way of approaching the difficulties in racial equality.

    C. He found motivation in the work of George Washington Carver, his first teacher.

    D. Booker T. Washington was motivated by a love of the North and the need to raise money for the Tuskegee Institute.

2. Based on the passage, which of the following sentences <u>best</u> describes the relationship between Teddy Roosevelt and Booker T. Washington?

    A. Roosevelt and Washington did not get along.

    B. Booker T. Washington taught Roosevelt how to raise money.

    C. Washington had Roosevelt visit his home on many occasions.

    D. Washington and Roosevelt admired each other and agreed on many issues.

3. In the passage, what two conflicts did Booker T. Washington have to resolve?

    A. 1) He convinced other black professionals that teaching at Tuskegee was a good job by writing a book about the Institute. 2) He had to raise money to keep the Institute growing by befriending Andrew Carnegie.

    B. 1) He first overcame the limits on former slaves by getting an education. 2) He had to overcome charges that he was too accommodating to the white leaders and stood by his promise to work toward economic equality for all citizens.

    C. 1) Overcoming poverty and 2) convincing Teddy Roosevelt that Washington was right about the importance of the peanut crop in Alabama.

    D. 1) He experienced conflict by being born in the South and so moved to New York. 2) He had to stand up to the other black leaders who said he was too harsh in his racial views.

DICTION AND SYNTAX

When someone writes, he or she wants to convey ideas accurately and in an interesting way to the reader. Once a writer has identified the audience and decided which tone and language would be appropriate, the writer will select certain words and phrases to reflect these decisions. The writer makes decisions about whether sentences will be written in simple or complex patterns.

In writing, **diction** refers to the author's choice of words, especially in regards to correctness, clarity, or effectiveness. **Syntax** involves the use of varied sentence structure and how the author uses it to best express meaning. Both diction and syntax are used by authors toward achieving a purpose.

STYLE EXPRESSED THROUGH SENTENCE FORMATION

Sentence formation or structure is an important part of **writing style** and the **author's purpose**. Some authors write in a style that uses short, simple sentences (a single independent clause containing a subject and a verb). Others use complex sentences, or sentences that contain an independent clause as well as subordinate clause(s). The following examples describe the same event. Compare the two examples for sentence structure, and discuss how that structure contributes to the writer's style and purpose.

Example 1: Simple Sentences: Swallows filled the trees. The noise was deafening.

Example 2: Complex Sentences: Hundreds of migrating swallows dropped from the sky and blended into nearby trees, causing a din that had residents shouting at each other to be heard.

Both of these styles describe something clearly and express the event well. One way is not necessarily better than the other. The two descriptions, however, vary in the imagery they provide and what they reveal about the story and the narrator. For example, the simple sentences could be setting up a scary scene, revealing less to create an eerie atmosphere; the descriptive complex sentences are lighter, almost like a journal.

For more explanation of simple and complex sentences, see the section on clauses in chapter 8.

It is a good idea to vary sentence structures in any essay you may write. Too many simple sentences can be boring and static and too many complex sentences can be too wordy and hard to follow. It's a good idea to incorporate both simple and complex sentences into your essay to keep it interesting. So mix it up!

The example below combines both simple and complex sentence structures. See if you can identify the simple and complex sentences.

Example: Simple and Complex Sentences: Hoping the disgust and dread he was feeling did not show on his face, Greg slowly stirred the glutinous green split pea soup his father had made. "Try it," his father gently commanded, watching him intently from across the small dining room table. Summoning all the courage he could muster, Greg held his breath and brought a small spoonful to his mouth. He took a bite. Greg swallowed hard, and the soup slid down his throat like phlegm, coating it with a slimy film. "So how is it?" his father asked. Ignoring the bitter aftertaste of the horrid soup, Greg smiled up at his father. "It's great, Dad."

Practice 3: Style and Sentence Formation

Read this passage. Then answer the questions that follow.

(1)Jay and Sue went out Saturday night. (2)It was their very first date. (3)Jay picked up Sue at six, before they headed to dinner. (4)After dinner, they saw a movie. (5)Sue had a great time, although she got into a bit of trouble coming home shortly after her curfew. (6)Luckily, she wasn't grounded, so she can go out with Jay again next weekend. (7)He has already asked her to go to a party.

1.   A. simple   3.   A. simple   5.   A. simple   7.   A. simple
      B. complex   B. complex   B. complex   B. complex

2.   A. simple   4.   A. simple   6.   A. simple
      B. complex   B. complex   B. complex

LITERARY DEVICES

Literary devices, such as **figurative language**, are used in literature to convey information in a creative way. Something may not be literally true, but it produces effective descriptions and images. As an example, think about the phrase, "He can't carry a tune in a bucket." No one can really carry a tune in a bucket. And if a tune could be carried in a bucket, that person might still have no clue as to how to do it. The phrase actually means that a person sings badly—off key and out of tune. The expression "can't carry a tune in a bucket" says the same thing as "sings badly and out of tune," but with more impact and with a vivid image. It also makes reading more enjoyable.

Following is a list of some of the common types of figurative language.

Figurative Language

Sound Devices   Some of the types of figurative language that authors can use are included in the category of **sound devices**. As the name implies, these are devices that have a particular sound to the ear, and they can create a mood or appeal to the senses. The types of figurative language included as sound devices include **alliteration**, **onomatopoeia**, **rhyme** and **rhythm**.

Onomatopoeia   words whose sound suggests their meaning. **Examples:** (1) splash, buzz, hiss, boom (2) "The *moan* of doves in immemorial elms; / And *murmuring* of innumerable bees," – Alfred Lord Tennyson.

Alliteration   **Alliteration** is the repetition of the same consonant sounds in lines of poetry or prose. **Examples:** (1) "Droning a drowsy syncopated tune,"– Langston Hughes (repetition of "d" sounds). (2) "I like to see it lap the miles, / And lick the valleys up," – Emily Dickinson (repetition of "l" sounds).

Rhyme   when words have the same sounds. **Examples:** (1) "Tyger! Tyger! burning bright / In the forests of the night" – William Blake (**bright** and **night** rhyme.) (2) "Happy the man who, safe on shore, / Now trims, at home, his evening fire; / Unmov'd, he hears the tempests roar, / That on the tufted groves expire" – Philip Freneau (**shore/roar** and **fire/expire**).

| Rhythm | the arrangement of stressed and unstressed syllables into a pattern. While rhythm is almost always found in poetry, quality prose writing also involves regular patterns that appeal to the reader. Read the following example out loud: "Vanishing, swerving, evermore curving again into sight, / Softly the sand beach wavers away to a dim gray looping of light." – Sidney Lanier |

Other Figurative Language

| Analogy | An **analogy** is an explanation or description of something unfamiliar or difficult to explain by comparing it with something familiar.

Example: Similes and metaphors are forms of analogy. |
| Metaphor | A **metaphor** is a direct comparison between two unlike things *without* using the words "like" or "as." **Example:** The sun is a big ball of fire. The moon is a luminescent pearl nestled in a cushion of stars.

An **extended metaphor** is when an item with several characteristics is compared with another item. The separate characteristics are compared with the characteristics of the second item. In her poem "The Fish," Elizabeth Bishop compares the skin of the fish she catches to old wallpaper. She compares several qualities of the two, including the colors, the patterns and the general appearance. |
Simile	A **simile** compares two things *using* "**like**" or "**as**." **Examples:** (1) "Sometimes I feel **like** a motherless child" African-American spiritual (2) "My love is **like** a red, red rose" – Robert Burns. (3) Free **as** a bird.
Allusion	 **Allusion** is a reference to a well-known place, literary or art work, famous person, or historical event. Today, these references are often related to current pop culture. In order for an allusion to work, the reader must be familiar with the work or item being referred to. For example, Pixar produced a popular movie called "Finding Nemo," about a father fish finding his son. The name Nemo is an allusion to Captain Nemo, the famous character in the novel *20,000 Leagues Under the Sea*.
Exaggeration (Hyperbole)	**Hyperbole** is the use of exaggeration to create an effect. **Examples:** (1) I was so surprised, you could have knocked me over with a feather. (2) I would rather die than eat brussels sprouts.
Understatement (Meiosis)	**Meiosis** is the opposite of hyperbole. It is a way of stressing the importance of an issue by minimizing the expression of it. For instance, if you were to describe a particularly chaotic evening you were facing tonight, you might list the three tests you have to study for, the soccer practice you have to attend, the projects you have due tomorrow, the band meeting that you are not supposed to miss, and the Spanish tape you have to listen to. And then, instead of stating the obvious by saying how busy you are going to be, you would instead understate that fact by saying "I guess I'm not going to be bored tonight." This **understatement** actually gives more impact to the idea that you are going to be extremely busy.

Imagery

Imagery is the use of words or phrases that evoke the sensations of sight, hearing, touch, smell, or taste. For example, Edgar Allan Poe opens "The Fall of the House of Usher" with "During the whole of a dull, dark, and soundless day in the autumn of the year, when the clouds hung oppressively low in the heavens..." Poe's word choices help the reader picture the day and perceive the mood.

Personification

giving human qualities to something not human. For example, (1) "As she sang softly at the evil face of the full moon." – Jean Toomer (2) "The oak trees whispered softly in the night breeze." – John Steinbeck. And Stephen Crane writes an extensive personification of fire in *The Red Badge of Courage*: "The smoke from the fire at times neglected the clay chimney and wreathed into the room, and this flimsy chimney of clay and sticks made endless threats to set ablaze the whole establishment."

Symbol

any object, person, place or action that has a meaning in itself and that also represents a meaning beyond itself, such as a quality, an attitude, a belief or a value. For example, a skull and crossbones is often a symbol that warns of poison. In Nathaniel Hawthorne's short story "The Minister's Black Veil," the black veil symbolizes secret sin.

Pun

A **pun** is a way of using words so that their meaning can be taken in different ways, which makes what is said humorous. William Shakespeare loved using puns. Sometimes he would use the humor of puns even in a tragic situation. One example of this takes place in *Romeo and Juliet*, when Mercutio, about to die of a stab wound says, "Ask for me tomorrow and you shall find me a grave man." The double meaning here is that a grave man is one who is serious, while Mercutio is implying he will be in his grave.

Rhetorical Devices

Parallelism

arranging an essay so that elements (tense, phrases, clauses, etc.) of equal importance are constructed in similar ways, creating balance. An example can be seen in the opening line of *A Tale of Two Cities by Charles Dickens:* "It was the best of times, it was the worst of times."

Repetition

using the same word or phrase several times for emphasis, as in this example from a speech by Winston Churchill: "We shall fight in France, we shall fight on the seas and oceans, . . .we shall fight on the beaches, we shall fight on the landing grounds. ."

Practice 4: Figurative Language

Read the following passage. For each numbered sentence, identify the figurative language it contains.

(1)I awoke to the buzz and whir of little flying things trying to breach the tent flap. (2)I realized what had awoken me, what made my eyes pop open, and what was now pulling me out of the tent. (3)The campground was awash with the aroma of sizzling bacon and fresh coffee, and my mouth began to water. (4)I was so hungry I could eat a horse. (5)Jessica was a morning angel floating between the fire pit and the cooler full of supplies, keeping an eye on everything at once. (6)I wrapped my sleeping bag around me, and went to sit by the fire, wide-eyed and expectant as a kid on Christmas morning.

1.

    A.   metaphor   C.   simile   E.   hyperbole

    B.   parallelism   D.   onomatopoeia   F.   imagery

2.

    A.   metaphor   C.   simile   E.   hyperbole

    B.   parallelism   D.   onomatopoeia   F.   imagery

3.

    A.   metaphor   C.   simile   E.   hyperbole

    B.   parallelism   D.   onomatopoeia   F.   imagery

4.

    A.   metaphor   C.   simile   E.   hyperbole

    B.   parallelism   D.   onomatopoeia   F.   imagery

5.

    A.   metaphor   C.   simile   E.   hyperbole

    B.   parallelism   D.   onomatopoeia   F.   imagery

6.

    A.   metaphor   C.   simile   E.   hyperbole

    B.   parallelism   D.   onomatopoeia   F.   imagery

CHAPTER 3 SUMMARY

Story structure is used to organize and build stories. A good writer uses **structural tools**, or devices, such as: **point of view and narrator, mood**, **tone**, **plot**, and **setting**.

The **point of view** is the perspective, or outlook, from which a writer tells a story. The **narrator** is the person who is telling about the dialogue and the action in the story.

Possible points of view are:

- **first person**: the narrator tells the story from the *I* point of view
- **second person**: the speaker uses the pronoun *you*
- **third person**: the speaker describes characters as *he, she,* or *they*
    - **omniscient**: narrator is capable of knowing, telling, and seeing all that happens
    - **limited:** the speaker knows only what is seen, heard, and felt by the thoughts and viewpoint of one character

The **setting** is the background for the action of a story. Setting includes **time**, **place,** and **general surroundings**.

The feeling created within the reader is called **mood**; **tone** is the writer's attitude toward a topic.

The parts of a **plot** are: introduction, conflict (internal and external), rising action, climax, falling action, and resolution.

Sequence is the order in which events happen in a story. The sequence may not go in a straight time order but may go back and forth in time with the use of **foreshadowing** and **flashbacks**.

Some different types of **character roles** or functions in a literary work are: **narrator, protagonist,** and **antagonist.**

Types of characters are: **flat** (one dimensional, minor character), **round** (multi-dimensional, major character), **static** (does not experience change or growth), and **dynamic** (undergoes significant change or personal growth).

Character traits are developed through the use of: **description, narration, dialogue, dialect,** and **actions.**

Figurative language is used to convey information in a creative way.

CHAPTER 3 REVIEW

A. Read each of the literary selections for content, and answer the questions that follow each one.

**Get up and Lock the Door
an old ballad, updated**

It was about November 11th
    And a happy time it was then,
That the good wife had sausages to make
    And she fried them in the pan.

The wind blew cold from east and north
    and blew onto the floor,
Said the good man to the good wife,
    "Get up and lock the door."

"My hand is busy with housework
    Good man as you may see,
If it were not locked for a hundred years
    It would not be locked by me."

They made an agreement between them
    They made it firm and sure,
That the one who spoke the first word
    Would get up and lock the door.

Then there came by two men - strangers
    At twelve o'clock at night
When they could see no other house
    But they could see their light.

They stood at the door and yelled,
    "May we come in and warm ourselves?"
We're cold down to the core."
    But neither one of them would answer
    nor get up and lock the door.

And first they ate the sausages
    and then they ate the bread,
And the good wife had many thoughts
    but kept them in her head.

Then one man to the other said,
    "Hey man, take my knife
You take off the old man's beard
    And I'll kiss the good wife

Then our good man got up
    An angry man was he,
"Will you kiss my wife before my eyes
    Don't you think I can see?"

Then the good wife got up
    Gave three skips on the floor,
"Good man you spoke the first word
    Get up and lock the door."

1. The main conflict in the selection is between

    A.   the two strangers.

    B.   the strangers and the wife.

    C.   the characters and the weather.

    D.   the husband and the wife.

2. What is the author's tone as revealed in the last stanza?

    A.   suspenseful

    B.   humorous

    C.   gloomy

    D.   dramatic

3. Who is the narrator of the selection?

    A.   the husband

    B.   the wife

    C.   one of the strangers

    D.   an unknown third person

Analysis of Literature

excerpt from *The Errand Boy* by Horatio Alger

Phil Brent was plodding through the snow in the direction of the house where he lived with his stepmother and her son, when a snowball, moist and hard, struck him just below his ear with stinging emphasis. The pain was considerable, and Phil's anger rose.

He turned suddenly, his eyes flashing fiercely, intent upon discovering who had committed this outrage, for he had no doubt that it was intentional.

He looked in all directions, but saw no one except a mild old gentleman in spectacles, who appeared to have some difficulty in making his way through the obstructed street.

Phil did not need to be told that it was not the old gentleman who had taken such an unwarrantable liberty with him. So he looked farther, but his ears gave him the first clue.

He heard a chuckling laugh, which seemed to proceed from behind the stone wall that ran along the roadside.

"I will see who it is," he decided, and plunging through the snow he surmounted the wall, in time to see a boy of about his own age running away across the fields as fast as the deep snow would allow.

"So it's you, Jonas!" he shouted wrathfully. "I thought it was some sneaking fellow like you."

Jonas Webb, his stepbrother, his freckled face showing a degree of dismay, for he had not calculated on discovery, ran the faster, but while fear winged his steps, anger proved

the more effectual spur, and Phil overtook him after a brief run, from the effects of which both boys panted. "What made you throw that snowball?" demanded Phil angrily, as he seized Jonas by the collar and shook him.

"You let me alone!" said Jonas, struggling ineffectually in his grasp.

"Answer me! What made you throw that snowball?" demanded Phil, in a tone that showed he did not intend to be trifled with.

"Because I chose to," answered Jonas, his spite getting the better of his prudence. "Did it hurt you?" he continued, his eyes gleaming with malice.

4. Which of the following <u>best</u> describes the relationship between Jonas and Phil?
   A. They are both bullies, but now they're fighting.
   B. They are neighbors who are used to teasing each other.
   C. They are friends who are angry at each other.
   D. They are stepbrothers who do not get along well.

5. Which of these sentences from the passage <u>best</u> illustrates Jonas's character?

    A. "You let me alone!" said Jonas, struggling ineffectually in his grasp.

    B. "Because I chose to," answered Jonas, his spite getting the better of his prudence.

    C. He heard a chuckling laugh, which seemed to proceed from behind the stone wall that ran along the roadside.

    D. "What made you throw that snowball?" demanded Phil angrily, as he seized Jonas by the collar and shook him

6. Based on the passage, which of the following sentences <u>best</u> describes the main conflict?

    A. Jonas is trying to teach Phil a lesson about snowball fighting.

    B. Each of the boys is resentful of the other one.

    C. Jonas is trying to get back at Phil for the way he has been treated.

    D. Phil is angry with his sneaky stepbrother Jonas.

The Cave

It was one of the coldest days of winter when the four high school seniors began their journey into the mountains. Chad, a football player; Doug, an apprentice auto mechanic; Steve, a deer hunter; and Mike, a computer whiz all had one thing in common: they ate together at lunch. For weeks, they had planned this trip. Steve's father owned about 600 acres of land near the Virginia border. The previous month, Steve had seen an old limestone cave he'd heard stories about and had been waiting for the best time to explore it. Winter break had just begun, so the boys were ready for high adventure.

After an hour's drive, they reached the edge of the forest that surrounded the cave. They parked Chad's SUV and unloaded the exit markers, rope, and helmets with cave lights attached. They carried their gear two miles through thick underbrush before reaching the cave's entrance. Mike yelled, "There's smoke coming out of that hole!"

"Will you hush, ya little book worm, don't ya know that caves are always warmer than the outside in the wintertime? That's just mist!" Steve said.

The cave entrance was slippery and muddy. Spiders crawled through the opening, and there were signs of bats regularly flying in and out at night. Once the boys passed the entrance, however, there were no more bugs.

"It sure is a lot warmer in here than outside," Doug muttered.

They crawled, jumped, and sloshed their way through the cave. Crystal stalactites and stalagmites decorated the cave floor and ceiling with stunning beauty. Chad reached out to grab one of the alluring crystal formations. "Don't you touch that!" Steve yelled. "I've heard talk from long ago that there's some sorta cave guardian here. The story's that the Guardian is supposed to be really mean and nasty, and it strikes whenever someone tries to steal parta the cave's formations." Chad dropped his hand, and the group continued crawling forward.

Slightly farther along, the passage opened up into a huge cavern. The ceiling soared 100 feet above. Beautiful crystal formations resembling amethyst and topaz sparkled under the light of their helmet lamps. Mike yelped when he tripped over a bone on the cave floor.

"Don't worry, Mike, it's probably some animal that crawled down here and died a long time ago," Steve said.

While the rest were occupied comforting Mike, Chad carefully examined a two foot long crystal formation. Unable to resist any longer, he reached up and broke off a shard. Suddenly, a low growl filled the cavern. "What was that?" everyone asked. Two yellow eyes shown through the darkness from a ledge near the ceiling.

A gravelly voice bellowed, "Get! Out!"

The group broke into a run. As Steve led everyone out of the cave, he yelled, "Don't look back! Whatever ya do, don't look back!" They could feel a presence behind them all the way to the cave's entrance. Once free from the darkness of the cave, the boys jumped, tripped, and ran through the forest as fast as they could. They were near exhaustion by the time they reached the SUV. Steve gasped, "Chad, get us outa here!" Chad fumbled for his keys and jumped in. Then, Steve heard something behind him. Turning around, he saw the Guardian coming at them. Steve told everyone, "Mike and I are gettin' near the car. When we see the Guardian, we'll run in front of the car. You run over the Guardian when it scurries in front of your car as it chases us."

Shaking with fear, Mike and Steve waited for the Guardian to catch up with them before they started racing to the SUV. As soon as the spider-like creature was in front of him, Chad floored the gas pedal, running over the Guardian. A flash of blue light flared from beneath the car, and the Guardian was nothing but a pile of big crab legs.

"Let's get outta here for good," Steve shouted as he jerked the door open and tumbled into the back seat.

7. Which of the following sentences <u>best</u> suggests a conflict in the passage?
   A. Once the boys passed the entrance, however, there were no bugs.
   B. "Don't worry Mike; it was probably some animal that crawled down here and died a long time ago," Steve said.
   C. They were near exhaustion by the time they reached the SUV.
   D. "Don't you touch that!" Steve yelled. "I've heard talk from long ago that there's some sorta cave guardian here, ..."

8. Which of the following sentences <u>best</u> describes the theme of the passage?
   A. An SUV is more reliable than friends in a difficult situation.
   B. Caves can be beautiful and educational places to visit.
   C. Strong bonds of friendship can overcome difficult obstacles.
   D. Caves and caving trips are very common in the mountains.

9. Which pair of nouns <u>best</u> describes the mood of this passage?

   A.   joy and happiness

   B.   suspense and resolution

   C.   pride and prejudice

   D.   trust and faith

10. The point of view in this selection is <u>best</u> described as

   A.   omniscient third person

   B.   second person

   C.   first person

   D.   limited third person

11. Which of the following sentences <u>best</u> describes the climax of the passage?

   A.   "A flash of blue light flared from beneath the car, and the Guardian was nothing but a pile of big crab legs."

   B.   "Unable to resist any longer, he reached up and broke off a shard."

   C.   "A gravelly voice bellowed, 'Get! Out!'"

   D.   "As Steve led everyone out of the cave he yelled, 'Don't look back! Whatever ya do, don't look back!'"

12. What is the <u>best</u> description of the setting of the passage?

   A.   a cave in the hot Arizona desert

   B.   deep in the rolling hills of Virginia

   C.   a cave in rainy, forested mountains

   D.   a cave in the muddy backwoods of the Rockies

13. Which of the following responses <u>best</u> describes the relationship between Steve and Mike?

   A.   As a confident outdoors person, Steve acts as a sort of big brother to Mike: fussing at or comforting Mike's fears.

   B.   Steve and Mike are always competing against each other for the leadership position of the group.

   C.   Mike willfully disobeys all of Steve's instructions and so brings the anger of the cave Guardian down on the group.

   D.   Mike is the brother of Steve's father, so Mike is Steve's uncle.

excerpt from *Frankenstein* by Mary Wollstonecraft Shelley

As the night advanced, a fierce wind arose from the woods and quickly dispersed the clouds that had loitered in the heavens; the blast tore along like a mighty avalanche and produced a kind of insanity in my spirits that burst all bounds of reason and reflection. I lighted the dry branch of a tree and danced with fury around the devoted cottage, my eyes still fixed on the western horizon, the edge of which the moon nearly touched. A part of its orb was at length hid, and I waved my brand; it sank and with a loud scream I fired the straw, and heath and bushes, which I had collected. The wind fanned the fire, and the cottage was quickly enveloped by the flames, which clung to it and licked it with their forked and destroying tongues.

14. Which of the following <u>best</u> describes the setting of this passage?
    A. The narrator is in the Arctic following someone.
    B. The setting is in a city at night.
    C. The story is placed in some countryside in the heat of day.
    D. The narrator is near someone's cottage as night is falling.

15. Which is the <u>best</u> example of foreshadowing from the selection?
    A. "A part of its orb was at length hid, and I waved my brand;"
    B. "a fierce wind arose from the woods and quickly dispersed the clouds that had loitered in the heavens"
    C. "the winds fanned the fire, and the cottage was quickly enveloped by the flames"
    D. "my eyes still fixed on the western horizon, the edge of which the moon nearly touched."

B. Read each excerpt in column A. On the line following each excerpt, write the letter of the word in column B which best describes the kind of literary device it is.

Excerpt	Literary Device
16. "Success is counted sweetest/ By those who ne'er succeed." – Emily Dickinson _____	a. **alliteration**
17. "The inherent vice of capitalism is the unequal sharing of blessing; the inherent virtue of socialism is the equal sharing of miseries." – Winston Churchill _____	b. **hyperbole** c. **repetition** d. **parallelism**
18. My brother, Mike, trampled the new lilies with his big Hobbit feet. _____	e. **metaphor** f. **rhythm**
19. I've told you a million times to be quiet in here._____	g. **simile**
20. "All the world's a stage, / And all the men and women merely players." –Shakespeare _____	h. **allusion** i. **personification**
21. "What lies behind us and what lies before us are tiny compared to what lies within us." – Ralph Waldo Emerson _____	j. **understatement**
22. "Love's stricken 'Why' is all that love can speak." _____	
23. After a big hurricane, Bill says to Sha Kira, "We've had a little wind tonight."_____	
24. "But soft! What light through yonder window breaks?" – Shakespeare (sound device) _____	
25. "A mass of wet grass, marched upon, rustled like silk." – Stephen Crane _____	

C. Read the following passage. Then, answer the questions about plot that follow it. The passage takes place during the American Civil War, as a young soldier waits with his regiment for the enemy to appear.

excerpt from *The Red Badge of Courage*
by Stephen Crane

There were moments of waiting. The youth thought of the village street at home before the arrival of the circus parade on a day in the spring. He remembered how he had stood, a small, thrillful boy, prepared to follow the dingy lady upon the white horse, or the band in its faded chariot. He saw the yellow road, the lines of expectant people and the sober houses. He particularly remembered an old fellow who used to sit upon a cracker box in front of the store and feign to despise such exhibitions. A thousand details of color and form surged in his mind. The old fellow upon the cracker box appeared in middle prominence.

Someone cried, "Here they come!"

There was rustling and muttering among the men. They displayed a feverish desire to have every possible cartridge ready to their hands. The boxes were pulled around into various positions, and adjusted with great care. It was as if seven hundred new bonnets were being tried on.

The tall soldier, having prepared his rifle, produced a red handkerchief of some kind. He was engaged in knotting it about his throat with exquisite attention to its position, when the cry was repeated up and down the line in a muffled roar of sound.

"Here they come! Here they come!" Gun locks clicked.

26. What is the flashback in the story?

27. Where does the flashback bring the reader and the character?

28. How does the flashback compare with the present moment of the story?

D. Read the following poem and answer the questions about figurative language.

There is no Frigate like a Book

1 There is no Frigate like a Book

2 To take us Lands away

3 Nor any Coursers like a Page

4 Of prancing Poetry—

5 This Traverse may the poorest take

6 Without oppress of Toll—

7 How frugal is the Chariot

8 That bears the Human soul.

– Emily Dickinson

29. Which of the following lines from the poem contain a *simile*?

    A. line 1   B. line 4   C. line 6   D. line 8

30. Which of the following lines contains an example of a *metaphor*?

    A. lines 1–2   B. lines 3–4   C. lines 5–6   D. lines 7–8

31. Which of the following lines from the poem contain *alliteration*?

    A. lines 1–2   B. lines 3–4   C. lines 5–6   D. lines 7–8

32. Write down the words that *rhyme* in this poem.

_____

33. **Short Answer.** Use your own paper to write your response.

    Explain what is being said about books in this poem and how the figurative language helps say it.

Chapter 4
Non-Print Text and Information Resources

This chapter addresses the following expectation(s) and their related indicators from **Core Learning Goal 1: Reading. Reviewing, and Responding to Texts**

Expectation 1.1	The student will use effective strategies before, during, and after reading, viewing, and listening to self-selected and assigned materials.
Expectation 1.3	The student will explain and give evidence to support perceptions about print and non-print works.

This chapter also addresses the following expectation(s) and their related indicators from **Core Learning Goal 2: Composing in a Variety of Modes**

Expectation 2.3	The student will locate, retrieve, and use information from various sources to accomplish a purpose.

In this chapter, you will learn how to understand non-print text and a variety of information resources. These are important for success in school and at work.

IMAGES

Do you recognize this picture?

Leonardo da Vinci's *Mona Lisa* is one of the most famous paintings in the world. To some people it is the first example that comes to mind when they think of art. To others, it represents a mystery—why is she smiling? **Images** can mean different things to different people. Sometimes, this is the power of images. Sometimes, this is a limitation.

TEXT

Text refers to written words. A short story is an example of text, as is a letter, a journal entry and an article in a magazine. Text can refer to words written on a piece of paper, read off of a computer monitor or printed on a movie poster. Anywhere a written word appears, that is text.

NON-PRINT TEXT

Paintings like the *Mona Lisa*, photographs, posters, art reproductions, cartoons, and stills from movie or film productions are all examples of **non-print text** or **images**. An **image** or **non-print text** means a physical likeness or representation that is shown without using words.

PURPOSE AND USE OF NON-PRINT TEXT

Non-print text can be a useful and powerful tool. Images, like words, can be used to inform, to entertain, to inspire, to prompt action, to symbolize, or to capture a moment in history. Images can sometimes show information in clearer or more effective ways than words can. Following are some ways that images are particularly useful for conveying ideas.

IMAGES USED TO SHOW WHAT WORDS CANNOT

Have you heard the saying, "A picture is worth 1,000 words"? The expression means that there are times when an image can show what words cannot describe, or that an image can say it more effectively. If you have ever shopped online for clothing or flipped through a catalogue looking for new electronic equipment, you have probably noticed the importance of photographs when a retailer is trying to sell something. Can you imagine buying a pair of jeans online with only the following information?

Denim, belt loops, front and back pockets, cotton blend, machine washable.

This describes the majority of jeans produced. How do you know that the jeans are today's style and not the style of five years ago? Few people would order an article of clothing without being able to see what it looks like. Often, the description of a product (the text) takes a backseat to the image of the product (the non-print text).

IMAGES USED AS REPRESENTATION

Sometimes an image is powerful because it serves as a **representation** or a symbol. Taken literally, the photograph to the right shows burning buildings. But taken in context, this image is much more than buildings afire. A photograph of the destruction of the World Trade Center represents to most Americans a national tragedy, enormous loss of life, and a startling new awareness of terrorist acts. Images depicting events like September 11 have meaning beyond the objects or people shown in the photographs.

IMAGES USED TO INSTRUCT OR INFORM

An image can play an important part in **instructing** or **informing**. A drawing in a history book might show a moment in history, such as this image of Christopher Columbus arriving in America. Information that the viewer can learn from this and other images of Columbus might include such historical details as clothing styles of the time, the structure of his ship, or the types of vegetation he encountered on the coastline where he landed.

Image Websites
http://images.google.com/ Google's image search feature brings images from all over the Web together. You can then link to the website where the original image was found to see it in context. http://www.bigfoto.com/ This site has free photos to download in categories from America to ships to food to nature

Practice 1: Purpose and Use of Non-Print Text

1. **Short Answer**. Read the description below. Use your own paper to respond in 2–3 sentences. Explain why a photograph would be a useful addition to this advertisement.

> For Sale:
>
> Red 2001 Ford
>
> 2-door, automatic, slight body damage, 90,000 miles, runs great, $2000

2. **Short Answer**. Look at the image below. Use your own paper to respond in 2–3 sentences. What is the artist trying to represent in the drawing below?

3. **Short Answer**. Look at the image below. Use your own paper to respond in 2–3 sentences.

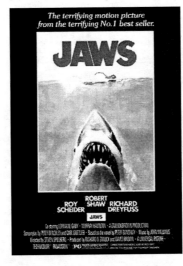

Why do you think this image was chosen for this movie poster?

USING NON-PRINT TEXT APPROPRIATELY

Images are more prevalent and accessible today than ever before. Twenty-four hour news stations cover topics around the world. The Internet offers millions of photographs and videos. Authors often add images to written text to prove or illustrate their point. Sometimes adding an image is the only way for an author to get his point across. Sometimes images detract from the point. What determines when an image is used appropriately? **A well-chosen image supports the point the author is trying to make and also takes into consideration who is reading the text.**

Practice 2: Using Non-Print Text Appropriately

1. **Short answer**. Look at the images below. Use your own paper to respond in 2–3 sentences.

Suppose you are trying to convince your family to get a dog. But, with all of the lawsuits involving dog bites, your parents are not enthusiastic. You do some research on the Internet and find several articles about what great pets dogs make and the benefits of having one. You decide to write your parents an email pleading your case. Which photo would be the better attachment to your email? Explain your answer.

Part of choosing an appropriate image is knowing to what **audience** the author is speaking. The audience is reading the author's words. Images can be interpreted in different ways depending on the audience or the context. Writers must always keep their audience in mind to avoid unintended responses that might hurt the **point**, or argument, they are trying to make. Look again at the photo of the snarling dog above. While it would certainly not help your case with your parents, the photo might be the perfect image for a different context. Imagine that your younger brother was bitten by an unleashed dog and you were starting a campaign to promote the enforcement of leash laws in your community. In that case, the snarling dog image best supports the reaction you intend from your audience.

TEXT AND NON-PRINT TEXT WORKING TOGETHER

Print and non-print text can work together to make a point and, in fact, often rely upon each other.

For example, look at the political poster. This is Rosie the Riveter, a cultural icon from World War II. Rosie represented the millions of American women who worked in the manufacturing plants that produced munitions while the men, who had traditionally done this kind of work, were at war. The image of Rosie was developed to convince women that they had a patriotic duty, as well as the ability, to serve their country in this way. Note how the text is crucial to the message of the poster. Alone, the image suggests a woman's strength. The text provides the motivation to work—together, the women can and do make a huge difference to the war effort.

Deciding whether to use printed text, non-print text, or both depends on many factors. What point is the author trying to make? Who is the audience? How does the audience already feel about the topic? What does the author intend for the audience to think or do after reading the text? The successful use of both print and non-print text depends on the author considering factors like these.

Practice 3: Text and Non-Print Text Working Together

Short Answer. Imagine that you are writing a short research paper on gazelles. Would you include images in your paper? Explain your decision in 2–3 sentences.

INFORMATION RESOURCES

Writing a report for school, seeing a movie, buying a new computer or video game, taking a vacation: What do all of these events have in common? They all benefit from a little research. Most research requires some type of information resource.

What are information resources? **Information resources** are texts and electronic media which supply information. In this section, we will discuss the following common information resources:

Dictionary	Internet	Newspapers	Periodicals
Thesaurus	Books	Encyclopedia	Electronic Catalog

Think about all the ways you use information resources: What resource would you look in to find descriptions of movies and time listings? What resource would you use to find information on vacationing in Disney World? What kind of research would you do before buying a new video game? Where would you find information for an essay on the dangers of smoking?

We live in an information society. There is an almost endless amount of information waiting for you to find it. Being able to find the exact information you are looking for is an important skill. Knowing what resource materials to choose and how to use them can help you find answers to your questions. This section will provide knowledge about information resources.

One of the most important skills related to information resources is knowing how to **cite**, or give credit to, your sources of information. Credit must be given to the original writers for information or ideas that come from other sources. See chapter 9 for a discussion about using resources.

You can use many types of resources when you are doing research for a speech or report. For example, if you were researching information about Hurricane Katrina, you might consult a magazine, a newspaper, or a Web site for your topic.

Now, let's learn more about some common information resources.

TYPES OF INFORMATION RESOURCES

DICTIONARY

A **dictionary** provides more than the meaning or meanings of a word. It also provides different forms of the word, such as the plural form or the past tense. A typical dictionary entry would tell what part of speech the word is and give a pronunciation key. Dictionaries often give examples of the word in a sentence. A dictionary entry also provides the origin of a word.

THESAURUS

A **thesaurus** provides a word's synonyms, words that mean basically the same thing. It may also provide antonyms, words that mean the opposite. A thesaurus is a useful resource text for improving both reading and writing.

THE INTERNET

The **Internet** can be a student's greatest resource or biggest waste of time. There are so many sites to explore that you can easily lose track of your original topic. You have to know how to find the right information and how to evaluate it for accuracy and value.

Using the Internet requires some skills similar to off-line research. For example, just as you would with other resource materials, you must select **keywords** to find the material you want. You also have to decide whether the material you find through your search is useful for your topic. Lastly, you have to keep a list of the sources where you found your material. You will need that list so that you can correctly cite those sources in your report.

BOOKS

Most books, including textbooks and literature collections, are organized into different **parts** to help the reader locate information. Below, you will find these parts in the order they appear in a book.

Title Page	The **title page** shows the title of the book, the author(s), the edition (if the book has been published before), the publishing company and the place of publication. Details on this page are important when you need to give credit for information you have found in the book. (The **copyright page** follows the title page, showing the book's publishing date and copyright restrictions.)
Table of Contents	The **table of contents** lists chapters, subheadings, and any supplemental headings found in the book, as well as the page numbers where they can be found. It is written to show the order of appearance from the beginning to the end. This page is usually titled as "Contents" and provides an overview of the content and organization of the book.
Appendix	The **appendix** (or appendix sections) contains material to provide the reader with additional information. This material might include charts, documents, tables, illustrations, and/or photographs. For example, your social studies book might have timelines, graphs, or historical maps in an appendix.

Glossary	The **glossary** is a dictionary of words found in the book. It usually contains all the important terms and words that were boldfaced or italicized in each chapter. There may be more than one glossary in the back of the book. For example, in a Spanish textbook you might find a glossary of grammar terms, a glossary of Spanish words, and a translation glossary of English words to Spanish words.
Index	The **index** is found at the end of the book and shows the topics found in the book as well as the page numbers where the topics appear in the book. The index items are arranged alphabetically.
Bibliography	The **bibliography** lists the different titles, authors, and publishing information for all the references and resources used to write the book.

NEWSPAPERS

Newspapers provide current information about local and world events. Most newspaper articles are written to be brief and purely informative, so they do not go into as much detail as magazine articles. Newspapers have both fact-based and opinion-based writing. **News reports** present information—facts, statistics, and statements by other people. They tell the *who, what, when, where, why,* and *how* of a specific event. **News features** also present information but reflect a reporter's opinion and personal style. Most newspapers now have Web sites on the Internet with current articles as well as archived copies of past articles.

ENCYCLOPEDIA

Encyclopedias are sets of books with entries about all kinds of topics. A general encyclopedia is arranged into volumes by the alphabet (for example, *A's* are in Volume 1). The subject entries inside each volume are also arranged by the alphabet. Entries cover a wide range of subjects such as people, places, historical events, science, and technology. Encyclopedia entries are meant to inform, meaning they provide facts without opinions. Libraries also have specialized encyclopedias with detailed material about specific topics such as art, music, literature, science, and technology.

When you are researching information in an encyclopedia, you must look for articles based on a **keyword**, much like you use for Internet searches. For example, if you were trying to find information about how car engines work, you might search under the following keywords: engines, automobiles, or cars.

Many encyclopedias now have online editions available on the Internet as well as CD-Rom versions to use in your computer. The information available from these sources is similar to the book version. However, these sources have the added benefits of references, or links, to other information sources as well as video and sound clips.

PERIODICALS

Magazines and journals are great resources for current information because these publications are issued weekly, semimonthly, monthly, or quarterly. They are also good for a variety of information because they contain articles from many different writers. Libraries classify magazines and journals as **periodicals** (published periodically—weekly, monthly, and so on).

Magazines usually offer many articles in a specific area of interest. They are written both to inform and to entertain. Magazine articles have much detail and background information and are written with a great deal of research. Magazine articles inform readers but can also express the writer's opinion. *People* is a popular magazine that features articles about celebrities and people of interest. It would be a good resource for information about the entertainment industry. *TIME* magazine contains articles on current events and politics. It would be a good resource for big news stories. Magazines are found in bookstores, grocery stores, libraries, and even on the Internet.

Journals are academic magazines that have information about specific areas of study. Since experts in each field write the articles, journals are considered unbiased, reliable sources of information. For example, the journal *Nature* features science articles and has the latest research in areas such as biology and geology. Journals are not usually found in bookstores, but they can be found in libraries and on the Internet.

ELECTRONIC LIBRARY CATALOG

Electronic Library Catalogs help you find a library's books and other materials. The computer catalog lets you search by *subject, author, title,* or *keyword,* and then shows you a list of material that matches your search. Each listing of an item or book will have the following information: author's full name, title of the book, place of publication, publisher's name, publication date, number of pages, brief facts about the book, and a call number. Every book will also show an **ISBN**. This stands for **International Standard Book Number**, and it uniquely identifies each publication. Use the short description of the book to decide whether it is the right material for your research, and then locate the book on the library's shelves using the call number.

Practice 4: Choosing the Right Resource Material

Choose the most appropriate resource material to find the information.

1. Alex is writing an essay and needs to find another word for *boring*.
   A. dictionary   B. Internet   C. thesaurus   D. encyclopedia

2. Michelle is working on a science project about bats.
   A. dictionary   B. newspaper   C. glossary   D. encyclopedia

3. Anthony is reviewing words for a vocabulary test.
   A. dictionary   B. Internet   C. thesaurus   D. encyclopedia

4. Latisha needs to bring in an example of a current event.
   A. newspaper   B. encyclopedia   C. journal   D. thesaurus

5. Lewis is writing about a baseball player's current season.
   A. encyclopedia   B. magazine   C. journal   D. dictionary

6. Maria wants to find a pen pal in a foreign county.
   A. encyclopedia   B. Internet   C. magazine   D. journal

7. Josh wants to find a scientific study on squid.
   A. encyclopedia   B. newspaper   C. magazine   D. journal

8. Hannah is looking for people's reactions to the state's new driver's license law.
   A. encyclopedia   B. newspaper   C. magazine   D. journal

CHAPTER 4 SUMMARY

Images can be useful and powerful tools. They can show what words cannot. They can become **symbols** and have meaning beyond what they show literally. They can describe things difficult to envision when reading a written description.

Images must be chosen carefully so that they support the text. An author must consider both his **point** and his **audience**, not only when writing but also when determining whether an image is a useful accompaniment to his text.

Text and **non-print text** can work powerfully together. They can provide proof of an author's point, helping to convince the audience to believe as the writer does. They can explain an image and give it new meaning. They can clarify ideas or information within a text. Images can be invaluable tools that provide and clarify information.

You can use many kinds of **information resources** for your research. Just make sure they are reliable, timely, and appropriate for your topic.

CHAPTER 4 REVIEW

A. Multiple choice

1. Which of the following is the best definition of a **representation**?

   A. a symbol   B. a photograph   C. an essay   D. an author

2. Which of the following are ways an image can be useful?
   A. to provide clarification of an idea in the text
   B. to convince the reader of the author's point of view
   C. to show what words cannot
   D. all of the above

3. Which is most effective?
   A. using text alone
   B. using images alone
   C. using both images and text together
   D. it depends on the context

4. Which of the following is an example of an audience?
   A. the author of a book.
   B. the publisher of a book
   C. the readers of a book.
   D. the sellers of a book

5. Images can do all of the following except:
   A. show what words cannot.
   B. be used as representation.
   C. be used to inform.
   D. contain only text.

6. The following are examples of printed text except:
    A. a movie poster.
    B. a music CD.
    C. a cartoon in a newspaper.
    D. a billboard advertisement.

B. Short answer

7. Evaluate the effectiveness of the photograph that accompanies this poem by Langston Hughes. Is the photograph a good accompaniment to the text? Explain your answer in 2–3 sentences.

Winter Moon
by Langston Hughes

How thin and sharp is the moon tonight!

How thin and sharp and ghostly white

Is the slim curved crook of the moon tonight!

C. Essay and photograph

Use the following essay and the photograph on the next page to answer the questions.

Essay

The pharmaceutical industry and the National Institutes of Health spend billions of dollars annually on medical research techniques that have been rendered obsolete by technological advances.

Adult stem cell research is key to our status as the world's leader in medical research. The continued use of animals to test the effectiveness of medications and health interventions for humans is akin to using smoke signals instead of email as a method of communication.

We have spent billions of dollars to cure cancer in mice, but so far have failed to replicate human cancer in any animal, let alone close in on a cure. All but a very few diseases are species-unique, and the only efficient and effective way to discover cures and create vaccines is through the use of the same species' cells, tissues and organs.

The use of animals as models for the development of human medications and disease almost always fails, simply because humans and animals have different physiologies.

Adult stem cell research is more effective than animal testing because there are no complications or failures related to tissue rejection. In fact, international researchers using adult stem cells—cells that are present in all growing human tissue—have shown success in treating cardiac infarction, Crohn's disease and thalassemia. The answers to the mysteries of Parkinson's and Alzheimer's will be found by using stem cells and other modern technologies, not by cutting up beagles.

It's time to insist that they stop harming defenseless animals and wasting our precious health care dollars so they can get busy saving our lives by embracing technologies that work.

(excerpts taken from *STOP ANIMAL TESTING* By Kelly Overton. ©2006 *The Baltimore Sun*)

Read this sentence from the second paragraph of the essay.

> Adult stem cell research is key to our status as the world's leader in medical research.

8. Which of these statements <u>best</u> explains why the author included this sentence in the essay?
   A. The author thinks stem cell research should only be used on adults.
   B. The author thinks that adult stem cell research is more effective that animal testing.
   C. The author wants to abandon all experimental testing.
   D. The author wants to stop embryonic stem cell research.

9. The author is trying to
   A. offend his audience.
   B. inform his audience.
   C. convince his audience to feel as he does.
   D. defend his thoughts against critics.

10. The author wants the audience to
   A. agree with him.
   B. support the use of adult stem cell research to help cure diseases.
   C. help stop animal testing.
   D. do all of the above.

Short Answer

11. How do you think someone who wants to stop animal testing would feel about the essay? How do you think someone who disagrees with the author would feel about the essay? Use your own paper to respond in 2–3 sentences.

Brief Constructed Response

12. Write a response that explains whether the photograph communicates ideas that are similar to the ideas found in the essay. In your response, be sure to describe how the author feels about animal testing, how he wants the writer to respond, and whether the photograph is a useful accompaniment to the text. Support your conclusions with appropriate details from both the essay and the photograph.

D. Directions. Choose the appropriate resource for finding the information required in each sentence.

13. Margaret is reading a new book and needs the definition for the word *assuredly.*
    A. dictionary   B. thesaurus   C. Internet   D. index

14. Sam wants to buy a used bicycle
    A. newspaper   C. dictionary
    B. encyclopedia   D. computer software

15. Kim is writing a paper about the recent discovery of a possible 10th planet.
    A. index   B. Internet   C. thesaurus   D. encyclopedia

16. Marco is researching the Nile River.
    A. journal   B. newspaper   C. encyclopedia   D. dictionary

17. Amanda wants to know about the next Jennifer Lopez movie.
    A. encyclopedia   B. magazine   C. journal   D. dictionary

E. Directions. Choose the appropriate section of a book for finding the information in each sentence.

18. Rico needs to see a map of colonial America.
    A. bibliography   B. appendix   C. index   D. title page

19. Tanya needs the definition of the word *allusion.*
    A. index   C. bibliography
    B. table of contents   D. glossary

20. Billy needs to know where and by whom his book was published.
    A. table of   B. index   C. title page   D. glossary
        contents

21. Erin would like to find which pages in her literature book have poems by Robert Frost.
    A. bibliography   B. index   C. title page   D. glossary

22. Joel would like to know where the articles in his book originally came from.
    A. bibliography   B. index   C. title page   D. glossary

ENGLISH

Chapter 5
Extending Meaning

This chapter addresses the following expectation(s) and their related indicators from **Core Learning Goal 1: Reading. Reviewing and Responding to Texts**

Expectation 1.2	The student will construct, examine, and extend meaning of traditional and contemporary works recognized as having significant literary merit.
Expectation 1.3	The student will explain and give evidence to support perceptions about print and non-print works.

EXTENDING MEANING OF A TEXT TO READER AND SOCIETY

In the preceding chapters, you have reviewed a number of strategies for reading and understanding a variety of texts. You have learned to develop the ideas presented in those texts by using prior knowledge, making predictions, drawing conclusions, and summarizing. Learning about how authors write for purpose and how they use diction and syntax, language and tone, figurative language, and non-print text also helps you understand the layers of meaning contained in what you read.

Now, we will go a step further by **extending the meaning** of a text. When you read, it is your interaction with the text that gives it a specific meaning (that's why a story or an article can mean one thing to you and another to your classmate). In addition to what a text means to you personally, its ideas and issues also relate (sometimes strongly, sometimes not) to the contemporary society and time in which we live.

LITERAL MEANING, AUTHOR'S PURPOSE, AND CONTEXT

First, make sure you understand the **literal meaning** of the text you are reading. Use the reading strategies from chapter 1 to help you get the full meaning. For example, if it is an old novel with archaic words or an article with technical terms, look up any words you don't know in a dictionary.

Next, determine the **author's purpose** for writing the text. What style and devices are used? Is the text meant to inform, persuade, or entertain?

Finally, consider the **context** of when, where, and by whom the text was written. How is the history of the time reflected, or how might it affect the author (including current affairs, if the text is contemporary)? What impact might culture make on the ideas in the text? Is there anything about the author's background that might play into how the text is written?

EXTENDING MEANING TO THE READER AND TO CONTEMPORARY SOCIETY

As you know working with chapter 2, authors have a purpose for writing a text, and so they usually intend for readers to have some thoughts or ideas or take some action after reading it. Consider the following example.

excerpt from *Walden* by Henry David Thoreau

I went to the woods because I wished to live deliberately, to front only the essential facts of life, and see if I could not learn what it had to teach, and not, when I came to die, discover that I had not lived. I did not wish to live what was not life, living is so dear; nor did I wish to practice resignation, unless it was quite necessary. I wanted to live deep and suck out all the marrow of life, to live so sturdily and Spartan-like as to put to rout all that was not life, to cut a broad swath and shave close, to drive life into a corner, and reduce it to its lowest terms, and, if it proved to be mean, why then to get the whole and genuine meanness of it, and publish its meanness to the world; or if it were sublime, to know it by experience, and be able to give a true account of it in my next excursion. For most men, it appears to me, are in a strange uncertainty about it, whether it is of the devil or of God, and have *somewhat hastily* concluded that it is the chief end of man here to "glorify God and enjoy him forever."

Literal meaning: From reading the passage carefully and using reading strategies, you see that the author describes wanting to live simply and naturally and find out what life is truly about.

Author's purpose: Thoreau was writing about nature and people's relationship to it. He felt people took it for granted in his time, and he wanted to show that one could get more out of life if the connection with nature was restored. He uses imagery in "suck out all the marrow of life" to describe wanting more than society offered, allusion when he refers to living "Spartan-like," and personification when he says he wants to "drive life into a corner, and reduce it to its lowest terms." Using these devices, Thoreau paints a picture of the passion and conviction behind his ideas.

Context: Thoreau moved to the woods to be close to nature and live without many of the constraints and expectations of his society. He studied nature, and his goal was to bring others to a greater understanding of our connectedness with and dependence on the natural world. He also felt that many people lived only to serve God, and although this is a praiseworthy ideal, Thoreau felt it needed thought, examination, and a broader look at how one can do that. He asked important questions of people in his time, like what does it cost to exist; what is the best way to live; and do we really need what we think we need?

Extend meaning to the reader: Decide what the passage means to you. Think about your opinions as you read Thoreau's words, your reaction to his ideas, and your existing thoughts about the topics he discussed.

Extend reading to contemporary society: Just as in Thoreau's time (perhaps more), we can forget about the world around us, that things are happening apart from our own everyday realities, and how nature is irrevocably connected to the man-made world. What relevance do Thoreau's words have for people in today's society?

When you extend the meaning of any text that you read, you apply what you learn to yourself and contemporary society. Taking the example above, what would be the best answers for the following questions?

1. After reading this text, a reader would most likely conclude that

    A. the author is depressed.
    B. the author is not a religious man.
    C. the author thinks country living is easier than city living.
    D. the author feels that many of our daily activities are not really living.

Using reading strategies, you can see that answer *A* is not supported; the language and style reveal that the author is excited and far from depressed. Answer *B* also is not supported, as Thoreau never denies religion but encourages an examined decision about how to live life. Answer *C* is never revealed in the text; the author talks about the creative advantages of living in the woods, but he never mentions the physical comfort. Answer *D* is the best choice for this question because it directly addresses one of the reasons Thoreau expresses for having left society to live in the woods: he wanted to "live deliberately" and not discover later that he "had not lived."

1. This passage would most likely encourage a reader to

    A. start writing in a diary.
    B. buy a cottage in the woods.
    C. think about whether his daily routine has meaning.
    D. develop a fund raising program at school to protect the environment.

While reading the passage might inspire any of the above reactions, the best answer is *C*. Thoreau made a point to say that a person must decide individually how to live, and this begins by thinking about it. Some of the other actions he mentions can certainly develop later on from that thinking!

Practice 1: Extending Meaning of a Text to Reader and Society

Read the following passages. Then choose the best answer to each question.

excerpt from *Apple Growing* by M.C. Burritt

The apple has long been the most popular of our tree fruits, but the last few years have seen a steady growth in its appreciation and use. This is probably due in a large measure to a better knowledge of its value and to the development of new methods of preparation for consumption. Few fruits can be utilized in as many ways as can the apple. In addition to the common use of the fresh fruit out of hand and of the fresh, sweet juice as cider, this "King of Fruits" can be cooked, baked, dried, canned, and made into jellies and other appetizing dishes, to enumerate all of which would be to prepare a list pages long. Few who have tasted once want to be without their apple sauce and apple pies in season, not to mention the crisp, juicy specimens to eat out of hand by the open fireplace in the long winter evenings. Apples thus served call up pleasant memories to most of us, but only recently have the culinary possibilities of the apple, especially as a dessert fruit, been fully realized.

1. In what way, if any, is the information in this text relevant in today's society?

   A. Everyone eats apples, so it offers useful information.
   B. No one has time to cook or bake these days, so it's not much use.
   C. With today's focus on healthy eating, this text offers ways to use a healthy food.
   D. People today have many choices of fruit, making this passage too narrow for modern audiences.

2. This passage would <u>most likely</u> encourage a reader to

   A. consider ways to prepare and eat apples more often.
   B. read further about the history of the apple.
   C. make a chart about types of apples.
   D. eat an apple pie.

excerpt from "The Spirit of 1906" by George W. Brooks, an eyewitness to the San Francisco earthquake

The first natural impulse of a human being in an earthquake is to get out into the open, and as I and those who were with me were at that particular moment decidedly human in both mold and temperament, we dressed hastily and joined the group of excited neighbors gathered on the street. Pale faced, nervous and excited, we chattered like daws until the next happening intervened, which was the approach of a man on horseback who shouted as he "Revere-d" past us the startling news that numerous fires had started in various parts of the city, that the Spring Valley Water Company's feed main had been broken by the quake, that there was no water and that the city was doomed.

This was the spur I needed. Fires and no water! It was a call to duty. The urge to get downtown and to the office of the "California" enveloped me to such an extent that my terror left me. Activity dominated all other sensations and I started for the office. As all street car lines and methods of transportation had ceased to operate it meant a hike of about two miles.

3. What aspect of human nature, true in the past as it is now, is expressed by the author?
   A. Without water, no one can put out a fire.
   B. Faced with danger, many people overcome fear and take action.
   C. People continue to move to California even thought it's not safe.
   D. It's important to get outside in an earthquake.

4. This passage would <u>most likely</u> encourage a reader to
    A. think about what he or she would do during a natural disaster.
    B. consider how his or her town would withstand a disaster.
    C. read the history of the San Francisco fire.
    D. dream about moving to California.

SYNTHESIZING INFORMATION

Reading various resources about a topic is like putting together a jigsaw puzzle, but the pieces for this kind of puzzle come from different boxes. As you read, you must decide how or if the pieces of information fit together and what ideas you can develop about the topic as a whole.

In chapter 4, you saw some of the information resources you can use. Some of these resources contain **primary sources** (firsthand accounts of an event), and some are mostly made up of **secondary sources** (written about the event from a distance of time and place). When reading the material, you will need to choose the resources which have the best information for your purpose, whether that is to understand a topic better, write a report, or create a presentation.

There are more options for finding informational material today than ever before. That is why the media says that we are living in the "Information Age."

EXAMPLE OF SYNTHESIZING MATERIAL

Suppose that you want to write a report on the women's issue of equal pay for equal work. The following three pages provide you with several different sources of information to read regarding the movement towards equal pay for equal work.

Examples of sources for a report about this issue include the following:

Summary of the Fair Pay Act introduced in 1999

Article by Jennifer Winters (1999) "Equal Pay Rights: the Struggle Continues"

Sample Table of Contents *Progress Towards Equal Pay for Women*

Key word search on "Glass Ceiling" from the Internet.

Bar graph "Disparities in Pay, 1980–1999"

Review all of the resources above, and read the articles for understanding. Think about where else you could find information for this issue. Also, think about how you would paraphrase and summarize this information so you could combine it with other sources and topics. Then, complete the practice section that follows.

The Fair Pay Act

The Fair Pay Act as introduced in 1999 amends the Fair Standards Act of 1938 by prohibiting discrimination in the payment of wages on account of gender (sex), race, or national origin. At the same time, this act also allows payment of different wages based on seniority or on a merit system. In addition, Section 5 of the Fair Pay Act empowers the court to fine employers who violate this act. Likewise, Section 6 of the act mandates that employers who are fined for violations will also fall under the scrutiny of the EEOC. This organization will require the employer to submit paperwork and preserve records indicating how the employer rewards personnel with pay raises. This proposed act adds strength to the consequences companies will pay for discriminating against employees on the basis of gender.

Chapter 5

Equal Pay Rights: The Struggle Continues (Introduction)

As early as the 1950s, women's groups organized and called attention to the issue of gender inequalities in pay. At this time, men held the top managerial positions in virtually every profession. Women were often told that being a homemaker was the only or best option available for fulfillment in life. Women who chose to work, moreover, faced an uphill battle in trying to get jobs that went beyond menial or clerical status.

In recent history, however, change has come at a more rapid pace. Women have entered the workforce in greater numbers. The number of women in the workforce has increased from 38 percent in 1960 to nearly 60 percent in 1997. In particular, women have entered the white collar professional jobs at increasingly higher rates. Because of higher attendance at universities and colleges across the nation, the number of women professionals has rapidly increased. Women now enjoy full participation in the professions of law, medicine, and management. In some cases, more women are enrolled in graduate programs than men!

Despite these great strides that have taken place in employment, there is a shrinking but still persistent difference between what women make and what men make for the same job. As a whole, the upward mobility of women has led to an increase in women's pay rates. However, the salary difference still hovers around 20 percent. The earnings of women in all ranks, in all professions, must be addressed.

One obstacle to closing this gap is the breaking of the "glass ceiling." The glass ceiling, however, is a real barrier that women experience as they try to move into the upper levels of company management. The upper levels are almost entirely controlled by men who tend to promote other men to the highest positions. Since these positions pay several times more annually than lower positions, this trend can explain some of the pay difference.

Fresh solutions are needed to close the continuing gender gap. Possible strategies to address the glass ceiling include sending a bill through Congress. In addition, women can start their own companies, becoming their own CEO's—starting at the top. Plans of action are needed and should be considered as soon as possible to address the wide gap in pay.

Equal Pay Rights: The Struggle Continues by Jennifer Winters c. 1999. published in New York by Goldwater Press.

> ## Selections from Internet Key Word Search on "Glass Ceiling"

Websites

1. The **Glass Ceiling** - Website offering articles and information on job discrimination, business articles, information for students, a large resource section, legal center, free business directory, family articles, literature
   *Society>Work>**Workplace Discrimination***
   [Translate]

2. **Glass Ceiling** on DataLine - DataLine engages people online about both corporate and academic glass ceiling lawsuits to enable interest and support for some of the plaintiffs for cases we have followed

   Society>People>Women>Women's Rights
   [Translate]

3. The **Glass Ceiling** Biographies - A biography of Clara Barton from "Shatter the **Glass Ceiling**," a working woman's magazine

   Health>Nursing>History>Clara Barton
   [Translate]

4. **Glass Ceiling** Business Directory - Free business directory covering national and international businesses

   Business>Directories>North America>United States
   [Translate]

News Article

webreview.com - Poll Results: New Paradigm, Same **Glass Ceiling**?—webreview.com—Cross-Training for Web Teams Home: Http://www.webreview.com/pub/1999/06/11/poll/ results.html New Paradigm: Same **Glass Ceiling**? Poll results: Does the same **glass ceiling** exist? More Articles about **glass ceiling** from webreview.com

[Translate]

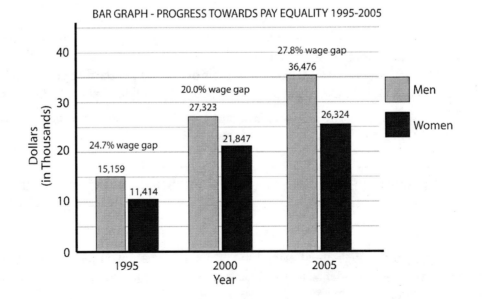

BAR GRAPH - PROGRESS TOWARDS PAY EQUALITY 1995-2005

Practice 2: Synthesizing Information

A. Choose the best answer for questions 1–6.

1. What power is given in section 5 of the Fair Pay Act as introduced in 2000?

    A. Employees who are fined will fall under the scrutiny of the EEOL.

    B. The EEOL will require employers to submit paperwork and preserve records indicating how the employer rewards personnel with pay raises.

    C. The court is empowered to fine employers who violate the Fair Pay Act.

    D. Discrimination is prohibited in the payment of wages on account of sex, race, or national origin.

2. Which of the following would be the <u>best</u> topic sentence for a report on the subject "Equal Pay for Women?"

    A. The struggle for equal pay for women has an important history and currently faces new challenges.

    B. The women's rights movement has gained momentum and notoriety.

    C. There are many resources available about the history of wage inequalities between men and women for the same work.

    D. News media sources have recently publicized many important statistics on wage inequalities between men and women.

3. Which of the following Web sites discusses lawsuits based on the Internet search?

    A. webreview.com

    B. the glass ceiling

    C. the glass ceiling biographies

    D. glass ceiling on DataLine

4. Based on the bar graph, what was the wage gap between men and women in 2000?
    A. 3.1%   B. 27.8%   C. 20.0%   D. 24.7%

5. Suppose you are going to write an outline of your report on the topic of equal pay for women. Which of the following is the <u>best</u> list of main topics for your outline?

    A. women's right to work, women's right to equal pay, women's right to healthy work environment

    B. the struggle for voting rights, the temperance movement, the Equal Rights Amendment

    C. previous struggles for equal pay rights for women, current progress towards equal pay, future solutions for breaking the glass ceiling

    D. equal rights for women, equal rights for minorities, equality in the workplace

6. Based on all the documents, which of the following statements <u>best</u> expresses the role of government in the issue of equal pay?

    A. The government has left the policies of equal pay to be resolved by the states.

    B. Since the issue is a social concern, the government has chosen to ignore it.

    C. The government takes harsh action against employers who report how many women are employed by them.

    D. The government has voted for legislation that makes unequal pay illegal.

B. Word Search. Look at the list of topics below, and then come up with five key word searches for each.

7. cloning, good/bad?

9. vegetarian nation, our future?

10. caffeine, a legal drug?

11. year-round schools, good/bad?

12. solutions to school violence?

13. Web music, legalize to burn on CDs?

COMPARING AND CONTRASTING

Comparing and **contrasting** is the process of looking for similarities and differences between two or more texts and the ideas and issues expressed in them. Comparing and contrasting is another effective way to analyze ideas and issues in a text or across texts.

One of the most important aspects of comparing and contrasting is to look for similarities or differences within the same category. A familiar way to express this idea is to make sure you are comparing "apples to apples" and "oranges to oranges" but not "apples to oranges." For example, consider the following sentence:

> This candy is tangy and sweet, but that candy is green.

This statement compares flavor and color which are two unrelated categories. We may be able to conclude that the writer likes sweet candy and does not like green candy, but we can't adequately compare the two candies because we don't know the color of the sweet candy, and we don't know the flavor of the green candy. Therefore, when comparing or contrasting two things or ideas, stay in the same category.

COMPARING AND CONTRASTING IDEAS IN A READING PASSAGE

Sometimes, finding similarities and differences in ideas that are described in a reading passage can be difficult. A strategy that can help you with comparing and contrasting is looking for signal words.

As you review a reading passage in order to answer questions about comparing and contrasting ideas, you can look for **signal words** that point to a similarity or a difference in the selection. Studying the following list of signal words will help you find similarities and differences in ideas discussed in reading passages.

Signal Words for Similarities and Differences

Similarities		Differences	
again	too	although	not as / not like
also	as well as	but	on the contrary
both	just as ... so too	contrary to	on the other hand
likewise	the same	despite	neither
once more		different from	regardless
similarly		even though	still
similar to		however	though
in the same way		in contrast	yet
like		in opposition	unlike
as		in spite of	whereas
in a related way		instead	while
parallel		nevertheless	conversely

Practice 3: Comparing and Contrasting in a Passage

Read the following passage. In the questions that follow, identify the signal words and whether they point to similarities or differences.

The **(1)main** interest of 17th century French colonizers in North America was trade in animal furs. Some furs were used for hats that were **(2)very** popular in France at the time. The Native Americans were valuable trading partners to the French, supplying animal pelts from beaver, otter, muskrat, and mink. **(3)Consequently**, the French saw no need to try to conquer them. **(4)Likewise**, the French did not destroy the forests because they wanted to maintain the habitat of the animals they valued so much. Because the northern areas of North America, where the French colonized, were sparsely populated, epidemics took less of a toll. **(5)Similarly**, the French **(6)tended** to see native peoples as equals, and they accepted intermarriage. The Native Americans were **(7)also** valuable to the French as allies in wars against the British.

(8)In contrast, the English colonies may be called "colonies of settlement" where settlers **(9)tried** to establish English society in the New World. They took control of the land and brought their own political and economic systems, **(10)as well as** crops and animals. The English came to the New World in much **(11)greater** numbers than the French, and they wanted control of more and more land, thus displacing great numbers of Native Americans. The Native Americans were **(12)not as** beneficial economically to the English **as** to the French, so the English saw them, **(13)instead**, as an obstacle to progress **(14)and** a nuisance.

1. A. compares   B. contrasts   C. neither
2. A. compares   B. contrasts   C. neither
3. A. compares   B. contrasts   C. neither
4. A. compares   B. contrasts   C. neither
5. A. compares   B. contrasts   C. neither
6. A. compares   B. contrasts   C. neither
7. A. compares   B. contrasts   C. neither
8. A. compares   B. contrasts   C. neither
9. A. compares   B. contrasts   C. neither
10. A. compares   B. contrasts   C. neither
11. A. compares   B. contrasts   C. neither
12. A. compares   B. contrasts   C. neither
13. A. compares   B. contrasts   C. neither
14. A. compares   B. contrasts   C. neither

15. Based on reading the passage as a whole, which statement is true?

    A. The entire passage focuses on similarities.

    B. The whole passage discusses differences.

    C. The first paragraph shows similarities while the second introduces differences.

    D. The first paragraph talks mainly about differences, while the second explores similarities

COMPARING AND CONTRASTING LANGUAGE AND TONE

At some point, you may be asked to compare and contrast the language and tone used in two different reading passages. **Language** refers to the words a writer uses. **Tone** is the way the writer uses those words to convey a certain attitude or feeling to the reader. Recall what you learned about tone in chapter 3. Language (what is said) and tone (how it is said) are often determined by the **author's purpose** and the intended **audience**—the person(s) who will read a text. Language and tone can provide important clues in helping you determine the theme and purpose of a text. You can review author's purpose in chapter 2.

To see how language and tone can differ, read and compare the letter below with the e-mail that follows.

4-17-07

Roy Wilson
Purrfect Pets
621 Oak Ridge Rd.
Towson, MD 21204

Dear Sir:

Because of my great love for animals, I am very interested in working at Purrfect Pets. I visit your store frequently as I purchase food and supplies to care for my several cats and dogs. I am always impressed by the cleanliness of your store and the care you show the animals.

During the school year, I will need to work part-time, but I will be available to work on nights and weekends as needed. Once school is out for the summer, I will be available to work full-time.

Please find enclosed my application and a list of references. I look forward to hearing from you soon.

Sincerely,

Tamika H. Jones

Tamika H. Jones

Hey Jack,

What's up?! I'm really psyched about workin' at the CD Emporium with you. I mean I don't have the job yet, but why wouldn't they hire me? By the way, when you're at work this afternoon, can you pick up a job application for me? Thanks! You're the best!

Does your sister still want to work at that stupid pet store? That would gross me out! Cleaning out all those cages with all the animal stuff in it. No thanks! Give me some cellophane-wrapped CDs any day. Catch you later. Thanks again.

T.J.

Extending Meaning

Did you notice the similarities and differences between the two letters? Both writers are seeking jobs. They also want to work where they enjoy what they are doing. The authors share a similar purpose, but their audiences are different.

Tamika is writing to the owner of the pet shop where she wants to work. She has chosen the language of a business letter to address her potential employer. She avoids dialect and slang terms, and her tone is formal and respectful. The language and tone of T.J.'s email, however, is very different because he is writing to a good friend and is asking a favor. Along with an informal tone, he uses slang terms and abbreviations that Jack will understand easily. Assuming that Jack will recognize T. J.'s style of language, T.J. uses neither his full name nor a salutation such as "sincerely" or "your friend."

The type of language and tone used in a text greatly affects how the reader will interpret it. Be aware of the language and tone you use in writing and in speaking. Also, study the following types and examples of language and tone to help improve your reading and writing.

Different Types of Language	
Informal	**Slang** is very informal language that enjoys a brief popularity and then generally becomes obsolete. It is often confined to a limited group of people. Examples: crib, dis, psych, yo' mama, word, peace, my bad, cool, dude, etc.
	Colloquial English refers to words that are appropriate in dialogue and informal writing but inappropriate in formal writing. Contractions, short words, and clichés may be used. Examples: You bet I'll be there! He's in so deep there's no way out! The apple never falls far from the tree.
	Nonstandardized English contains grammar and usage that do not follow the standard rules for English. The pronouns or verbs are nonstandard.
Formal	**Standardized American English** is the English that is most widely accepted in the United States. It is the language of educated people. The grammar used in standardized English becomes the model for all to follow.

Practice 4: Language and Tone

You are running as a representative for your class on the student council. You want to write a short announcement to your friends and to the school faculty that explains why you are running for this office. How would your language and tone differ for these two audiences? Explain your answer. Then write a short announcement for each audience.

COMPARING AND CONTRASTING UNIVERSAL THEMES WITHIN AND BETWEEN TEXTS

When reading and discussing (or writing) about literature, often you will need to compare and/or contrast the universal themes in a single piece of literature or in more than one piece of literature. A theme in literature is the message(s) [or insight(s)] into life that an author communicates through the images, characters, and plot. It is rarely stated directly in a literary work. In *Romeo and Juliet,* one of the themes is nothing can separate two teenagers in love.

Certainly the first thing to examine is the universal theme or themes present in each individual piece of literature. If you are discussing a single piece of literature, you need to consider each character and how that character is related to the plot and theme. How do the characters relate to each other? Sometimes, within a single piece of literature, one character may represent or be involved in one particular theme, while another character represents a different theme. By considering these questions, you will then have the points of discussion that will be your basis for comparison and contrast.

If you are comparing two or more pieces of literature, such as a poem and a story, there are additional questions to explore. What are the similarities and differences in the way the characters in each piece are related to the theme? Answering some or all of the preceding questions should provide you with material for comparison and contrast.

COMPARING AND CONTRASTING CONFLICT IN TWO OR MORE TEXTS

Sometimes you may be asked to discuss the conflicts in two or more pieces of literature or texts. The pieces may have many similarities, or they may be very different. In order to have some points to compare and contrast, you will want to look carefully at the conflicts in each text. Consider the types of conflict, internal or external, and the details about each conflict. Which characters are involved? To what extent does the conflict impact and affect the plot of the story? Once you have determined the facts about the conflict in each text, consider how the various texts are related and different from each other.

Practice 5:   Comparing and Contrasting Universal Themes and Conflict

A. Read the synopsis of "The Gift of the Magi," and answer the questions that follow.

Synopsis of "The Gift of the Magi" by O. Henry

A young married couple named Jim and Della live in a rented room in New York. Times are hard, and they are poor. Jim recently had to take a cut in pay, and the couple can barely pay rent and buy groceries.

Tomorrow is Christmas, and Della wants to buy Jim a gold chain for his gold watch. Jim is very proud of his watch, which is one of the few possessions the couple has that's worth anything. Della, on the other hand, is most proud of her beautiful long hair, which Jim loves as well. But she really wants to buy that gold chain though she's managed to save only $1.87. She decides to sell her hair for $20 to a woman who makes wigs.

Extending Meaning

Della now has enough to buy the chain, which costs $21. She comes home with her purchase, prepares Jim's dinner, and waits for him to come home, a little bit worried that he will be shocked when he sees her beautiful hair has been cut off.

When Jim comes home, he does look shocked, and he stares at Della's short hair in a way that scares her a bit. She explains how she sold her hair to buy a nice Christmas present for him. Jim assures her that nothing can change his love for her, and he explains that he is so shocked because he, too, wanted to give her a nice Christmas present. He gives her the gift, which Della unwraps to see that Jim has bought a set of beautiful combs for her hair.

She had seen these expensive combs in a shop before…but how did Jim afford them? Della then gives Jim the beautiful gold chain. When she asks Jim to put it on his watch, Jim surprises her: he has sold the watch to buy her the beautiful combs.

At the end of the story, O. Henry tells readers that this couple is like magi, the wise men who brought the original Christmas gifts to the babe in the manger. He tells us that they truly are wise.

1. Which of the following is <u>not</u> a universal theme expressed in this story?

    A. It is better to give than to receive
    B. A person's identity is created by the things he owns.
    C. The greatest gift is making a sacrifice for another
    D. Loving another person is a greater reward than pride in possessions.

2. Which of these sayings <u>best</u> expresses one of the themes of this story?
    A. A gift must come from the heart.
    B. All that glitters is not gold.
    C. Beauty comes from within.
    D. Money can't buy you love.

3. Which of the following is <u>not</u> a conflict presented in this story?
    A. Della trying to figure out how to buy the gold chain
    B. Jim considering whether he likes Della's new haircut
    C. the couple wanting to buy each other nice gifts but having no money
    D. All of these are conflicts presented in the story.

B. Think about some of your favorite short stories, fairy or folk tales, movies, and novels. Choose at least three works and create a chart like the one illustrated below. One title has been filled in as an example.

	The Wizard of Oz	(Title of Work)	(Title of Work)
Universal theme and Main conflict	longing to go home man vs. man, Dorothy vs. Wicked Witch and others		
Work with same universal theme	*The Odyssey*		
Main conflict in above work	primarily man vs. man, Odysseus against various people he meets on his journey		
Additional works that are related by similar theme and/or conflict	*E.T.* (longing to go home)		

CHAPTER 5 SUMMARY

Extending the meaning of a text involves understanding and the applying the ideas and issues expressed to the reader and to contemporary society.

Synthesizing information from sources means bringing different parts together to create something that's complete. In reading, being able to synthesize information is important for displaying understanding of **different documents**.

Comparing and **contrasting** is the process of looking for similarities and differences between two or more objects, characters, or ideas. One of the most important aspects of comparing and contrasting is to look for similarities or differences **within the same category**. There are several areas of written materials that can be compared and contrasted, including ideas, language, tone, and theme.

CHAPTER 5 REVIEW

Read the following scene from a 1906 story by O. Henry. Then answer the questions that follow.

excerpt from a short story by O. Henry

This scene from the story "The Coming-Out of Maggie" takes place at a private dance held by the "Give and Take" Athletic Association. Two young men are about to fight over Maggie.

Some fine instinct that Rome must have bequeathed to us caused nearly everyone to turn and look at them—there was a subtle feeling that two gladiators had met in the arena. Two or three Give and Takes with tight coat sleeves drew nearer.

"One moment, Mr. O'Sullivan," said Dempsey. "I hope you're enjoying yourself. Where did you say you lived?"

The two gladiators were well matched. Dempsey had, perhaps, ten pounds of weight to give away. The O'Sullivan had breadth with quickness. Dempsey had a glacial eye, a dominating slit of a mouth, an indestructible jaw, a complexion like a belle's, and the coolness of a champion. The visitor showed more fire in his contempt and less control over his conspicuous sneer. They were enemies by the law written when the rocks were molten. They were each too splendid, too mighty, too incomparable to divide preeminence. One only must survive.

"I live on Grand," said O'Sullivan, insolently; "and no trouble to find me at home. Where do you live?" Dempsey ignored the question.

"You say your name's O'Sullivan," he went on. "Well, 'Big Mike' says he never saw you before."

"Lots of things he never saw," said the favorite of the hop.

"As a rule," went on Dempsey, huskily sweet, "O'Sullivans in this district know one another. You escorted one of our lady members here, and we want a chance to make good. If you've got a family tree let's see a few historical O'Sullivan buds come out on it. Or do you want us to dig it out of you by the roots?"

1. After reading this text, a reader would <u>most likely</u> feel that

   A. O'Sullivan and Dempsey are old friends.
   B. O'Sullivan is rich and Dempsey is poor.
   C. Dempsey is threatening O'Sullivan.
   D. Dempsey is afraid of O'Sullivan.

2. This excerpt is from a story about a plain girl who becomes popular because she finally has a handsome date for a dance. However, "O'Sullivan" is really Italian (a fact he tries to hide) and does not fit in with the Irish community (a fact that Dempsey discovers). Knowing this context, what might reading this story <u>most likely</u> encourage a reader to do?

   A. attend a dance
   B. think about why people date
   C. learn Irish dances
   D. read about immigrant relations

Extending Meaning

Read the following interview. Then answer the questions that follow.

Dating in Different Countries

American men and women must find their own spouses, and no one else can do it for them.

This concept is very difficult for young people in India to understand, as you can tell from the following interview with two Indian teenage girls.

"Don't you want to be able to choose your own husbands?" I asked.

"No! Never!" the girls answered vehemently. Nisha, a very beautiful girl with wide, almond-shaped eyes went on to say, "I don't want to worry about whether I'll get married or not. I know I'll get married. I know my parents are better judges of character than I am. I am too young to make such a decision. When my parents choose someone for me, I know it will be someone who will be able to support me, and someone whom my family already likes and respects.

"What if I lived in America and I chose a boy my family didn't like? Before it was over, everyone might be against me. There might be bad feelings at home with my parents because of my choice, and if I argued with my husband, who would support me?"

It was Rasheeda's turn. "It seems the American system would be very humiliating for me. I would have to spend a lot more time making myself beautiful and attractive and try to figure out ways to get boys to notice me. And if the boy I liked didn't notice me, maybe I would feel like a failure as a person. I would have to compete with other girls to be the prettiest—it seems so demeaning and stressful. And what if I were shy? Would I get married?"

"Possibly not," I answered honestly. "But there's certainly no shame in being single."

Nisha asked the hardest question, "In America, does the girl get to choose? Isn't it the boy who chooses anyway?" A good question.

3. After reading this interview, a reader would most likely be encouraged to

    A. learn more about arranged marriages.

    B. join an online dating service.

    C. read about family relationships in other cultures.

    D. consider the disadvantages of dating.

4. Review both the excerpt from the O.Henry story and the interview with the Indian girls. Which idea best expresses a theme in both passages?

    A. Dating can often be difficult.

    B. Culture has great influence on relationships.

    C. Parents are wiser than their children.

    D. Misunderstandings are common when dating.

Chapter 5

Read the following information for understanding, and then answer the questions which follow.

List of materials: Keyword search on "Shark Attacks" from the Internet

Newspaper article by B.E. Wares (2001) "In the Eye of the Shark"

"West Regional Beach Safety Guide"

Product Information for *Shark-Away Watt Wand*

Selections from Internet Key Word Search on "Shark Attacks"

- Shark Research Program at the University of Florida Museum of Natural History

Pages include shark biology, ecology, conservation, and research. **Shark** attack statistics, **shark** breaking news, great white **sharks** and megamouth . . .

URL: http://www.flmnh.ufl.edu/fish/sharks/sharks/sharks.htm • Related Pages • Translate

- The Relative Risk of **Shark Attacks** to Humans

ISAF. **Shark** Selections . . . IUCN/SSG Home. Great White Home. Megamouth Home. In the news . . .

URL: http://www.flmnh.ufl.edu/fish/sharks/attacks/relarisk.htm • Translate

Topic: Shark Attacks

- White **Shark** Central-Not your ordinary tribute to the White **Shark**

White **Shark** Central-Tons of pictures, cool links, the latest shark news, listing of **shark attacks**, and General facts

URL: http://www.geocities.com/RainForest/Andes/2771/index.html • Related Pages • Translate

"In the Eye of the Shark" editorial by B. A. Wares

     Here's a new idea: put yourself into a shark's skin. Do you dare to enter the world where they must glide alone and hungry? Imagine you feel the emptiness of a creature for whom there is no free lunch, no supermarket, and no way to beg for even a single fish scale. You're that animal. Cast your gaze through the waters: the waters that grow dimmer and lose oxygen every day. You, as the shark, don't realize that it is pollution from some very profitable corporations that is suffocating and blinding you. You only know hunger and want. Now you feel the tugs and swishes in the water which signal food, life. You move with silent purpose towards the food. You feel the weight of the water moving against your skin as the food bobs in front of your eyes. Your eyes see little through the murky water, little but the food you must have to live, and the urge to live is stronger than the pull of tides. Now the moment is here, and you open your mouth to grasp the food that comes from your place in the ocean; as a meat-eater your place is to eat the weak and misshapen. Your eyes must close against the struggling food. You see even less than before. There are flashes of pain as you hold to food that will sustain your life. The ache of hunger is gone, and you move to deeper, clearer water.

Listen people: fearing and condemning sharks won't change their needs or their natures. We, as intelligent beings, must simply take our chances or stay out of the water.

West Regional Beach Safety Guide

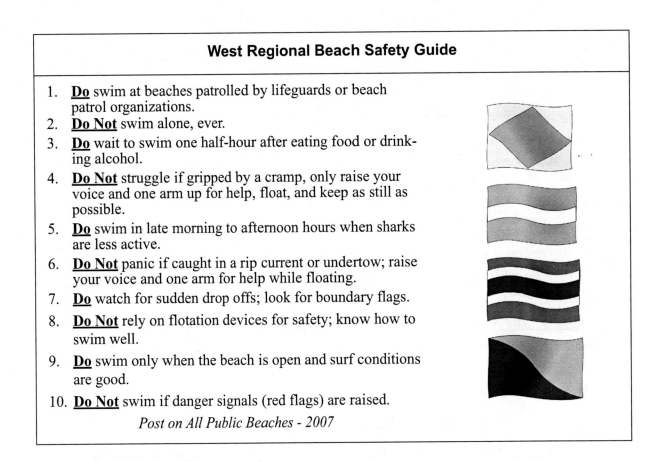

1. **Do** swim at beaches patrolled by lifeguards or beach patrol organizations.
2. **Do Not** swim alone, ever.
3. **Do** wait to swim one half-hour after eating food or drinking alcohol.
4. **Do Not** struggle if gripped by a cramp, only raise your voice and one arm up for help, float, and keep as still as possible.
5. **Do** swim in late morning to afternoon hours when sharks are less active.
6. **Do Not** panic if caught in a rip current or undertow; raise your voice and one arm for help while floating.
7. **Do** watch for sudden drop offs; look for boundary flags.
8. **Do Not** rely on flotation devices for safety; know how to swim well.
9. **Do** swim only when the beach is open and surf conditions are good.
10. **Do Not** swim if danger signals (red flags) are raised.

Post on All Public Beaches - 2007

Shark-Away Watt Wand: Product Information			
Maximum Watt Wand for Large Sharks	**Lead Wrapped for Maximum Insulation**	**Maximum Dimensions** Length 17 ft Diameter 10 in	**Maximum Batteries Required:** 1 9-Volt
Serious Watt Wand for Middle-Size Sharks	**Duct Tape Wrapped for Serious Insulation**	**Serious Dimensions:** Length 10 ft Diameter 7 in	**Serious Batteries Required:** 2 AA
Essential Watt Wand for Mid and Small Size Sharks/Rays	**Plastic Wrap Wrapped for Essential Insulation**	**Essential Dimensions:** Length 7 ft Diameter 5 in	**Essential Batteries Required:** 3 AAA

NOTE: Wands are legal only in the North Sea. Must be over 21 to use. Use at your own risk.

- This company can not be held responsible for misuse of wand, any abuses of the wand, or any failure of the wand to work. The wand is most effective during the waning of the moon.
- The company advises the use of heavy rubber gloves while operating. There are no warranties for parts. If not satisfied with this product, you will receive a full apology, but expect no money back.

5. Based on the materials, which of the keywords below would be <u>best</u> for continuing the research for the issue of shark attacks?

A. west regional

B. white shark

C. watt wand

D. relative risk

6. Which of the following statements <u>best</u> summarizes the findings of the materials about shark attacks?

A. The flags that fly on a beach help to scare away sharks as well as people who would like to swim despite the warnings.

B. There is no reason to fear sharks since there are many inventions that now enable people to swim in the ocean without thinking about dangers.

C. Humans have taken good care of the oceans and beaches, and sharks should be taken care of as well by open-shore patrolling, keeping the sharks away from our beaches.

D. A shark's nature and people's desire to swim lead to risk of attack, but there are other dangers on the beach, including rip currents and dangerous inventions.

7. Review the article "In the Eye of the Shark" and the product information for the Shark-Away Watt Wand. Which statement <u>best</u> describes the language used in these materials?

   A. Both are formal.

   B. The article is formal, and the product information is informal.

   C. The article is informal, and the product information is formal.

   D. Both are informal.

8. Considering all of these materials, which would provide the most appropriate information for an article about how to avoid the danger of shark attacks?

   A. the "White Shark Central" Web site

   B. the article, "In the Eye of the Shark"

   C. the West Regional Beach Safety Guide

   D. the product information for the Shark-Away Watt Wand

Chapter 6
Writing Skills: Usage and Conventions

This chapter addresses the following expectation(s) and their related indicators from **Core Learning Goal 3: Controlling Language**

Expectation 3.3	The student will use capitalization, punctuation, and correct spelling appropriately.

There are various rules for appropriate **usage and conventions** in Standard American English Some common ones are reviewed in this chapter. For detailed information about spelling and grammar, it is important to have a good **dictionary** and **grammar guide** which you should ask your teacher to recommend. For more review and practice, refer to American Book Company's ***Basics Made Easy: Grammar and Usage Review,*** available at www.americanbookcompany.com.

PUNCTUATION AND CAPITALIZATION

The appropriate use of punctuation is an important key to understanding. Punctuation signals how words, phrases, and sentences relate to one another and when a reader should pause.

END PUNCTUATION

End punctuation signals the end of a sentence. The mark used at the end of a sentence also indicates how that sentence should be read.

1. A **period** ends a declarative sentence (a simple statement of fact or argument).

    Example: I knew that he was going to run for office**.**

2. A **question mark** comes after a question. Questions are often signaled by inversion of the subject and verb (for example, *you do* becomes *do you* to form a question), or by starting with a question word such as *how, why, who, where,* or *when.*

    Example: How did you know that**?**

3. An **exclamation point** ends an imperative statement, like a command, or a sentence meant to convey excitement or urgency.

    Example: He can't keep a secret from me!

COMMAS

1. **Commas** help **separate the parts of a list** of three or more words or phrases.

    Example: Remember that we need to get crepe paper, glue, paint, and some nails before going to the float-building party tonight.

    - The choice of whether to use a **final comma before the conjunction** in a list is a matter of style, for which there are style guides (for example, American Book company uses the *Chicago Manual of Style*, which says the final comma should be used because it adds clarity). Ask your teacher what style you should be using.

2. They **show the relationship between related independent clauses** (complete sentences) when joined by a conjunction.

    Example: They wanted to take a vacation at the beach, but they didn't schedule far enough ahead for a good hotel near the shore.

3. They **set off nonrestrictive elements** (not essential to the meaning of a sentence) from the rest of the sentence. A *nonrestrictive element* is a phrase or clause that adds something but is not necessary to understanding a sentence, while a *restrictive element* is essential and not set off by commas.

    Example, nonrestrictive: We knew something was up when Larry, who has a sense of style, came to the club wearing plaid and stripes!

    Example, restrictive: Anyone who has a sense of style can see that most plaids and stripes don't mix.

4. A comma usually **follows an introductory word, phrase, or clause**.

    Examples: Furthermore, the way that you enunciated made your speech easy to follow. After giving concrete examples, you finished with a strong conclusion. Given the well-prepared presentations you provided, you've earned an A in Speech.

5. Commas are used to **separate added comments or information** as well as transitional elements such as conjunctive adverbs.

    Example: We are, however, pleased you've joined us even though your new position, as we all know, is not quite as exciting as traveling the world with your previous employer.

6. They also set off **direct address, tag questions, interjections,** and **opposing elements**.

    Example 1, direct address: Sabrina, please come here.

    Example 2, tag question: You're not going to eat that, are you?

    Example 3, interjection: We grabbed our bikes and, wow, did we pedal fast!

    Example 4, opposing element: Rudy said to go right, not left, when you get to the corner.

138

7. They also are used to **set off direct quotations**. You would not use a comma after the quotation if it is a question or an imperative.

> **Example 1:** "When the going gets tough," Milo joked, "I usually take a nap."

> **Example 2:** She exclaimed, "I can't stand it!" and promptly turned and left.

8. Commas are used **between date and year** as well as **after the year**, and **between address, city, and state** as well as **after the state**.

> **Example 1:** She was born on July 14, 1888, and lived for nearly 100 years.

> **Example 2:** His address was 627 Charring Road, Hampstead, New Hampshire, for more years than I can remember. Then he moved to Boulder, Colorado, and we didn't hear from him much.

COLONS

1. A **colon** is often used to **introduce a list** (when the statement before the colon is an independent clause). It also can be used for **particular emphasis on what comes after the colon**, and it can be used **before a phrase or clause that restates or explains the first clause**.

> **Example 1:** She had everything she needed for the trip: a warm sleeping bag, a lightweight tent, a camp stove, mosquito repellent, and her trusty compass.

> **Example 2:** There was only one word for what he had become by selling secrets: traitor.

> **Example 3:** Sheila had her own opinion about the new sofa: She didn't like it.

Note that in Examples 1 and 2, there is **no initial capitalization** used in what follows the colon. Example 3 does use initial capitalization because what follows the colon is an **independent clause**; this is, however, a matter of style—some styles do not use initial capitalization after a colon at all—so ask your teacher which style you are supposed to use.

2. Colons have other specific uses. They are used **after a greeting in a formal letter**, to **set off hours from minutes** in writing the time, and to **separate chapters and verses of the Bible**. Finally, as you can see each time the word **Example:** is used, colons also are used to **signal that something is coming that pertains to a designation**.

> **Example 1:** Dear Mr. Bennigan:

> **Example 2:** 2:45 pm

> **Example 3:** Please read Genesis 2:15.

SEMICOLONS

1. A **semicolon** can be used to **join two independent clauses** that are closely related. When a semicolon is used this way, no coordinating conjunction is needed. In other words, it acts like a comma plus *and* or *but* between sentences.

> **Example:** Manny couldn't study at the library; it was always closed by the time he got off work.

2. A semicolon can serve as a **stronger division than a comma**—becoming a "super comma"—when commas are already being used for other purposes. This includes linking an independent clause with a transitional phrase or conjunctive adverb, or in lists which already contain commas.

> **Example:** We brought the books, all 300 volumes, to the sale on time; yet, we weren't allowed to set up our table until someone had checked them all in!

QUOTATION MARKS

1. **Quotation marks** are used to signify a **direct quote**, indicating that whatever lies within the quotation marks was said or written exactly as it appears. Do not use quotation marks when making an indirect quote or paraphrasing (conjunctions like *that*, *if*, *who*, *what*, and *why* often introduce indirect quotes).

> **Example of direct quote:** Janet said, "I just don't get the plot of this novel."

2. Also use quotation marks to indicate the **title of a short work of literature** like a story, speech, or article.

> **Example:** My favorite poem by Edgar Allan Poe is "The Raven."

3. It is standard to use double quotation marks ("like this"); single quotation marks ('like this') are used only for a quote within a quote or to indicate the title of a short work within a quote.

> **Example:** "We just read 'The Story of an Hour' by Kate Chopin," she told me.

4. **Periods and commas always stay within the end quotation marks.** The choice of whether other punctuation stays inside or goes outside the end quotation marks depends upon whether the mark is part of the quote or not.

> **Example 1:** As loudly as he could, he yelled, "Look out below!" (Here, the exclamation point is part of the quoted sentence, so it stays within the quotation marks.)

> **Example 2:** Did I hear you say, "You can have a cookie"? (Here, the question mark is part of the surrounding sentence, so it goes outside the quotation marks.)

ELLIPSES

1. **Ellipsis** (plural *ellipses*) means "omission" in Greek. An ellipsis appears as three dots (…) in Standard American English. Understandably, ellipses are used **when something is being omitted**, usually from quoted material. For instance, when you write a paper, you may want to cite something from a piece of literature but omit a lengthy description in the middle; you would use an ellipsis to show where you left something out.

> **Example:** "He was prodigiously pleased by her outspoken heartiness … The speech made him her friend; it couldn't well help it." (excerpted from *The American Claimant*, by Mark Twain)

2. Additionally, an ellipsis is sometimes used to **indicate a pause or an unfinished thought**.

> **Example:** Dracula never drinks…wine.

HYPHENS

1. A **hyphen** is used to join words, word parts, and numbers. It can also show the division of word syllables, as when words need to be broken across lines.

2. A hyphen **connects a prefix and a proper noun or proper adjective**. It also serves to **connect prefixes** that have not become one in our lexicon with words that follow them or which would become ambiguous or hard to read if they were joined (a current dictionary can help you learn which words have melded with certain prefixes).

    Examples: pre-Colombian, post-Impressionist, anti-hero / antifreeze, ecosystem / eco-awareness

3. A hyphen **joins two or more nouns that are used as one word**, such as great-grandfather, sister-in-law, or secretary-treasurer.

4. A hyphen **unites a compound adjective** (an adjective formed by two separate words) that comes before a noun.

    Examples: an even-tempered man, a well-deserved raise, an up-to-the-minute news report

5. A hyphen is used in writing out the **numbers twenty-one through ninety-nine**. A **fraction used as an adjective** needs a hyphen. A fraction used as a noun does not need a hyphen.

6. A hyphen shows a word has been broken into syllables and continued on the next line. The word must always be broken between syllables.

APOSTROPHES

1. An **apostrophe** shows **possession**. If the person or thing to which possession is attributed is singular, you will use an apostrophe followed by an "s"; if plural, then the apostrophe follows the "s." This does not apply to plurals which don't end in an "s."

    Examples: the book's pages, Mary's guitar, the Jones' dog, the children's game

2. An apostrophe indicates a **contraction**, a combination of two words that leave out certain letters. The places for the missing letters are marked with apostrophes (') as in *I'm* (I am), *wouldn't* (would not), and *you'll* (you will / you shall). There are lists of common contractions available in grammar books and on the Internet.

3. The apostrophe also shows **other omissions**, as in some long words, phrases, or numbers.

    Examples: government / gov't   rock and roll / rock 'n' roll
    six of the clock / six o'clock   1970s / '70s

4. Apostrophes can also be used to form **certain plurals**, where simply adding an "s" may be confusing. This includes plurals of letters (**Examples:** dot your i's and cross your t's), though capital letters usually do not need an apostrophe (**Examples:** I got all As last semester, so Mom bought me some new CDs); it also includes symbols (**Example:** email addresses use @'s before their domain names).

CAPITALIZATION

1. An **initial capital** letter is used at the beginning of a sentence. This is called *sentence case*. Also capitalize the **first word of a direct quotation when it is a complete sentence**.

    Examples: We went to the library. The librarian asked, "How long will you need these books?"

2. In *title case*, capital letters are used on **all words in the title** of a work, except prepositions and articles (unless they come at the beginning of the title).

    Examples: *The Son of the Wolf*, by Jack London
    "Extracts from Adam's Diary," by Mark Twain

3. Always capitalize the **singular first-person pronoun**, *I*; always capitalize **proper nouns** (names of people, places, and things) and **adjectives formed by proper nouns**; always capitalize names of **days and months**; always capitalize **language and country names**, as well as **races and nationalities**.

    Examples: That's what **I** said: The Jones twins are in the Japanese garden again. I wish their parents were back from France; they have not been home since March.

4. Capitalize **family relationship only when they refer to a specific person directly**, substituting for that person's name. Capitalize **titles** that come before a proper name.

    Examples: I think that Mom could out-bake *other kids' moms* any day. Don't you think so, Sis? If you don't believe me, ask Professor Sawyer; she raves about her oatmeal cookies, which *my dad* really likes too.

If you or your teacher feel you need more practice with English grammar, usage, and conventions, please consult American Book Company's ***Basics Made Easy: Grammar and Usage Review***, available at www.americanbookcompany.com.

Practice 1: Punctuation and Capitalization

Read the following sentences. In each set of sentences, choose the one that is correctly punctuated and capitalized.

1. A. Could someone tell me, why the windows are rolled down while its raining outside?
    B. Could someone tell me why the windows are rolled down, while it's raining outside.
    C. Could someone tell me why the windows are rolled down while its raining outside!
    D. Could someone tell me why the windows are rolled down while it's raining outside?

2. A. Bela will meet you at 621 Franklin Street, Hagerstown Maryland, on March 25, 2008 to discuss the deal.
    B. Bela will meet you, at 621 Franklin Street Hagerstown, Maryland, on March 25, 2008 to discuss the deal
    C. Bela will meet you at 621 Franklin Street, Hagerstown, Maryland, on March 25, 2008, to discuss the deal
    D. Bela will meet you at 621 Franklin Street, Hagerstown, Maryland on March 25, 2008 to discuss the deal

3.   A.   She must have gone to the store otherwise she would have taken the dog with her.

      B.   She must have gone to the store; otherwise she would have taken the dog with her.

      C.   She must have gone to the store; otherwise, she would have taken the dog with her.

      D.   She must have gone to the store, otherwise, she would have taken the dog with her.

4.   A.   "Have you read "Paul's case" by Willa Cather?", the teacher asked.

      B.   "Have you read "Paul's Case" by Willa Cather," the teacher asked.

      C.   "Have you read 'Paul's Case' by Willa Cather?" the teacher asked.

      D.   "Have you read 'Paul's case' by Willa Cather?" the teacher asked.

5.   A.   The 1950's began a period of realism in American literature paving the way for such authors as John Updike, Eudora Welty, and Ralph Ellison.

      B.   The 1950s began a period of realism in American literature, paving the way for such authors as John Updike, Eudora Welty, and Ralph Ellison.

      C.   The 1950's began a period of realism in American literature, paving the way for such authors as John Updike; Eudora Welty; and Ralph Ellison.

      D.   The 1950s began a period of realism, in American literature, paving the way for such authors as, John Updike, Eudora Welty, and Ralph Ellison.

PRONOUN FORMS

A **pronoun** is a word that takes the place of a noun. Words such as **I**, **we**, **us**, **them**, **their**, **you**, and **it** are all examples of pronouns.

There are three basic types of pronouns: **nominative**, **objective**, and **possessive**.

1. **Nominative pronouns** are used whenever a pronoun is used as a subject.

> **Example:** Amy and **I** are going water skiing.

In this example, **I** is part of the subject, so the pronoun **I** has to be nominative.

2. **Objective pronouns** are used when the pronoun answers the questions, "What?" or "Whom?" after the action verb.

> **Example:** I heard **him** in the courtyard.

In this example, **him** answers the question, "Heard whom?" so the pronoun is in the objective case.

3. **Possessive pronouns** are used to show ownership or attachment.

> **Example:** **His** watch is very expensive.

In this example, **His** answers the question: Who owns the watch?

Personal Pronoun Forms		
Nominative	**Objective**	**Possessive**
I	me	my, mine
you	you	your, yours
she	her	her, hers
he	him	his
it	it	its
we	us	our, ours
they	them	their, theirs
who	whom	whose
whoever	whomever	

Some people confuse their pronouns. Remember how the pronoun is used in the sentence to determine the correct form.

> **Example: Carlotta** and **me** are going swimming today.

In this sentence, **me** is incorrectly used. Because the pronoun is part of the subject, it is a nominative pronoun. **I** should replace **me**.

Practice 2: Pronoun Forms

Read the following passage. For each blank in the passage, choose the pronoun form that belongs there.

> My mom is really great. She took my friends and (1)____ to the mall for the Back-to-School sale. Mom drove (2)____ and helped (3) ____ find the stores we needed. My friend Kelly bought (4)____ a giant cookie as a thank-you. When Mom ducked into a store, we all took a bite, even though it was (5)____! Besides all the notebooks and pencils (6)____ needed, (7)____ also looked for a dress for my date with Chad. (8)____ are going to a nice restaurant next weekend. When (9)____ shopping bags were full, we headed home. Mom said she didn't mind my friends being along and that she really likes (10)____. I'm glad to have such a cool mom.

1. A. I
   B. me

2. A. us
   B. we

3. A. us
   B. we

4. A. her
   B. she

5. A. her
   B. she

6. A. I
   B. me

7. A. us
   B. we

8. A. Him and I
   B. Him and me
   C. He and me
   D. He and I

9. A. us's
   B. we's

10. A. they
    B. them

PRONOUN ANTECEDENTS

The **antecedent** of a pronoun is the word to which a pronoun refers.

In the following example, **them** refers to the antecedent, **Smoky Mountains**.

antecedent   pronoun

Example 1: Before we visited the **Smoky Mountains**, we studied **them** in our science class.

In the next example, **her** refers to the antecedent, **Paula**.

antecedent   pronoun

Example 2: **Paula** cleaned **her** room after the party.

Practice 3: Pronoun Antecedents

Read the passage below. For each pronoun in boldface, choose the correct antecedent.

Example: Although the plums were ripe, **they** tasted bitter.

A. although	B. plums	C. were	D. ripe

The correct answer is *B, plums*. *They* replaced the word plums in the clause which describes their taste.

An old Hebrew folktale tells a story about fate:

One day, King Solomon's servant came to see (1)**him,** breathless from running.

"Please! Let (2)**me** borrow your fastest horse!" the servant said to the King. "I must be in a town ten miles south of here by nightfall!"

Because (3)**he** was very curious, the King asked why.

The shuddering servant, whose voice shook, answered: "I just met Death in the garden! Death looked (4)**me** in the face, and if I stay, (5)**he** will claim me!"

The King granted the servant what (6)**he** wanted. "My fastest horse has hooves like wings. Take (7)**him**." As the servant rode away, the horse kicked up dust with (8)**its** hooves.

Then King Solomon walked into the garden. As the sun set, (9)**it** cast soft rays on the trees and flowers. The King saw Death sitting there with a perplexed look on (10)**his** face.

"What's this?" asked King Solomon, scratching his head.

Death said to the king, "Tonight I'm supposed to claim (11)**your** servant, and I just now saw (12)**him** in the garden. But I'm supposed to claim him in a town ten miles south of here! Unless he had a horse with hooves like wings, how could he get there by nightfall . . .?"

1.
   A. one   B. day   C. King Solomon   D. servant

2.
   A. a horse   B. servant   C. said   D. King

3.
   A. horse   B. servant   C. curious   D. King

4.
   A. servant   B. voice   C. Death   D. face

5.
   A. servant   B. voice   C. Death   D. face

6.
   A. King   B. granted   C. servant   D. wanted

7.
   A. King   B. servant   C. horse   D. hooves

8.
   A. servant   B. horse   C. dust   D. hooves

9.
   A. King Solomon   B. garden   C. sun   D. rays

10.
   A. sun   B. King   C. Death   D. look

11.
   A. Death   B. the King   C. the servant   D. tonight

12.
   A. Death   B. the King   C. the servant   D. the garden

PRONOUN-ANTECEDENT AGREEMENT

Here's a trick for help with pronoun-antecedent agreement:

Pronoun-antecedent agreement can be complicated, or *it* may be complicated.

In the rule above, "it" is a pronoun that replaces the lengthy **antecedent** phrase "Pronoun-antecedent agreement." The pronoun is singular and gender-neutral, like the noun it replaces, so they are said to agree. But consider these more complicated grammar constructions with pronoun-antecedent agreements.

Pronouns agreeing with compound antecedents, which happens when two or more nouns are joined by the conjunction *and*. In this instance, the pronoun must be plural.

>**Example:** <u>Senators</u> *and* the <u>president</u> alike must agree on *their* agenda for the diplomatic trip.

Because two parties — in this case, the president and the senators — must agree on something, the pronoun is plural. (They already agree with themselves.) But when the compound antecedent comes after *each* or *every*, the pronoun becomes singular.

>**Example:** *Each* <u>rock</u> and <u>tree</u> has *its* charm and story to tell.

The pronoun is the singular *its* (instead of the plural *their*) because, while the rocks and trees have something in common, the use of *each* implies the individual stories would be told separately.

Having pronouns agree with collective-noun antecedents has two possibilities for construction. **1)** When a collective noun refers to *individual* members of a unit, the pronoun will be <u>plural</u>. **2)** When a collective noun refers *to the complete unit*, the pronoun will be <u>singular</u>.

>**Example:** The *herd* of bison scattered towards *their* favorite places at the river.

>**Example:** The *herd* of bison thundered past us in tight formation, protecting *its* young.

Having pronouns agree with indefinite-pronoun antecedents mostly depends on the logic of the text. Some indefinite pronouns like "one" will always take the singular pronoun, while some indefinite pronouns like "several" always takes the plural pronoun. Then others, like "some," depend on the context.

>**Example:** *One* of the horses threw *its* shoe during the race.

>**Example:** *Several* of the children left for *their* field trip carrying cameras.

>**Example:** *Some* of the lawyers offered *their* free time to help with the debate team.

>**Example:** *Some* of the music needed *its* tempo tweaked.

DEMONSTRATIVE PRONOUNS AND ADJECTIVES

This, that, these, and ***those*** are demonstrative words that can be used as either pronouns or adjectives. Demonstrative words are used to point out specific persons, places, things, or ideas. When they are used alone, they are **demonstrative pronouns**.

This is used to point out a singular object that is close by.

>**Example 1:** **This** tastes very good!

These is used to point out a plural object that is close by.

>**Example 2:** **These** are the only donuts we have left.

That is used to point out a singular object far away.

>**Example 3:** **That** is my book propping the door open.

Those is used to point out a plural object that is far away.

Example 4: "Heidi, can you pick **those** up and bring them here?" her father asked.

This, *that*, *these*, and *those* can also be used as adjectives. They are **demonstrative adjectives** when they are followed by the noun they describe.

Example 1: **This** hamburger tastes very good.

Example 2: **These** donuts are the only ones we have left.

Example 3: Do you see **that** book over there by the door?

Example 4: "Heidi, can you pick up **those** keys and bring them here?" her father asked.

Practice 4: Demonstrative Pronouns and Adjectives

Read the following passage, and choose the correct answer to fill in the blank with the appropriate demonstrative pronoun or demonstrative adjective.

It was spring cleaning time at the house, and Mama was on a rampage! "_____(1) doors over there could use another coat of paint," she shouted to my brother. "And take _____(2) cleaning supplies out of my hands before I drop them."

He answered, "_____(3) is no fun."

Mama headed to the garage. Turning to Dad, she said, "I am going to sell _____(4) old motorcycle of yours; it's just taking up space here." Dad and I looked at each other.

"But _____(5) bike was going to be mine soon," I whined.

"Don't get any of _____(6) ideas," Mama snapped at me. "Motorcycles aren't safe!"

I guess _____(7) was the end of the discussion!

1. A. this   B. that   C. these   D. those

2. A. this   B. that   C. these   D. those

3. A. this   B. that   C. these   D. those

4. A. this   B. that   C. these   D. those

5. A. this   B. that   C. these   D. those

6. A. this   B. that   C. these   D. those

7. A. this   B. that   C. these   D. those

Verb Tense Consistency and Agreement

Verb Tense Consistency

The **tense** of the verbs you use in your writing helps readers know when something took place and the relationship of actions of events to one another. Within a sentence, paragraph, story, or book, changes in verb tense help readers understand the time relationships among events. But unnecessary or inconsistent shifts in tense can be confusing.

First, let's briefly review the most commonly used tenses and participles.

1. **Present tense** is used to express an action or condition occurring now, always, or repeatedly.

    Example: Ray Bradbury **writes** primarily science fiction and fantasy. I **am** a big fan and **read** his work regularly.

2. **Past tense** expresses a previous action or connection.
    Example: Mark Twain **wrote** *The Adventures of Huckleberry Finn*, which we **read** and **discussed** in class last year.

3. **Future tense** indicates action that will take place at a later time.
    Example: I wonder what Stephen King's next novel **will be**. Whatever it is, someone probably **will make** it into a movie soon after its release.

4. **Present perfect tense** signals an event that began in the past and either ended in the past or continues to the present.
    Example: Leila **has seen** several film adaptations of *Pride and Prejudice*. She **has decided** that none of them is as good as the book.

5. **Past perfect tense** indicates actions completed by a specific time in the past or before some other past action occurred.

    Example: **Example:** By the beginning of the 20th century, Naturalism **had become** a popular literary movement.

Verb Tense Shifts and How to Fix Them

> **Example 1:** *The Scarlet Letter* **contains** symbolism that readers **used** to help them understand the story.

Contains is present tense, which in this context means that the condition is ongoing. *Used* is past tense but should be present (*use*) to agree with the first verb and because readers in any time frame can and do take this action.

> **Example 2:** In 1836, Ralph Waldo Emerson **has published** *Nature*, in which he **claims** it **was** possible to reach a spiritual state not through religion but by relating to the natural world.

There are several tense shifts in this sentence. First, with a past date provided, we know that these actions took place previously, so the main tense of this sentence should be past tense. *Has published* is present perfect and not appropriate for the action of publishing that clearly took place at a fixed time in the past; it should be simply *published*. *Claims* is present tense, which certainly can be used to express an idea that endures in literature, but it does not agree with *was*. We could change *was* to *is*; however, to attain true consistency in this sentence, the best choice is to change *claims* to *claimed*.

SUBJECT-VERB AGREEMENT

In addition to consistency in tense, there needs to be **agreement between subject and verb** in all cases. You have undoubtedly learned to conjugate most regular and irregular verbs at some time in school. However, there can be some tricky cases. In the following examples, the subject is bold and the verb is underlined.

> **Example 1, simple agreement:** the **dog** barks, her **cousins** listen

> **Example 2, compound singular subjects:** **Josh and Davey** want some ice cream *(but)* Neither **Mrs. Rampling** nor **I** want to go. (An interrupter like *or* or *nor* renders separates the subjects, unlike *and* which joins them, so they do not become plural.)

> **Example 3, subject separated from verb:** A **bushel** of apples is keeping the doctor from our door.

> **Example 4, subject plus prepositional phrase:** The **teacher**, along with all of the students, does not want to miss the pep rally tomorrow.

> **Example 5, collective nouns:** The **jury** deliberates on the verdict *(acting as a group);* sometimes the **jury** disagree and a verdict cannot be reached *(acting as individuals)*.

> **Example 6, indefinite pronouns:** Of the two choices, **neither** *(choice)* appeals much to me. **Both** *(choices)* are rather unpleasant.

> **Example 7, subject following verb:** Under the bed are **boxes** filled with memories.

> **Example 8, title used as subject:** *Children of the Frost* is a collection of stories by Jack London.

Practice 5: Verb Tense Consistency and Agreement

Read the following sentences. Fill in the blanks with the appropriate verb form and tense, chosen from the list below the question.

1. Each of the rare stamps _____ a dollar or more.
   A. cost   B. costs   C. costed   D. can cost

2. They _____ all of the strawberries before lunch; later they _____ most of the blackberries, too.
   A. eat   C. have eaten   F. eat   H. have eaten
   B. ate   D. had eaten   G. ate   J. had eaten

3. I like rock 'n' roll, but rhythm and blues really _____ my favorite music.
   A. is   B. was   C. has been   D. had been

4.   The mass production of books _____ after the invention of the Gutenberg Press.
     A.   begin   B.   begins   C.   began   D.   has begun

5.   "The Eyes of the Panther" _____ a successful story for Ambrose Bierce back in 1892.
     A.   is   B.   was   C.   are   D.   were

6.   Milford found that he _____ a protégé without knowing it; the young man apparently
     A.   take on   B.   took on   C.   has taken on   D.   had taken on

_____ into his life and his work while Milford _____ the other way.
     F.   sneaks   H.   has sneaked   L   looks   N.   was looking
     G.   sneaked   J.   had sneaked   M.   looked   O.   has been looking

VERB FORMS

Following are two lists containing examples of some common forms of verbs. The first list below contains **regular verbs**. The second list contains **irregular verbs**. When you are unsure of the correct verb form of a word, look up the word in the dictionary and the irregular verb forms will be shown.

Notice in the chart that **regular verbs** strictly follow the rules to form other tenses. The endings on the first example have been bolded to emphasize them. Note that some endings change the spelling, for example in *fry*, but these usually follow the regular rules of spelling.

Regular Verb Forms					
Verb	3rd Person Singular Form	Plural Form	Past Tense	Present Participle	Past Participle
call	call**s**	call	call**ed**	call**ing**	call**ed**
fry	fries	fry	fried	frying	fried
plan	plans	plan	planned	planning	planned
work	works	work	worked	working	worked

Irregular Verb Forms					
Verb	3rd Person Singular Form	Plural Form	Past Tense	Present Participle	Past Participle
be	is	are	was/were	being	been
do	does	do	did	doing	done
eat	eats	eat	ate	eating	eaten
freeze	freezes	freeze	froze	freezing	frozen
know	knows	know	knew	knowing	known
read	reads	read	read	reading	read
run	runs	run	ran	running	run
see	sees	see	saw	seeing	seen
sing	sings	sing	sang	singing	sung
speak	speaks	speak	spoke	speaking	spoken
teach	teaches	teach	taught	teaching	taught
think	thinks	think	thought	thinking	thought
write	writes	write	wrote	writing	written

PRESENT PARTICIPLE

The present participle is used when a writer wants to point out an action that is continuous, was continuous or will be continuous or in progress. The present participle is formed by adding -*ing* to a verb.

    Example 1: has been continuous - I **was being** my usual self at the party.

    Example 2: is continuous - He **is studying** for his medical exam.

    Example 3: will be continuous - She **will be working** as a nurse.

PAST PARTICIPLE

The past participle is used when an action has been completed. Some form of *be* or *have* must be used with a past participle to form a complete verb in a sentence.

    Example 1: Da Vinci **had worked** hard on the *Mona Lisa*.

    Example 2: I **have been** at this school for two years.

Practice 6: Verb Forms

Read the following passage. Choose the answer that fills in or identifies the correct verb form for each question.

> *The whole town _____ worried when Joey fell down the well. But when they pulled him out after a few hours, the rescuers _____ him looking healthy and calm. We all felt relieved that he was alright. Waiting to see what would happen had been very nerve-wracking!*

1. In the first sentence, what is the correct verb form to fill in the blank?

    A. were   B. was   C. has been   D. had been

2. The verb you put in this blank is a(n)
    A. an action verb.   C. a helping verb.
    B. a linking verb.   D. none of the above.

3. In the first sentence, **fell** is
    A. an action verb.   C. a helping verb.
    B. a linking verb.   D. none of the above.

4. In the second sentence, **pulled** is
    A. an action verb.   C. a helping verb.
    B. a linking verb.   D. none of the above.

5. In the second sentence, what is the correct verb form to fill in the blank?
    A. find   B. finds   C. finded   D. found

6. The main verb in the second sentence is
    A. pulled.   B. out.   C. found.   D. looking.

7. In the third sentence, which verb, if any, is not used in its correct form?
    A. feeled   C. was
    B. relieved   D. All the verb forms are correct.

8. In the last sentence, **had been** is a(n)
    A. regular verb.   C. present participle.
    B. irregular verb.   D. past participle.

SPELLING

Naturally, **spelling** is important so that readers can understand the words you mean to use. The English language borrows heavily from other languages, so the rules of spelling vary greatly, mainly due to the different origins of the words. Good ways to improve spelling skills include studying the roots of English words, reading continually to increase vocabulary, and looking up new words in the dictionary. Following are some spelling rules that also are useful to learn. There are other rules that will help you with spelling, and if you or your teacher feel that you need more practice with spelling, consult American Book Company's *Basics Made Easy: Grammar and Usage Review* book, available at www.americanbookcompany.com.

Affixed words are words that have had a **prefix** (group of letters placed before a root word) or **suffix** (group of letters placed after a root word) added. Knowing how to use affixes helps you spell words that use them. Here are some common affixes and spelling rules to use with them.

Prefix	Meaning	Example	Suffix	Meaning	Example
de-	take away	derail	-dom	place or state	kingdom
bi-	two	bipolar	-ism	doctrine/belief	atheism
inter-	between	international	-acy	state or quality	accuracy
un-	not	unstoppable	-able, ible	capable of being	livable
dis-	apart, away	disorder	-ful	having a quality	bashful
il-, im-	not	immature	-ious, ous	of or with	delicious
pre-	before	preheat	-less	without	colorless

1. Use *i* before *e*, except after *c*, or when a word is pronounced "ay" as in *reign*.

    Examples: friend, receive, eight, perceive

Exceptions: Most of the time, Rule 1 provides the correct spelling of a word. Yet there are some exceptions in such words as *foreigner, forfeit, height, leisure, neither, science, scientific, seizes,* and *weird.*

2. When prefixes are added to root words, the spelling of the root word does not change.

    Examples: dis + satisfied = dissatisfied, un + noticed = unnoticed

3. When a suffix starting with a vowel is added to a word ending in a silent *-e*, such as *receive* and *smile*, the *-e* is dropped, making words such as *receiving* and *smiling*.

Exception 1: The *-e* is not dropped when it would change the meaning of the root word. (dye + ing = dyeing, not dying)

Exception 2: The *-e* is not dropped if the *-e* clarifies pronunciation. (flee + ing = fleeing, not fleing)

Exception 3: The *-e* is not dropped if the sound *c* or *g* must be kept soft. (courage + ous = courageous, not couragous)

4. When a suffix starting with a consonant is added to a word ending in a silent *-e*, the *-e* is usually kept, such as in *largely* and *excitement*.

5. When a suffix is added to root words ending in *-y*, change the *y* to an *i*, as in *silliness* and *dutiful*. Keep the *-y* if the suffix being added is *–ing* (flying), if the root word has a vowel before the *–y* (stayed), and in some one-syllable base words (shyer).

6. If a word ends in a consonant + vowel + consonant, and the suffix begins with a vowel, double the final consonant or the root word. This also applies if the word contains only one syllable or an accented ending syllable. Otherwise, do not double the last consonant in the root. (stop + er = stopper; begin + ing = beginning)

7. English words that have French, Greek, Latin, or Italian roots form the plural according to their language.

Examples

Singular	Plural	Singular	Plural
analysis	analyses	fungus	fungi
basis	bases	medium	media
beau	beaux	phenomenon	phenomena
crisis	crises	criterion	criteria
syllabus	syllabi	datum	data

HOMONYMS

Problems in understanding what's written also arise if a word is spelled correctly but is not the appropriate word for the context. Such errors occur with **homonyms**, words that sound alike but mean different things depending on their spelling. Below are a few commonly misused homonyms.

bare, lacking covering   **bear**, large carnivore; verb meaning to withstand or hold

brake, stop abruptly   **break**, a rest; verb meaning to smash

hear, to listen   **here**, direction

knew, past tense of know   **new**, original, not old

roll, to turn over   **role**, position or character

their, possessive pronoun   **there**, direction   **they're**, contraction of they are

where, direction   **wear**, what you do with clothing

Practice 7: Spelling

Select the word in each list that is not spelled correctly.

1.
A. health   B. moved   C. Southwest   D. autum

2.
A. floral   B. thirdy-eight   C. worker   D. money

3.
A. scant   B. connection   C. ajust   D. ignorant

4.
A. withold   B. repeat   C. grand   D. cancel

5.
   A. mathmatics   B. wrist   C. charity   D. transportation

6.
   A. frightened   B. happenning   C. going   D. swimming

In the following sentences, choose the appropriate homonym to fill in the blank.

7. I didn't _____ that Jessica was going away.
   A. know   B. no

8. He made a gesture that Robert couldn't _____.
   A. sea   B. see

9. Lucy wandered around the huge house for _____.
   A. days   B. daze

10. Haley asked me if I _____ make some tea.
    A. wood   B. would

11. There are _____ many letters _____ to count!
    A. to   F. hear
    B. too   G. here
    C. two

12. Unfortunately, my father refused to cosign the _____, so I can't _____ the house.
    A. loan   F. buy
    B. lone   G. by

CHAPTER 6 SUMMARY

Recognize and use appropriate **usage and conventions** of Standard American English. This includes these general areas; for more detail, review all of the ideas and rules covered in the chapter.

Capitalization and punctuation signal how words, phrases, and sentences relate to one another; which words may have specific meanings; how sentences should be read; and when a reader should pause.

Verb form and tense help readers understand how an action is being expressed and the time relationships among events; unnecessary or inconsistent shifts in tense can be confusing. In addition, a **verb needs to agree with its subject** in all cases.

Correct **spelling** allows readers to understand the words you mean to use. Learning the rules of spelling as well as the meanings of affixes and root words will improve your skills. In addition, it is important to know commonly misused **homonyms**, words that sound alike but have different meanings and spellings.

CHAPTER 6 REVIEW

A. Read the following passage, then answer the questions about punctuation that follow.

> My brother-in-law's business is for sale; are you interested? Great, lets go and see him. We'll go through the tunnel around the park and down Melcher Street. He acted as though he already had an offer but I wonder? I read an article in the paper called How Long Does it Take to Sell a Business, and it sounds like he may have a few months to go.

1. Is there any punctuation that needs to be corrected in the first sentence?
   A. remove the apostrophe after *law*
   B. change the semicolon after *sale* to a comma
   C. change the question mark at the end to an exclamation point
   D. no change needed

2. Is there any punctuation that needs to be corrected in the second sentence?
   A. change the comma after *Great* to a semicolon
   B. insert an apostrophe in *lets* (let's)
   C. insert a comma after *go*
   D. no change needed

3. In the third sentence, are any corrections needed?
   A. insert a colon after *go*
   B. place commas after *tunnel* and *park*
   C. replace the period at the end with an exclamation point
   D. no change needed

4. In the fourth sentence, are any corrections needed?
   A. place a comma after *though* and change the question mark to an ellipsis
   B. insert a semicolon after *offer*
   C. place a comma after *offer* and change the question mark to an ellipsis
   D. no change needed

5. What is the correct way to punctuate the final sentence?
   A. I read an article in the paper called, "How Long Does it Take to Sell a Business," and it sounds like he may have a few months to go.
   B. I read an article in the paper, called "How Long Does it Take to Sell a Business", and it sounds like he may have a few months to go.
   C. I read an article in the paper called, 'How Long Does it Take to Sell a Business,' and it sounds like he may have a few months to go.
   D. no change needed

Chapter 6

B. For the following passage, choose the <u>pronoun</u> that correctly completes the sentences. Then, select the type of pronoun it is.

(6)It isn't often that you and _____ have a chance to chat. (7)Our families should let _____ get together more often. (8)While the rest of _____ go to the movies, (9)we can have a cola and catch up on _____. (10)_____ do you think of (11)_____ idea?

6.
A. me, possessive   B. I, nominative   C. me, objective   D. I, possessive

7.
A. us, possessive   B. we, nominative   C. us, objective   D. we, objective

8.
A. them, objective   B. they, possessive   C. them, nominative   D. they, objective

9.
A. something, demonstrative   C. anything, interrogative
B. much, relative   D. everything, indefinite

10.
A. Where, indefinite   C. Why, demonstrative
B. What, interrogative   D. When, relative

11.
A. those, indefinite   C. these, relative
B. that, demonstrative   D. that, interrogative

C. Read the passage, and choose the answers which appropriately fill in the blanks, paying attention to subject-verb agreement and consistency of verb tenses.

Mathematics _____(12) my favorite subject, so I was thrilled to learn about an internship at Maryland's largest engineering firm. I didn't hear anything after applying, until one day, as I was about to leave, the phone _____(13). Though the intern program _____(14) advertised well, just five of us _____(15) for the orientation last Friday. We first _____(16) the boss that afternoon; later, I hoped we _____(17) a good impression.

12. A. is   B. are   C. was   D. were
13. A. is ringing   B. rings   C. rang   D. will ring
14. A. is   B. was   C. has been   D. had been
15. A. show up   B. showed up   C. have shown up   D. had shown up
16. A. will meet   B. met   C. have met   D. had met
17. A. will make   B. made   C. have made   D. had made

Writing Skills: Usage and Conventions

D. Read the passage below. For each blank, choose the <u>correct verb</u> to use, and then identify the <u>form and tense</u> of that verb.

      The clever invention, the cell phone, _____(18) a threat in moving cars. Driving and talking on a cell phone _____(19) like playing Russian roulette with a rocket launcher. The cell phone is the trigger, and your car _____(20) as well be the rocket. Yes, our nation's highways are like battlefields, but now we must _____(21) for a law that is a total disarmament. _____(22) you join me in this quest for peace? If you don't, you could find someday that you _____(23) the victim of this dangerous diversion.

18. **correct verb**
    A. pose   B. poses   C. hinder   D. hinders
    correct tense
    F. present tense   G. past tense   H. future tense   J. present perfect
    correct form
    K. action verb   L. linking verb   M. helping verb   N none of these

19. **correct verb**
    A. was   B. were   C. is   D. are
    correct tense
    F. present tense   G. past tense   H. future tense   J. past perfect
    correct form
    K. transitive verb   L. intransitive verb

20. **correct verb**
    A. could   B. might   C. should   D. will
    correct form
    F. action verb   G. linking verb   H. helping verb   J. none of these

21. **correct verb**
    A. call   B. calls   C. called   D. calling
    correct form
    F. action verb   G. linking verb   H. helping verb   J. none of these

22. **correct verb**

  A. Are
  B. Did
  C. Does
  D. Will

  correct tense

  F. present tense
  G. past tense
  H. future tense
  J. future perfect

  correct form

  K. action verb
  L. linking verb
  M. helping verb
  N. none of these

23. **correct verb**

  A. become
  B. are becoming
  C. have become
  D. has become

  correct tense

  F. present tense
  G. past tense
  H. present perfect
  J. past perfect

E. Read the passage and identify spelling errors, if any, in each sentence.

(24)His beutiful new client entered the room like an acrobat, with perfect balance and grace. (25)He made small talk, knowing that if he filled out a contract now, he'd misspell his own name, which was not acceptible; he would need to separate his feelings from this business opportunity. (26)She asked all the relevant questions, and together they decided on a schedule, including an occasion during which he could stake out the sematary where she had been accosted. (27)The look on her face was enough to acquit her of any wierd story telling, and he completely believed she was committed to finding a solution. (28)Her jew-lery had disappeared mysteriously that night, and she'd come to him because he was the only person with the knowledge and equipment to get to the bottom of it.

24.

  A. beutiful
  B. acrobat
  C. perfect
  D. balance

25.

  A. misspell
  B. acceptible
  C. separate
  D. opportunity

26.

  A. relevant
  B. schedule
  C. occasion
  D. sematary

27.

  A. acquit
  B. wierd
  C. believed
  D. committed

28.

  A. jewlery
  B. mysteriously
  C. knowledge
  D. equipment

Writing Skills: Usage and Conventions

F. In the following passage, choose the appropriate homonyms to fill in the blanks.

What are you going to _____ **(29)** tonight? I'm just going in jeans. I can't wait to see *Terror in the Attic 2*; some people thought the first movie was really scary, but it has little _____ **(30)** on me. I thought it was hilarious when they decided to _____ **(31)** that creature they found, not realizing that's what would make it come to life. _____ **(32)** always doing goofy things like that in horror movies.

29.
   A.   wear   B.   where

30.
   A.   affect   B.   effect

31.
   A.   berry   B.   bury

32.
   A.   Their   B.   There   C.   They're

Chapter 7
Controlling Language

This chapter addresses the following expectation(s) and their related indicators from **Core Learning Goal 2: Composing in a Variety of Modes**

Expectation 2.2	The student will compose texts using the prewriting, drafting, revising, and editing strategies of effective writers and speakers.

This chapter addresses the following expectation(s) from **Core Learning Goal 3**: Controlling Language

Expectation 3.1	The student will demonstrate the understanding of the nature and structure of language, including grammar concepts and skills, to strengthen control of oral and written language.

SIMPLE SUBJECTS AND SIMPLE PREDICATES

- A sentence must contain a simple subject and a simple predicate.
- A simple subject is a word or group of words that tells what the sentence is about.
- The simple predicate is a verb or group of verbs that asks or says something about the subject or tells what the subject is doing.

In the following examples, the simple subject is bolded, and the simple predicate is underlined.

> **Example 1:** **Flipper**, the movie star dolphin, <u>swam</u> in the ocean.
>
> **Example 2:** **Life** <u>is</u> but a dream.
>
> **Example 3:** **Carol** and **Julie** <u>are hiking</u> in the Rocky Mountains.

In Example 3, when two or more subjects perform the same action, the verb tense becomes plural (are hiking, not is hiking).

Sentences that are questions must be turned into a statement to determine the simple subject and predicate.

Example 4: Do you want to jump off this rock?

Rearranged: You <u>do want</u> to jump off this rock.

Verb forms that include two or more words, such as <u>is lying</u> in Example 5, are often split apart when asking a question.

Example 5: Why <u>is</u> the **cat** <u>lying</u> on the new carpet?

Practice 1: Simple Subjects and Simple Predicates

Read the following passage, and answer the questions about simple subjects and simple predicates.

(1)The watch dogs have been eating more than usual. (2)That big dog is going to bite someone if he escapes. (3)Carrie and Lynn don't train the dogs very well. (4)Brutus, the leader of the pack, loves to eat leftovers. (5)How would you like to deal with those beasts?

1. The simple subject of this sentence is
   A. watch.　　　　B. dogs　　　　C. watch dogs.　　　D. eating.

   The simple predicate of this sentence is

   F. have.　　　　　　　　　　　H. have been eating.
   G. have been.　　　　　　　　　J. have been eating more.

2. The simple subject of this sentence is
   A. That.　　　　B. big　　　　C. That big　　　D. dog.

   The simple predicate of this sentence is

   F. is going.　　　　　　　　　　H. going.
   G. is going to bite.　　　　　　　J. bite.

3. The simple subject of this sentence is
   A. Carrie and Lynn.　　　　　　C. Lynn.
   B. Carrie.　　　　　　　　　　D. dogs.

   The simple predicate of this sentence is

   F. don't train the dogs very well.　　H. don't train.
   G. don't train the dogs.　　　　　　J. don't.

4. The simple subject of this sentence is
   A. Brutus, leader of the pack.　　C. leader.
   B. Brutus.　　　　　　　　　　D. leftovers

   The simple predicate of this sentence is

   F. loves.　　　　G. loves to eat　　　H. to eat　　　J. eat

164

5. The simple subject of this sentence is
    A. How would you like.
    B. How would you.

    C. How.
    D. you.

    The simple predicate of this sentence is

    A. would.
    B. would you.

    C. would like.
    D. would you like to deal.

MODIFIERS: ADJECTIVES, INFINITIVES AND PARTICIPLES

ADJECTIVES

Adjectives are words that describe nouns and pronouns. A word is an adjective when it answers the questions *which, how many,* or *what kind.*

> **Example:** The beautiful aquarium contains a rare kind of seaweed.

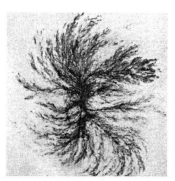

In this example, the word *beautiful* refers to the aquarium and answers the question, "What kind of aquarium is it?" Also, the word *rare* describes the seaweed and answers the question, "What kind of seaweed is this?" So, the adjectives in this sentence are *beautiful* and *rare.*

Note: Adjectives can also be formed by adding the suffixes -able, -ful, -ish, -less, or -y to nouns and verbs.

> **Example:** The *selfish* customer took the Beanie Baby out of the shopping cart of a *helpless* child.

In this example, the word *selfish,* formed by adding -ish to self, describes what kind of customer is in the store. The word *helpless,* formed by adding the suffix -less to help, describes the child in the cart.

**Remember: Possessive pronouns such as *his, her, its, our,* and *their* can be used as adjectives. The articles *a, an,* and *the* are adjectives. In addition, *this, that, these,* and *those* can be adjectives.

Practice 2: Adjective Identification

For each sentence below, choose the answer that identifies an adjective in the sentence.

1. Jerry took his yellow ATV and ran it through the muddiest part of the woods.

    A. ATV B. through C. muddiest D. part

2. Tim's girlfriend, Tamara, stared at all the animals in the pet store.

    A. Tim's B. animals C. in D. store

3. "If I had a dollar bill for every time I heard that remark, I'd be a millionaire!" Richie said.

    A. a B. bill C. millionaire D. Richie

4. I left the costume party disappointed about not winning first prize.
   A. party   B. disappointed   C. winning   D. first

5. "Just wait till Grandma hears how you broke her new vase!" Jake said to his big brother, Ed.
   A. Just   B. how   C. big   D. brother

6. Jacinda joyously played in the yellow daffodils and warmed her beaming face in the sun.
   A. joyously   B. the   C. daffodils   D. face

ADVERBS

An **adverb** is the part of speech used to modify many different kinds of words. Adverbs can modify verbs, adjectives, or other adverbs. Frequently, adverbs end in **-ly**. For example, *lovely, truly,* and *softly* are adverbs. However, be aware of adverbs that do not end in -ly such as *soon* and *well*.

Adverbs modifying verbs — If an adverb describes a verb, it will answer one of these four questions: *Where? When? In what manner? To what extent?*

> **Example:** Does the musician really understand what he is getting into?

In this example, the adverb, *really*, answers the question, "*To what extent* does the musician understand?"

> **Example:** Is the storm going to hit our area tomorrow?

In this example, the adverb, *tomorrow*, answers the question, "*When* could the storm hit?"

Adverbs modifying adjectives—If an adverb describes an adjective, it answers the question, "To what extent?"

> **Example:** With her husband's death, she is now a very wealthy widow.

In this example, the adverb, *very,* answers the question "*To what extent* is the widow wealthy?"

Adverbs modifying other adverbs—If an adverb describes another adverb, the adverbs will appear together, and the first adverb will answer the question "To what extent?" for the second adverb.

> **Example:** The stunt men ride their high-powered motorcycles more cautiously than before.

In this example, the adverb, *more*, answers the question, "*To what extent* do the stunt men ride their motorcycles cautiously?"

Practice 3: Adverb Identification

Read the following sentences. Choose the answer that correctly identifies the adverb in each sentence, if there is one.

1. Stephen King's description of the clown in his novel, *It,* is frightening.
   A. King's   B. the   C. his   D. no adverb

2. What should we do today, Amelia?
   A. What   B. do   C. today   D. no adverb

3. Terry prepared the apple turnovers quickly.
   A. the   B. prepared   C. apple   D. quickly

4. He had to clean his gun extremely well after the soldier jammed it.
   A. his   B. extremely   C. after   D. no adverb

5. We ate the cookies ravenously when they came out of the oven.
   A. ravenously   B. when   C. oven   D. no adverb

6. Kerri Fisher's pet rabbit, Fluffy, was finishing a cut carrot.
   A. pet   B. finishing   C. cut   D. no adverb

INFINITIVES

An **infinitive** is formed by placing the word *to* in front of the base form of a verb. The infinitive can be used in a sentence as a noun, adjective, or adverb. Because of its versatility, the infinitive is often needed when constructing sentences.

You will need to ask yourself what the purpose of the infinitive is in each sentence in order to distinguish it as a noun, an adjective, or an adverb.

> **Example:** As a **noun**: I need <u>to time</u> the cooking of the meat for exactly thirty minutes.

In this sentence, the infinitive *to time* is used as the object of the sentence. <u>Usually,</u> infinitives are not used as subjects of sentences.

> **Example:** As an **adjective**: She needed a house <u>to call</u> her own.

In this sentence, the infinitive *to call* is an adjective describing the noun, house.

> **Example:** As an **adverb**: The guest showed his cards <u>to prove</u> he wasn't cheating.

The infinitive *to prove* in this sentence acts as an adverb by answering the question, "Why did he show his cards?" Thus, the infinitive acts as an adverb modifying the verb, showed.

Practice 4: Find the Infinitive

Read the following sentences in which the infinitives are underlined. Then, choose the answer that correctly identifies whether the infinitive acts as a noun, an adjective, or an adverb.

1. You had better file your tax return if you want <u>to stay</u> out of trouble.
   A. noun   B. adjective   C. adverb

2. It will cost too much <u>to redecorate</u> the room.
   A. noun   B. adjective   C. adverb

3. The new student was looking for someone <u>to eat</u> with over lunch.
   A. noun   B. adjective   C. adverb

4. The club members had <u>to agree</u> to a unanimous decision.
   A. noun   B. adjective   C. adverb

5. George Golding needs a new glove to play baseball.
   A. noun   B. adjective   C. adverb

6. The band gave a longer concert to surprise their fans.
   A. noun   B. adjective   C. adverb

PARTICIPLES

Participle—a word that is formed from a verb but is used as an adjective.

There are four different kinds of participles: past participle, present participle, perfect participle, and passive participle.

Past participle—to make a verb into a past participle, simply add *-en* or *-ed* to the base form of the verb or use a special spelling for irregular verbs.

    Example: eat = eaten, starve = starved, bleed = bled, read = read

    Example: The sunken living room looks great in your house.

Here, the word *sunken* acts as an adjective describing *living room*.

Present participle—to make a verb into a present participle, add *-ing* to the verb.

    Example: skate = skating, fly = flying, drive = driving

    Example: Growing restless, the travelers left the airport.

Here, the word *growing* acts as an adjective describing the noun, *travelers*.

Perfect participle—to make a verb into a perfect participle, place the word h*aving* in front of the past participle form of the verb.

    Example: "say" becomes "having said," "yell" becomes "having yelled," and "crawl" becomes "having crawled."

    Example: Having flown to Paris, Billy felt lost because he couldn't speak French.

Here, the words *having flown* act as an adjective modifying *Billy*.

Passive participle—to make a verb into a passive participle, place the words *having been* in front of the past participle form of the verb.

    Example: "make" becomes "having been made," "solve" becomes "having been solved" and "write" becomes "having been written."

    Example: Having been carved out of onyx, the statues were shiny and smooth.

Here, the words *having been carved* act as an adjective modifying *statues*.

Practice 5: Participles

Read the sentences below. In each, identify the participle and the noun it modifies.

Having dropped out of an airplane, Daffy Duck landed on a bale of straw.

1. What is the participle in this sentence?
    A. having
    B. having dropped
    C. landed
    D. landed on

2. What noun does it modify?
    A. airplane
    B. Daffy Duck
    C. bale
    D. straw

My physical education teacher, Ms. Nguyen, made us exercise on inflated mattresses.

3. What is the participle in this sentence?
    A. made
    B. made us
    C. inflated
    D. on inflated

4. What noun does it modify?
    A. physical
    B. teacher
    C. exercise
    D. mattresses

The dancing puppet made me laugh until my stomach hurt.

5. What is the participle in this sentence?
    A. dancing
    B. made
    C. laugh
    D. hurt

6. What noun does it modify?
    A. puppet
    B. me
    C. my stomach
    D. stomach

Having been awarded a Nobel prize, the physicist became instantly famous.

7. What is the participle in this sentence?
    A. Having
    B. Having been
    C. Having been awarded
    D. awarded

8. What noun does it modify?
    A. Nobel prize
    B. physicist
    C. instantly famous
    D. famous

VERBAL PHRASES

A **phrase** is a group of words acting together as a unit. A **verbal phrase** does not serve as a verb in the sentence; instead, it functions as a noun, adjective, or adverb. There are three types of verbal phrases: **infinitive**, **participial**, and **gerund**. The verbal phrases are underlined in the examples below.

Infinitive phrases start with an infinitive which is followed by any objects and/or modifiers.

> **Example:** Everyone wanted to see clearly.

> *Everyone* is the subject, *wanted* is the verb, *to see* is the infinitive, and *clearly* is an adverb modifying the infinitive.

Controlling Language

Participial phrases are made up of a past or a present participle plus any objects and/or modifiers. Participial phrases always function as adjectives within a sentence

> **Example:** The woman <u>carefully arranging the flowers</u> is my wife.

> *Woman* is the subject, *is* is the verb, *arranging* is the present participle, with *the flowers* being the direct object and *carefully* being a modifying adverb within the participial phrase.

Gerund phrases consist of a gerund (a verbal ending in *-ing* that functions as a noun) and any objects and/or modifiers. It functions as a noun in a sentence.

> **Example:** I dream of <u>traveling the world</u>.

> *I* is the subject, *dream* is the verb, *traveling* is the gerund, and *the world* is its direct object.

The participial phrase and the gerund phrase can look deceivingly similar. After all, a gerund takes the same form as a present participle. Just remember that a **participial phrase serves as an adjective** in a sentence, and a **gerund phrase functions as a noun** (just as a gerund itself does).

Practice 6: Identifying Verbal Phrases

Read the passage based on *The Sketch Book of Geoffrey Crayon, Gent.*, by Washington Irving. Then choose the answer that identifies each underlined clause or phrase.

> Further **(1)**<u>reading and thinking</u>, made me more decided. I visited various parts of my own country; and had I been merely a lover of fine scenery, I should have felt little desire **(2)**<u>to see the sights anywhere else</u>, for on no country had the charms of nature been more lavished. Her oceans of liquid silver; her mountains, with their bright colors; her valleys, with afternoon storms **(3)**<u>thundering in their solitudes</u>; her boundless plains, waving with green; her broad, deep rivers, rolling in solemn silence to the ocean; her trackless forests, **(4)** <u>where vegetation puts forth all its magnificence</u>; her skies, with the magic of summer clouds and glorious sunshine—no, **(5)**<u>never need an American look beyond his own country</u> for the beauty of natural scenery… I had, besides all this, a strong desire **(6)**<u>to see the great men of the earth</u>. We have, it is true, our great men in America: every city has an ample share of them. I have mingled among them in my time, and been almost withered by the shade into which they cast me; **(7)**<u>for there is nothing so humbling</u> to a small man as the shade of a great one, particularly the great man of a city. But I was anxious to see the great men of Europe; for I had read that all men degenerated in America. A great man of Europe, thought I, must therefore be as superior to a great man of America, as a peak of the Alps to a highland of the Hudson; and this idea I confirmed by **(8)**<u>observing the swelling importance</u> of many English travellers among us, who, I was assured, were very little people in their own country. I will visit this land of wonders, thought I, and see the gigantic race from which I come.

1.
A.	infinitive phrase	B.	participial phrase	C.	gerund phrase	D.	not a verbal phrase

2.
A.	infinitive phrase	B.	participial phrase	C.	gerund phrase	D.	not a verbal phrase

3.

A.	infinitive phrase	B.	participial phrase	C.	gerund phrase	D.	not a verbal phrase

4.

A.	infinitive phrase	B.	participial phrase	C.	gerund phrase	D.	not a verbal phrase

5.

A.	infinitive phrase	B.	participial phrase	C.	gerund phrase	D.	not a verbal phrase

6.

A.	infinitive phrase	B.	participial phrase	C.	gerund phrase	D.	not a verbal phrase

7.

A.	infinitive phrase	B.	participial phrase	C.	gerund phrase	D.	not a verbal phrase

8.

A.	infinitive phrase	B.	participial phrase	C.	gerund phrase	D.	not a verbal phrase

CONJUNCTIONS

Conjunction—the part of speech connecting words or groups of words to one another.

There are four types of conjunctions—each with their own uses. These types include *coordinating conjunctions, subordinating conjunctions, correlative conjunctions,* and *conjunctive adverbs.*

Coordinating Conjunctions—used to join two or more of the same parts of speech such as nouns, pronouns, verbs, adjectives, adverbs, prepositions, conjunctions, as well as phrases or clauses. Here is a list of some frequently used coordinating conjunctions. Notice that the first letter of each word spells out "**boys fan.**"

B	O	Y	S	F	A	N
but	or	yet	so	for	and	nor

Example: Alice *and* Jim toured the oldest house in town.

Example: The children were crawling *or* jumping their way through the obstacle course.

Example: I really wanted to see the concert, *so* I camped out in line before the doors opened.

Controlling Language

Correlative Conjunctions—also join similar elements of a sentence. However, these conjunctions come in pairs. The main correlative conjunctions are:

both....and	if....then	either...or	just as...so
neither...nor	not only....but also	whether...or	

Example: *If* I get this degree, *then* I can work in any modern television studio.

Example: *Neither* my mother *nor* my father knows how to drive a car with a manual transmission.

Subordinating Conjunctions—come before adverb clauses and show a relationship between an adverb clause and another clause. The subordinating conjunctions include these examples:

after	because	in order that	than	until
although	before	once	that	when
as	even though	provided	though	where
as much as	if	since	unless	while

Example: My kids left the house a mess *because* they had to get to school on time.

Example: My uncle took a trip around the world *after* he won the lottery.

Conjunctive Adverbs—conjunctions which are also adverbs that connect independent clauses. Common conjunctive adverbs are listed below:

also	furthermore	likewise	next	then
anyway	however	meanwhile	now	therefore
besides	incidentally	moreover	otherwise	thus
consequently	indeed	namely	similarly	
finally	instead	nevertheless	still	

Example: Oliver decided to end his search for the exotic plant; *consequently*, he had more time to devote to his family.

Example: King Sargon knew he ruled a great, powerful nation; *moreover*, he did not fear attacks from other countries.

Chapter 7

Practice 7: Identifying Conjunctions

Read the following passage in which the conjunctions are underlined. Identify the type of conjunction used in each sentence.

(1)Billy, Ralph, and Alice took a walk on the wild side by dressing like clowns. (2)It wasn't Halloween; however, Alice knew about a costume party. (3)It didn't matter that she didn't know the host well; besides, who would recognize them? (4)Either they would have a great time, or they would get kicked out. (5)If the party wasn't fun, then they would leave anyway. (6)Billy had borrowed his brother's car; consequently, they were at the party in no time. (7)As much as Billy hated to borrow anything, having a car was much better than taking the bus—especially in costume! (8)Everyone at the party had on cool costumes, although there weren't many with a group theme. (9)The threesome had arrived just in time, because the contests were starting. (10)Ralph ended up winning for best homemade costume with his wild Blinky the Clown suit, while the group took third place for coordinated costume effort!

1.
  A. coordinating conjunction   C. subordinating conjunction
  B. correlative conjunction   D. conjunctive adverb

2.
  A. coordinating conjunction   C. subordinating conjunction
  B. correlative conjunction   D. conjunctive adverb

3.
  A. coordinating conjunction   C. subordinating conjunction
  B. correlative conjunction   D. conjunctive adverb

4.
  A. coordinating conjunction   C. subordinating conjunction
  B. correlative conjunction   D. conjunctive adverb

5.
  A. coordinating conjunction   C. subordinating conjunction
  B. correlative conjunction   D. conjunctive adverb

6.
  A. coordinating conjunction   C. subordinating conjunction
  B. correlative conjunction   D. conjunctive adverb

7.
  A. coordinating conjunction   C. subordinating conjunction
  B. correlative conjunction   D. conjunctive adverb

8.
  A. coordinating conjunction   C. subordinating conjunction
  B. correlative conjunction   D. conjunctive adverb

9.
    A.   coordinating conjunction   C.   subordinating conjunction

    B.   correlative conjunction   D.   conjunctive adverb

10.
    A.   coordinating conjunction   C.   subordinating conjunction

    B.   correlative conjunction   D.   conjunctive adverb

CHAPTER 7 SUMMARY

A sentence must contain a **simple subject** and a **simple predicate**. A simple subject is a word or group of words that tells what the sentence is about. The simple predicate is a verb or group of verbs that asks or says something about the subject or tells what the subject is doing.

Adjectives are words that describe nouns and pronouns. A word is an adjective when it answers the questions *which*, *how many*, or *what kind*.

An **adverb** is the part of speech used to modify many different kinds of words. Adverbs can modify verbs, adjectives or other adverbs.

An **infinitive** is formed by placing the word *to* in front of the base form of a verb. The infinitive can be used in a sentence as a noun, adjective or adverb.

Participle is a word that is formed from a verb but is used as an adjective. There are four different kinds of participles:

- **past participle:** add **-en** or **-ed** to the base form of the verb or use a special spelling for irregular verbs
- **present participle:** add **-ing** to the verb
- **perfect participle:** place the word *having* in front of the past participle form of the verb.
- **passive participle:** place the words *having been* in front of the past participle form of the verb.

Verbal Phrases are groups of words acting as a unit which function as nouns, adjectives, or adverbs in a sentence. They include infinitive phrases, **participial phrases**, and **gerund phrases**.

Conjunction is the part of speech that connects words or groups of words to one another (remember **BOYSFAN**). Types of conjunctions include:

- **coordinating conjunctions** that join parts of speech
- **correlative conjunctions** that join similar elements of a sentence
- **subordinating conjunctions** that come before subordinate clauses
- **conjunctive adverbs** that connect independent clauses

CHAPTER 7 REVIEW

A. Read the following passage and identify the simple subject and simple predicate in each sentence.

(1)Our friend, Lisa, is taking a trip to Europe with her class. (2)All of the kids are flying out on Sunday. (3)Can I go with Lisa?

1. What is the simple subject in sentence 1?
   A. Our friend   B. friend   C. Lisa   D. Europe

   What is the simple predicate in this sentence?
   F. is   G. taking   H. is taking   J. trip

2. What is the simple subject in sentence 2?
   A. All   B. kids   C. all of the kids   D. Sunday

   What is the simple predicate in this sentence?
   F. of the   G. are   H. flying out   J. are flying

3. What is the simple subject in sentence 3?
   A. I   B. Can I   C. with them   D. them

   What is the simple predicate in this sentence?
   F. Can   G. I   H. go   J. go with

B. Identify the adjective in each sentence in the passage below.

(4)The performer just looked at the ground. (5)The audience gratefully applauded the talented magician. (6)As a boy, he had made a name for himself as the class clown. (7)Now, he was making a decent living doing tricks on stage.

4.   A. The   B. performer   C. just   D. ground

5.   A. gratefully   B. applauded   C. talented   D. magician

6.   A. name   B. form   C. himself   D. class

7.   A. making   B. decent   C. tricks   D. stage

C. Read the following passage. Then identify the adverb in each sentence, if there is one.

(8)Going to the state fair was the most fun we've had this year! (9)Priscilla was barely able to stand up after getting off the roller coaster. (10)In the cages, a hyena was cackling loudly to the left of a lion. (11)We all visited the recently added funhouse several times.

8.

   A. state   B. fair   C. most   D. no adverb

9.

   A. barely   B. off   C. roller   D. no adverb

10.

   A. The   B. loudly   C. left   D. no adverb

11.

   A. all   B. visited   C. recently   D. several

D. For the following passage, identify whether the underlined infinitive acts as a noun, an adjective, or an adverb.

(12)Shannon knew <u>to have</u> a camcorder was a big expense. (13)She spent her allowance <u>to buy</u> one that was on sale. (14)<u>To remember</u> how many scenes she had shot, she kept a little notebook with her. (15)She captured so many funny incidents, she had several <u>to send</u> in to that funny video show. (16)Shannon's likely <u>to win</u> a prize on that show!

12.

   A. noun   B. adjective   C. adverb

13.

   A. noun   B. adjective   C. adverb

14.

   A. noun   B. adjective   C. adverb

15.

   A. noun   B. adjective   C. adverb

16.

   A. noun   B. adjective   C. adverb

D. Read the following passage and identify the underlined verbal phrases.

(17)Bryan loved to spend the afternoon <u>running</u> around town. (18)He was happy **to compete** in the track meet, and broke a school record in the 50 yard dash. (19)The people <u>watching</u> stood up and cheered. (20)Bryan was proud of <u>running</u> a good race.

17.
  A.   infinitive phrase
  B.   participial phrase
  C.   gerund phrase
  D.   not a verbal phrase

18.
  A.   infinitive phrase
  B.   participial phrase
  C.   gerund phrase
  D.   not a verbal phrase

19.
  A.   infinitive phrase
  B.   participial phrase
  C.   gerund phrase
  D.   not a verbal phrase

20. .
  A.   infinitive phrase
  B.   participial phrase
  C.   gerund phrase
  D.   not a verbal phrase

E. In each sentence of the passage below, identify the participle and the noun it modifies.

> **(21)**Having been given recess for an hour, the children played hide-and-seek. **(22)**When we saw Davey's hiding place in a high tree limb, we gasped. **(23)**The handyman brought out his telescoping ladder and climbed to rescue Davey.

21. What is the participle in this sentence?
  A.   Having
  B.   Having been given
  C.   Having been
  D.   played

  What is the noun it modifies?

  A.   recess   B.   hour   C.   children   D.   hide-and-seek

22. What is the participle in this sentence?
  A.   saw   B.   hiding   C.   high   D.   gasped

  What is the noun it modifies?

  A.   we   B.   Davey's   C.   place   D.   limb

23. What is the participle in this sentence?
  A.   brought   B.   brought out   C.   telescoping   D.   climbed

24. What is the noun it modifies?
  A.   handyman   B.   ladder   C.   rescue   D.   Davey

F. Identify the types of conjunctions used in the following passage (conjunctions are underlined).

(25)I will stick by my principles <u>whether</u> my friends want me to <u>or not</u>. (26)There are many opportunities to spend time with my friends; <u>however,</u> I know I don't have to say "yes" every time they want to go somewhere. (27)Niyesha and Yolanda are going to the mall, <u>but</u> I don't feel like going there today. (28)<u>Not only</u> do they spend too much time window shopping, <u>but</u> they <u>also</u> spend too much money! (29)<u>Even though</u> I'm seventeen, I know the value of saving for the future. (30)I've had a savings account since I was 10, <u>so</u> there's a nice sum in there now. (31)Most of my friends have <u>not</u> saved much money, <u>nor</u> do they plan to. (32)<u>Although</u> it's fun to spend now, it's also important to think about future needs.

25.
A. coordinating conjunction
B. correlative conjunction
C. subordinating conjunction
D. conjunctive adverb

26.
A. coordinating conjunction
B. correlative conjunction
C. subordinating conjunction
D. conjunctive adverb

27.
A. coordinating conjunction
B. correlative conjunction
C. subordinating conjunction
D. conjunctive adverb

28.
A. coordinating conjunction
B. correlative conjunction
C. subordinating conjunction
D. conjunctive adverb

29.
A. coordinating conjunction
B. correlative conjunction
C. subordinating conjunction
D. conjunctive adverb

30.
A. coordinating conjunction
B. correlative conjunction
C. subordinating conjunction
D. conjunctive adverb

31.
A. coordinating conjunction
B. correlative conjunction
C. subordinating conjunction
D. conjunctive adverb

32.
A. coordinating conjunction
B. correlative conjunction
C. subordinating conjunction
D. conjunctive adverb

Chapter 8
Conventions in Sentences and Paragraphs

This chapter addresses the following expectation(s) and their related indicators from **Core Learning Goal 2: Composing in a Variety of Modes**.

Expectation 2.2	The student will compose texts using the prewriting, drafting, revising, and editing strategies of effective writers and speakers.

This chapter also addresses the following expectation(s) and related indicators from **Core Learning Goal 3: Controlling Language.**

Expectation 3.1	The student will demonstrate understanding of the nature and structure of language, including grammar concepts and skills, to strengthen control of oral and written language.

When you write an essay or prepare oral presentations, you need to pay attention to the big ideas and how they address an assignment <u>and</u> to the structure, conventions, style, and words you use. There is much to think about!

Thus, as you are prewriting, drafting, revising, and editing, keep in mind the steps reviewed in this chapter and the next (chapter 9, "Writing the Essay").

In this chapter, you will learn some of the steps to use that can improve your writing and oral presentation skills. You have already reviewed grammar and usage in chapters 6 and 7. This chapter builds on those concepts and provides more about constructing effective sentences and paragraphs.

SENTENCE CONSTRUCTION

The basic construction in sentences must be complete and sturdy. **Simple sentences (independent clauses)** and **compound sentences** (two or more independent clauses joined by *and, but, or*) should be used appropriately and varied. **Conjunctions** should hold the elements together, and run-ons must be avoided. **Fragments** must be corrected and **parallels** drawn to keep things equal. **Misplaced modifiers** deserve and should receive logical placement. See the following sections on how to improve these sentence construction elements.

CLAUSES

An **independent clause** is a group of words that has a subject and predicate and can stand on its own as a sentence. An independent clause on its own forms a *simple sentence*. A **dependent clause** also has a subject and predicate but depends on the main clause (for example, joined to it with a subordinating conjunction). When two or more clauses are joined, this is a *compound sentence*; a simple sentence with a dependent clause becomes a *complex sentence*, and a compound sentence with a dependent clause becomes a *compound-complex sentence*.

PHRASES

A **phrase** is a group of words that cannot stand on its own but modifies or further explains something in a clause. For examples of verbal phrases, see chapter 7.

RUN-ONS

When two independent clauses are joined but lack a conjunction, this is called a **run-on**. The sentence has two ideas in tandem, making it sound rushed.

There are three common methods to correct and improve run-on sentences:

- using a comma and conjunction between the two clauses
- using a semi-colon between the two clauses
- using a period after the first clause and a capital letter for the second to make the clauses two separate sentences.

See the following example and its three improvements.

> **Example:** The space shuttle may not be ready for launch **in late summer, it may even be delayed till the fall of this year**.

> **Correction 1:** in late summer, *and* it may even be delayed untill the fall of this year

> **Correction 2:** in late summer; it may even be delayed till the fall of this year

> **Correction 3:** in late summer. *It* may even be delayed till the fall of this year

FRAGMENTS

View of Beijing, China

A **fragment** is a serious sentence error that is fairly straightforward and easy to "hear" in text. A sentence fragment is missing either a subject or verb. To correct these fragments, merely add the missing part. A less common example of a sentence fragment is a clause which begins with a subordinating word and is not a question. Add another clause to the subordinate one or combine the subordinate clause to a nearby independent clause to create a complete sentence.

Example: Changes in the business culture of emerging, modernizing China.

Correction: Changes in the business culture of emerging, modernizing China allow employees and managers to think outside the historic box.

Example: Making the Chinese economy vibrant and nimble in its reactions to the global market.

Correction: The change in culture is making the Chinese economy vibrant and nimble in its reactions to the global market.

Example: Because China is experiencing change and a revitalization of the economy.

Correction: Because China is experiencing change and a revitalization of the economy, the global market is experiencing change as well.

PARALLELISM

Think of a log cabin which has logs of differing lengths and angles so that the cabin leans or teeters in uneven lines. Likewise, a sentence will seem disjointed or uneven if the elements within the structure are not **parallel**. These elements may be items in a series, joined phrases, joined clauses, verb forms and so on. To make elements in the sentence parallel, simply use the same form for all repeated items in the sentence. In the following examples, note the balance in the sentence elements.

Example: Today's headlines encompass stories of <u>union upheavals</u>, <u>tragic occurrences</u>, and <u>civil reactionaries</u>. (all have a disturbing effect)

Example: Local union leaders are voting *either* <u>to remain</u> with the national organization *or* <u>to disband</u> the local chapter completely. (choice of actions)

Example: News reporters closely scrutinized the unfolding drama, *and* many took unprecedented risks near the harrowing scene. (cause and effect)

Example: Scores of citizens <u>took</u> part in the peace march *yet* <u>released</u> pamphlets urging calm in the streets. (series of actions)

MISPLACED AND DANGLING MODIFIERS

Using **modifiers** (words, phrases or clauses) correctly adds color to writing and expands a reader's understanding of the text. Using the same modifiers in the wrong place causes confusion. Modifiers need to be placed next to the word(s) they modify and should not be used where they may be ambiguous (possibly modifying words both before and after them). To improve a sentence with a misplaced or dangling modifier, move the modifier closer to the word(s) to be modified. See the following examples of misplaced modifiers and corrections:

Example: We took photos of the <u>Stanley Steamer motor car</u> with our friends <u>displayed</u> at the famous Stanley Hotel in Colorado.

Correction: We took photos of our friends with the <u>Stanley Steamer motor car</u> <u>displayed</u> at the famous Stanley Hotel in Colorado.

Example: <u>Spouting white steam from side vents</u>, we photographed the Durango train's <u>engine</u>.

Correction: We photographed the Durango train's <u>engine spouting white steam from side vents</u>.

Example: (ambiguous): The silver mine's tour director said <u>when she finished</u> she would take requests for western music.

Correction: The silver mine's tour director said she would take requests for western music <u>when she finished</u>.

SENTENCE EFFECTIVENESS

An ingredient in the recipe for writing a good essay is mixing in different kinds of sentences. This is called **sentence variety**; it means using sentences of different lengths and structures. Simple sentences get your meaning across easily. More complicated, or complex, sentences add interest to your essay. Using both forms gives your essay sentence variety.

COMBINE SENTENCES

Combining sentences is a good way to add variety to your sentence structure. A paragraph with short, simple sentences may be easy to understand, but it is not very interesting to read. Read the following paragraph.

> Katrina was a hurricane. The hurricane struck the coast in Louisiana. The hurricane struck at night. The hurricane had high winds and rain. The hurricane caused major flooding. The hurricane caused a lot of damage. The hurricane destroyed many houses. The hurricane destroyed businesses. The hurricane caused many injuries. The hurricane caused many deaths.

This paragraph has good, solid information. The sentences are short and easy to read, but the flow of the paragraph is choppy. This takes away from the impact of the information. Creating some longer sentences would improve the flow and the impact of the paragraph.

The hurricane struck the coastal Louisiana town in the middle of the night. The high winds and rains caused extensive flooding and damage as it swept through the town destroying homes and businesses. Numerous injuries were reported in addition to many deaths.

Both paragraphs tell the same story, but the second one is more interesting to read. The sentence variety has added interest and impact. The writer created longer sentences by combining, or putting together, some of the short sentences. Sentence combining is done in many ways:

- **Use a semicolon** to combine two equally important, related sentences.

  The hurricane had high winds and rain; therefore, it caused extensive flooding and damage.

- **Use a conjunction** to compare or contrast two ideas in a sentence.

  The hurricane caused not only major property damage, but also numerous injuries.

- **Use a series** to combine three or more similar ideas.

  The hurricane struck the coastal town causing major flooding, extensive damage, multiple injuries, and many deaths.

- **Use a relative pronoun** to introduce less important ideas.

  The hurricane, which struck in the middle of the night, left a path of destruction in the coastal Louisiana town.

- **Use an introductory phrase or clause** for less important ideas.

  Because it struck in the middle of the night, the horrible extent of the hurricane damage was not apparent until morning.

USE DIFFERENT BEGINNINGS

In the English language, the most common sentence structure includes subject, verb, and object, in that order. Adjectives, adverbs, and different phrases are often added to the middle or end of this structure. Using this same structure over and over can become boring and may even irritate readers. To add variety to sentences, start some with a part of speech other than the subject. Look at the following examples:

Begin with an adverb:

  Replace "The hurricane's winds suddenly blew the roof off the house."

   with "Suddenly, the hurricane's winds blew the roof off the house."

Begin with a prepositional phrase:

  Replace "The governor saw many destroyed homes on a tour of the damage."

  with "On a tour of the damage, the governor saw many destroyed homes."

Begin with a participial phrase:

  Replace "The hurricane swept through the town, leaving a trail of destruction."

  with "Leaving a trail of destruction, the hurricane swept through the town."

These examples show how to add a variety of sentence structures to your essay. The examples also show how a modifier is best understood when it is placed near the noun or verb it is modifying.

EXPAND WITH DETAILS

Expanding a sentence with details is a great way to add variety to your sentences. It will also improve your writing by making it more vibrant. You can add more details to a basic sentence in five ways:

Add adjectives or adverbs:
> The **high-speed** winds **effortlessly** tore off the roof.

Add prepositional phrases:
> We sat **with our ears covered in the basement** until the storm passed.

Add participial phrases:
> **Holding our breath**, we hoped our home would endure the storm.

Add subordinate clauses:
> **When we finally came up from the basement,** we discovered what was left of our home.

Add relative clauses:
> Our home, **which had been in our family for generations**, was in rubble.

USE A QUESTION OR EXCLAMATION

Replacing a simple, quiet sentence with an explosive or questioning one will add emotion to your writing. Using an exclamation mark (!) adds excitement. Using a question mark (?) adds to a reader's curiosity. Sentence variety is part of the recipe for good writing. Compare the following examples:

> **Example:** I didn't like it when my childhood home was destroyed by the hurricane. It was the worst feeling I've ever experienced.

> **Example:** How would you like having your childhood home destroyed by a hurricane? It's the worst feeling I've ever experienced**!**

186

Chapter 8

Practice 1: Sentence Construction

This practice allows you to assess the correctness and effectiveness of sentence construction. In choosing responses, use the expectations set by standard written English for sentence construction.

In the sentences below, part of the sentence or the whole sentence is underlined. Beneath these sentences you will find four ways of re-phrasing the underlined part. Choose the response that best expresses the meaning of the original sentence. Your choice should create the most effective sentence—clear and precise, without awkwardness or ambiguity.

1. <u>Nell promised after juggling five pine cones at once she could use</u> three lit torches and a pine branch in her routine.

   A. leave as is
   B. After juggling five pine cones at once, Nell promised she could use
   C. Nell promised after juggling five pine cones, at once, she could use
   D. After she juggled five pine cones, Nell promised, at once, she could use

2. <u>From seventy feet away, Dennis watched the fireworks display so he</u> would be safe.

   A. leave as is
   B. From seventy feet away, Dennis watched the fireworks display; so he
   C. So he would be safe, Dennis the fireworks display watched from seventy feet away
   D. Dennis watched the fireworks display from seventy feet away, so he

3. The new car models <u>all have GPS tracking systems, satellite radios and an ice dispenser serving</u> cubed or crushed ice.

   A. leave as is
   B. each have GPS tracking systems, satellite radios and an ice dispenser now serving
   C. all have GPS tracking systems, satellite radios and ice dispensers serving
   D. they all have GPS tracking systems, satellite radios and an ice dispenser which serves
   E. all having GPS tracking, satellite systems radio and ice dispenser serving

4. <u>Mailing a personal or professional letter through the local, traditional</u> blue collection box.

   A. leave as is
   B. Few people have been mailing personal or professional letters through the local, traditional
   C. Mailing a personal or professional letter through the local but traditional
   D. Resulting from public restraint, mailing a personal or professional letter through the local, traditional

5. The mythological status of <u>Johnny Appleseed is grounded in reality, he planted orchards</u> across the states which stand even today.

    A. leave as is
    B. Johnny Appleseed is grounded in reality, because he planted orchards
    C. Johnny Appleseed is grounded in reality planting orchards
    D. Johnny Appleseed is grounded in reality; he planted orchards

6. <u>Offering a sanitized version of the Roald Dahl story, "Charlie and the Chocolate Factory," many audience members went out to rent the Gene Wilder/Willy Wonka movie.</u>

    A. leave as is
    B. Though really only a sanitized version of the Roald Dahl story "Charlie and the Chocolate Factory," many moviegoers nonetheless turned out for the Gene Wilder movie.
    C. Offering the Roald Dahl story, "Charlie and the Chocolate Factory," many audience members renting a sanitized version of the Gene Wilder/Willy Wonka movie
    D. Many audience members went out to rent the Gene Wilder/Willy Wonka movie that offered a sanitized version of the Roald Dahl story, "Charlie and the Chocolate Factory."

WORD CHOICE

Choosing words is partly a matter of **style**, partly a matter of **tone,** and partly a matter of audience. These three elements, as well as the topic of a text and the appropriateness of the words themselves, guide the writer to correct word choices. You read in chapter 2, under "Author's Purpose," how these elements influence a text, and now you will focus on using them when you write. Here are some additional word choice considerations to keep in mind as you write.

WORDINESS

Word choice also concerns how succinct or how wordy a piece of text may be. Generally, writers need to avoid **wordiness** for clear, concise writing. To this end, positive sentences are clearer for readers than negative ones, and dropping common empty phrases like "the fact that" fosters concise writing.

> **Example:** <u>At this moment in time</u>, gas prices have reached an unprecedented high.
>
> **Correction:** Gas prices <u>today</u> have reached an unprecedented high.
>
> **Example:** <u>To make a long story short</u>, the perceived global hoarding of oil, <u>which is at a crisis level</u>, is pricing energy beyond the reach of many third world nations.
>
> **Correction:** The perceived global hoarding of oil, <u>now at crisis levels</u>, is pricing energy beyond the reach of many third world nations.
>
> **Example:** <u>In spite of the fact</u> that this market report has been compiled <u>for the purpose of</u> educating consumers about choices in alternative energy, no one is listening.
>
> **Correction:** <u>Although</u> this market report has been compiled <u>to</u> educate consumers about choices in alternative energy, no one is listening.

AVOID TRITE EXPRESSIONS AND CLICHÉS

Trite expressions and **clichés** are phrases or ideas that have been overused. Sometimes, such a figure of speech describes a situation in a succinct and understandable way, such as when someone knows it takes hard work to succeed and sums it up with the cliché, "No pain, no gain!" In everyday speech, we may use such expressions, but in writing, they are overly familiar and not as descriptive as finding original and vivid wording to describe an idea or feeling. When you find yourself using worn out expressions, replace them with more descriptive language.

> **Example: Cliché:** He's a chip off the old block.
> **Vivid description:** He resembles his father not only in looks but in mannerisms and ambition.
>
> **Cliché:** You're like a bull in a china shop.
> **Vivid description:** Be more careful so you don't break all the dishes in the kitchen.
>
> **Cliche:** I'm a happy camper about the test!
> **Vivid description:** I'm relieved and thrilled with my grade on the test!

Practice 2: Word Choices

In the sentences below, part of the sentence or the whole sentence is underlined. Beneath these sentences you will find four ways of rephrasing the underlined part. Choose the response that best expresses the meaning of the original sentence. Choose A if you think the original is correct. Choose one of the others if it is an improvement. Your choice should create the most effective sentence—clear and precise, without awkwardness or ambiguity.

1. The <u>Pentagon cannot hardly ever say it will be completely accurate</u> in its security predictions.

   A. leave as is
   B. Pentagon cannot say it will be completely accurate
   C. Pentagon cannot hardly say it will be completely accurate
   D. Pentagon hardly never can say it will be completely accurate

2. This summer's <u>heat wave arrived in the western planes of the Rock-ies</u> during July.

   A. leave as is
   B. heat wave arrived in the Rockies, its western plains,
   C. heat wave arrived in the western plains of the Rockies
   D. a wave of heat arrives in the western plains of the Rockies

3. Lewis and Clark experienced the flat plains of Kansas and the peaks of Colorado, and <u>these are the wonders described in their detailed</u> journals.

   A. leave as is
   B. described these wonders in their detailed
   C. this is the wonder described in their detailed
   D. Lewis and Clark described them in their detailed

4. <u>Having that rainy-day fund is my ace in the hole.</u>
    A. leave as is
    B. My rainy-day fund is really handy.
    C. Having money in the bank for emergencies gives me a secure feeling.
    D. Having dough socked for any contingency is the only way to fly.

5. A well-orchestrated <u>field trip may ascend the conscientiousness of students</u> and chaperones.
    A. field trip may higher the conscientiousness of students
    B. field trip may raise student consciousness
    C. field trip may raise the conscience in students
    D. field trip may raise the consciousness of students

ACTIVE AND PASSIVE VOICE

Some issues of the Maryland test concern the use of **standard English** and **active voice**. As students of writing, you have heard many times that a written essay should follow the rules of standard English. The use of standard English depends upon the **author's purpose** of the essay. If the essay is formal and informative, the use of standard English is required. If, on the other hand, it is a casual essay meant to entertain, then a more **colloquial**, or informal language is acceptable. That is why some questions will ask you to consider the author's purpose before determining the best language for a paragraph.

Refer back to chapter 2 where you learned about **language**, **tone**, and **voice** under the discussion of "Author's Purpose."

Active and **passive voice** pertain to the way an action is described. When a writer describes an action in an active voice, the subject comes first and performs the action: *Jane took the test twice*. In contrast, the passive voice focuses on the object of the action first, and then describes the action as what was done to the object: *The test was taken by Jane twice*. Conventional standard English for essays requires active voice as the preferred mode of expressing ideas. Active voice states a point more directly and effectively than passive voice does. The following explanation contains some examples of passive and active voice.

Passive	Active
The aria by Puccini was sung by Maria Callas.	Maria Callas sang the aria by Puccini.
The launch of the space shuttle from Cape Canaveral was controlled by N.A.S.A.	N.A.S.A. controlled the launch of the space shuttle from Cape Canaveral.
The test is being prepared for by all 10th grade students in the county.	All 10th grade students in the county are preparing for the test.
An admission of guilt was finally made by the defendant.	The defendant finally admitted his guilt.

When the subject and verb are paired together in **active voice**, the action is much more direct and dynamic.

In the passive voice, syntax is "switched"— instead of subject-verb-object, it is object-verb-subject. This produces a slower thought process and reads awkwardly.

Example: The newest Driver's Ed class *will be taken* by our school's juniors first.

The Driver's Ed class is not performing the verb — it will not be taking something. The junior class is the subject. Clues to this passive voice construction include the use of the word *by* after the verb, and the use of past participle verbs (in this case *taken*) with the auxiliary verbs to be.

Correction: Our school's juniors *will take* the newest Driver's Ed class.

Practice 3: Active and Passive Voice

In the sentences below, part of the sentence or the whole sentence is underlined. Beneath these sentences you will find four ways of re-phrasing the underlined part. Choose the response that best expresses the meaning of the original sentence.

1. After lunch, the prize for the best barbecue recipe will be awarded by the judge.

    A. leave as is
    B. awarded the prize for the best barbecue recipe by the judge.
    C. the judge will award the prize for the best barbecue recipe.
    D. the award for the prize barbecue recipe took place by the judge.

2. The next working road trip will be taken to Catonsville by our chorus ensemble.

    A. leave as is
    B. To Catonsville is where our chorus is taking its next working road trip.
    C. Our chorus ensemble takes its next road trip working at Catonsville.
    D. Our chorus ensemble will take its next working road trip to Catonsville.

3. Raspberries grow equally well in Atlanta and Seattle most likely because of similar rainfall and if they are harvested daily by gardeners, a fresh home supply is guaranteed.

    A. leave as is
    B. and if it's harvested daily by gardeners, a fresh home supply are guaranteed.
    C. and if harvested daily by gardeners, a fresh home supply is guaranteed.
    D. and if gardeners harvest them daily, a fresh supply is guaranteed.

4. Plagued by music piracy, powerful anti-sharing legislation is a measure that most rock bands would embrace while still advocating personal freedoms.

    A. leave as is
    B. anti-sharing legislation that is a measure that most rock bands would embrace while still advocating
    C. most rock bands would embrace powerful anti-sharing legislation while still advocating
    D. powerful anti-sharing legislation is a measure that most rock bands would embrace while advocating

TRANSITIONS AND THE FLOW OF IDEAS

Ideas have to flow smoothly from one to another. This entails using **clear connectors** and **transitional devices** within and between sentences and paragraphs. Jolting a reader from one idea to the next and leaving the reader to make connections is not a characteristic of good writing. The goal of a reader is to comprehend and analyze ideas, not to figure out what the author could possibly mean by a number of disjointed thoughts. If your car bounced you around on normal roads to the point of giving you a headache, you would have the suspension fixed. In writing, the suspension apparatus needed for a smooth ride consists of techniques such as those listed in the following table.

Transitional Technique	Examples
Using transitional terms	therefore, while, on the other hand, in contrast, furthermore, yet, in spite of, etc.
Using introductory phrases	*By making literature available to common people*, Caxton's press influenced the class structure in British society.
Combining sentences	(1)Caxton's press changed the reading habits of common people. (2)The reading habits of the common people affected the press by placing greater demand on it.
	While Caxton's press changed the reading habits of the common people, that change in the people had a reciprocal effect on the press by placing greater demand on it for more stories.
Inserting sentences to clarify context	**Unclear**: Only selected segments of society were literate at that time.
	Clarified: *Before Caxton's printing press, hand-scripted texts were relatively rare and had an exclusive readership.* Only selected segments of society were literate at that time.

Practice 4: Transitions

This sample passage contains typical mistakes in transitional techniques. Read the two paragraphs. Then read the questions pertaining to them. A discussion following the example question explains the answer. Complete questions 1 through 4 on your own.

excerpt 1 from Sample Passage

(1)Before William Caxton set up the first printing press in England in 1476, the only writing available to literate people was handwritten. (2)They were labor intensive and time consuming products. (3)These manuscripts were relatively few in number. (4)They were accessible to only a small segment of society. (5)They could be read only by the educated classes. (6)Only the nobility and the clergy were literate. (7)All other members of society belonged to the class of laborers and they were generally uneducated and they were known as "commoners." **(8)**A new merchant class was beginning to emerge in Europe, men who had a basic degree of education, as well as some expendable cash.

(9) The new middle class demanded books, especially good, entertaining stories. **(10)** Caxton had a receptive market for his product. **(11)**But what would he print for them? **(12)** Whatever came from Caxton's press it was bound to have a profound effect on the collective experience, language and psychology of that society. **(13)**They were the first "mass produced" writings in Anglo-Saxon society, they were bound to shape culture and ideas.

Example: In the context, which is the best way to revise and combine sentences 2 and 3? (reproduced below)

They were labor intensive and time consuming products. These manuscripts were relatively few in number.

A. leave as is

B. As they were labor intensive and time consuming products, they were manuscripts that were relatively few in number.

C. They were labor intensive and time consuming products. They were also relatively few in number.

D. As labor intensive and time-consuming products, these manuscripts were relatively few in number.

The answer is *D*. The sentences needed to be combined using an introductory phrase: "As labor intensive and time-consuming products..." *B* sounds as if it might be correct because "As" should not be used in place of "because." If the word "because" were used in *B*, it would have been an acceptable answer.

Conventions in Sentences and Paragraphs

1. In the context, which is the <u>best</u> way to revise the underlined portions of sentence 7? (reproduced below)

   All other members of society belonged to <u>the class of laborers and they were generally</u> <u>uneducated and they were known as "commoners."</u>

   A. All other members of society belonged to the class of laborers. And they were generally uneducated and they were known as "commoners."
   B. All other members of society belonged to the class of laborers: they were generally uneducated and they were known as "commoners."
   C. All other members of society belonged to the class of laborers who were generally uneducated and they were known as "commoners."
   D. All other members of society belonged to the class of laborers, and were generally uneducated and were known as "commoners."

2. Which sentence would be <u>most</u> appropriate to precede sentence number 9?
   A. The new middle class demanded reading material.
   B. Caxton's import from Germany of Gutenburg's invention began a revolution in literacy.
   C. Caxton's import from Germany made book production easier.
   D. The new middle class were primarily merchants and traders.

3. Which is the <u>best</u> revision to make to the beginning of sentence 12?
   A. leave as is
   B. Whatever it was came from Caxton's press it was bound to have a profound effect
   C. Whatever came from Caxton's press was bound to have a profound effect
   D. Whatever came from Caxton's press had a profound effect

4. In the context, which is the <u>best</u> way to revise the underlined portions of sentence 13? (reproduced below)

   <u>They were the first "mass produced" writings in Anglo-Saxon society, they were</u> <u>bound</u> to shape culture and ideas.

   A. leave as is
   B. As the first "mass produced" writings in Anglo-Saxon society, they were bound to shape culture and ideas.
   C. They were the first "mass produced" writings in Anglo-Saxon society, being bound to shape culture and ideas.
   D. As the first "mass produced" writings in Anglo-Saxon society, so they were bound to shape culture and ideas.

194

WORKING WITH PARAGRAPHS

A **paragraph** is a series of related sentences that make a single point about one subject. Focusing and developing one central idea is called coherence, and all paragraphs should be coherent.

- **Choose one subject:** A paragraph is too brief to discuss more than one subject.

- **Make a single point:** To "make a point" is to tell readers something that you want them to know. Usually, you will state your point in the **topic sentence** of your paragraph. The topic sentence often begins a paragraph, though it may also be at the end or in the middle.

- **Relate other sentences to the topic sentence:** Though you *state* your point in the topic sentence, you must *make* your point by providing **supporting details**. Other sentences in the paragraph provide readers with information and evidence to explain your topic sentence. If the topic sentence does not end the paragraph, a **concluding sentence** can bring the paragraph to a close, and if appropriate, lead into the next paragraph.

An easy way to understand the structure of a paragraph is to compare it to a table. The topic sentence is like the table top. Just as the table top's purpose is to provide a flat surface for writing or eating, the topic sentence's purpose is to give the reader a broad view of the topic. Of course, without legs, the table top will not stand. In a similar way, the topic sentence must be supported by details, examples, and explanations. Finally, a table that rocks on an uneven floor makes people wonder if objects they place on it will fall off. Similarly, a paragraph that does not provide a clear conclusion may leave the reader wondering if the writer has left out some important ideas.

Writing a well-organized paragraph may seem difficult, but do you realize that you talk in paragraphs every day? Here is an example of a paragraph spoken by a cheerleading coach at the season's first practice.

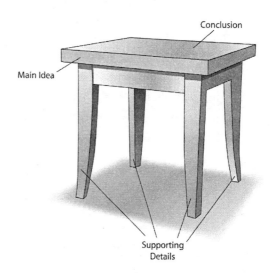

> *Gather around here and listen up!* ***If you really want to be cheerleaders, you have to be ready to stretch yourselves to the limit!*** *Be sure you really want to do this, people! You will need to be at practice every day after school. There will be no time for any other extracurricular activities! All of you must be ready to give of yourselves and endure pain as you never have before! You will also need to rely on each other. Some of you will be learning how to trust someone else for the first time in your lives. Above all, cheerleading will bring out your character and show you what you're made of. Now, if you still feel up to the task, I want to see you here tomorrow evening at five o'clock, ready to work hard.*

Though spoken, the coach's instruction is like a well-written paragraph. It states the main idea in a topic sentence (indicated in bold) and then supports that idea by describing how the cheerleaders will need to "stretch themselves." The coach concludes by challenging the cheerleaders to action. The speech has overall **coherence** in that all the ideas and sentences relate to one another.

Practice 5: Paragraph Structure

All of the sentences in each series make a paragraph, but they may not be in order. For each sentence, identify the topic sentence, supporting detail, and concluding sentence.

   A.   Constantly surrounded by beeping faxes, ringing cell phones, and flashing computer screens, many business people are sitting down at the end of the day to enjoy some quiet time with knitting needles and a big ball of yarn.

   B.   Men and women with fast-paced, high-powered careers are turning to knitting as a way to unwind.

   C.   So, as you speed through modern society, remember, knitting isn't just for Grandma anymore!

   D.   Besides the peace and quiet, these knitting professionals say they find it refreshing to focus on the process of creating something, instead of looking only at deadlines and finished products.

1.   The topic sentence is letter_____.

2.   Letter ____ is a supporting sentence.

3.   Letter____ is a supporting sentence.

4.   The concluding sentence is letter____.

   A.   As she climbed the stairs, her nose was filled with the musty smell of old things.
   B.   She walked to the door of her old refuge: the attic.
   C.   Times at home had always been happy, but now Sheila needed a break.
   D.   The memories of good times made the present situation seem bearable.
   E.   Sheila dusted off an old picture frame and found a picture of her mother, smiling.

5.   The topic sentence is letter_____.

6.   Letter ____ is a supporting sentence.

7.   Letter____ is a supporting sentence.

8.   Letter____ is a supporting sentence.

9.   The concluding sentence is letter____.

A. With the sale of each bike, he offered a monthly maintenance program.

B. These regular check-ups kept the bikes in good working condition and brought customers back to the store where they could see new products he was selling.

C. The success of Alek's young business shows the importance of keeping customers happy.

D. His work in other bicycle shops had shown him that a successful business is based on quality products and good service.

E. With several years experience under his belt, Alek Siegers established a successful bicycle shop in Aspen, Colorado.

10. The topic sentence is letter_____.

11. Letter ____ is a supporting sentence.

12. Letter____ is a supporting sentence.

13. Letter____ is a supporting sentence.

14. The concluding sentence is letter____.

A. While Brad, Katya, and Willy were strolling down Eighth Street, they heard a disturbing noise.

B. They looked up and saw an elderly woman calling out from a second floor window, "Help me, please."

C. The look on the woman's face propelled the three teens up the stairs to her door.

D. The woman could not speak but brought them to the kitchen where her husband lay on the floor.

E. Immediately, Katya called 911, while Brad checked the man's pulse, and Willy tried to reassure the woman.

F. Within minutes, police officers arrived and commended the teens for their quick thinking.

15. The topic sentence is letter_____.

16. Letter ____ is a supporting sentence.

17. Letter____ is a supporting sentence.

18. Letter____ is a supporting sentence.

19. The concluding sentence is letter____.

A.   Training involves many hours of lifting weights and running sprints.

B.   Without this preparation, performance will drop and injuries are more of a risk.

C.   Like the other athletes you see at the Olympics, javelin throwers deserve respect.

D.   The javelin is not a very heavy object, but throwing it long distances requires great arm and leg strength.

E.   Javelin throwing may look easy on TV, but in reality, it is a very demanding sport.

20. The topic sentence is letter_____.

21. Letter _____is a supporting sentence.

22. Letter_____ is a supporting sentence.

23. Letter_____ is a supporting sentence.

24. The concluding sentence is letter_____.

ORGANIZING PARAGRAPHS

Once you have a topic sentence, a list of supporting details, and a concluding sentence, you must decide how you want to organize your paragraph. Just like the table we discussed at the beginning of this section, a paragraph is not put together haphazardly. It has structure and organization to make it stand. And just like there are different types of tables, there are different ways to organize paragraphs, such as **time order**, **spatial order**, **order of importance**, and **contrasting ideas**.

CHRONOLOGICAL ORDER (TIME)

Chronological order is especially important when you are writing a narrative. A story doesn't make sense when the events are not presented in the proper sequence. Here is an example:

> *I arrived after the speaker had begun her presentation. As I was running down the hill, I remembered that I had left my car keys on the kitchen table. When I started the car, I saw the clock, and I knew I was going to be late. I had to go back and get my keys.*

The lack of organization in this paragraph makes it very difficult to follow the story line. See below how organizing the passage in a time sequence makes it much easier to read and understand.

> *As I was running down the hill, I remembered that I had left my car keys on the kitchen table. I had to go back and get my keys. When I started the car, I saw the clock, and I knew I was going to be late. I arrived after the speaker had begun her presentation.*

You can also use chronological order to organize other types of writing, including writing to inform, also called expository writing.

SPATIAL ORDER

When you describe a scene or a location, you can sometimes use **spatial order** to arrange your ideas in a paragraph. Imagine yourself holding a camcorder and moving it in every direction. You can order your observations from **top to bottom**, **left to right**, **clockwise**, **near to far**, **front to back**, **inside to outside**, **east to west**, **north to south**, etc., and all of these directions *reversed* (e.g., **bottom to top**).

Spatial order can also be an effective way to organize other kinds of writing, as you can see in the following example of persuasive writing.

> *It's time for the city to clean up Jones Park. As visitors enter the park, they are greeted by a broken sign that is smeared with graffiti. Next, they pass the pond where they must hold their noses because of the smell of decaying trash. If visitors make it past all of this, they reach the playground in the middle of the park. Here they find swings with ripped seats hanging limp beside slides with broken steps. The park, in its current state, is a hazardous waste area that must be cleaned up.*

ORDER OF IMPORTANCE

The most common way to organize a paragraph is in **order of importance**. All of the details you include in your paragraph should be relevant to the topic and important to the reader. Some details, however, you will want to emphasize more than others. You can emphasize a certain idea by placing it either at the beginning or at the end of a paragraph. The following letter provides a good example.

> *Dear Aunt Jenny,*
>
> *I would really like to spend the summer with you because I have never spent much time in Oregon. Also, I am interested in earning some extra money for my college savings, and many jobs are available in your area. Most importantly, I really enjoy our short visits when we get together over the holidays, and I want to spend more time with you so we can be closer.*
>
> *Please write back soon, and let me know what you think.*
>
> *Love,*
>
> *Kelly*

In this letter, Kelly begins with a simple wish that may be of some interest to her aunt. Aunt Jenny would be more likely to respect Sandra's second reason. However, Kelly's desire for a closer relationship will make the greatest impression upon her aunt's decision.

Sometimes you will want to start off with the most important idea. Other times you will want to "save the best for last." The decision is yours based upon your audience, topic, and personal preference.

CONTRASTING IDEAS

Sometimes writing assignments require that you choose one side of an issue or topic and convince the reader of the validity of your position. One good way to do this is to **contrast** your position with its opposite. In this kind of contrasting, you will point out differences and show why your position is better.

Example: If someone is trying to convince his or her family to get a cat as a pet, instead of a dog, he or she might point out contrasting facts such as a cat not needing to be taken for walks, being able to snack from a bowl of food without a regular feeding time, and being content on its own for longer than a dog, which needs constant attention and affection.

CHAPTER 8 SUMMARY

Sentence construction must be complete and sturdy, with effective use of **conjunctions** and proper placement of **modifiers**. Avoid **run-ons** and **fragments**, and strive for **parallelism**.

Word choice should be clear and precise. Focus on appropriate **style** and **tone**, with a sense of **audience**. Avoid **wordiness** and **chichés**.

When a writer describes an action in an **active voice**, the subject comes first and performs the action. Grammar in the **passive voice** is *switched*—instead of subject-verb-object, it is object-verb-subject.

Use **clear connectors** and **transitional devices** between sentences and paragraphs.

Paragraphs should be **coherent** and can be **organized** according to time, space, importance, or contrasting ideas.

CHAPTER 8 REVIEW

A. Read the passage and answer the questions that follow.

Taboos for Dummies

(1)There is a growing opportunity for test dummies (people who volunteer for research studies). (2)The area of scientific and industrial research has expanded in a time when no one wants to see animals used as test subjects. (3)Mostly the studies are for mundane items such as a new, organic honey based toothpaste, but sometimes they are set up for important but risky vaccination trials. (4)Others simply sound interesting.

(5)One of the most intriguing studies is one about taboos. (6)The word taboo comes from the Polynesian language. (7)The word was introduced to the English speaking culture by the British explorer James Cook in 1771. (8)Taboo means the prohibition (ban) of an action or use of an object or food. (9)In the original sense of a taboo, the prohibition was tied to religious teachings identifying those aspects of the world that was seen as unclean or profane as opposed to clean or sacred. (10)It is a blending or blurring of actions or objects in the two categories that produces a reaction of disgust. (11)Generally, the prohibition includes the idea that defiance of the taboo will result in trouble for the offender, such as illness, loss or injury. (12)They would ordinarily be regarded as accidents or bad luck, but to believers in taboos they are regarded as punishments for breaking some taboo.

(13)Sir James G. Frazer wrote a comprehensive treatise on the subject of taboos from a mythological basis and on a global scale in his work *The Golden Bough*. (14)Sigmund Freud, in his book *Totem and Taboo*, put forth an explanation for the taboos which seem to exist without logic. (15)His idea was that they represent the forbidden fruit, something that is perceived to be as desirable (subconsciously, of course) as it is seen to be deplorable.

(16)For the taboo research, a research team gathered test subjects, both a control group and a test group. (17)The premise of the test is that any perversion or blurring of what is seen as clean and healthy with something seen as unclean and unhealthy produces an extreme reaction of disgust in humans. (18)Some of the taboos seem logical, for example, those against certain foods that may spoil easy.

(19)During the test, the researchers gave the test group certain tasks to perform. (20)On the surface, the tasks seemed innocent enough. (21)The subjects were asked to drink from a cup of water. (22)Then, they were told to spit into a cup of water and drink from it. (23)The reaction to the second request was a typical display of distaste. (24)There was a mixing of clean water with a body fluid, which is normally seen as unclean. (25)Another task involved apple juice and a clean bed pan. (26)The subjects were asked to drink the apple juice from a newly unwrapped bed pan. (27)Even though logically the subjects knew the pan was clean, they had strong negative reactions to the request.

(28)Yet another task for the research subjects involved an insect. (29)The test subjects were asked to drink white grape juice. (30)Then, they were asked to drink the grape juice with a cockroach laying in the juice. (31)The reaction to this was strong and immediate.

(32)The subjects were grossed out and put physical space between themselves and the cup; they were verbal in either strong denials or jokes and laughter. (33)That is a typical defense that humans use to place themselves apart from the "other." (34)The "other" is anything unexpected and unfamiliar.

(35)It is important to remember that taboos are tied to cultural beliefs; in many cultures, the taboo against the eating of insects does not exist. (36)In the ancient Greek culture, the practice was common: Aristotle mentioned in a text that cicadas were a favorite of his, and in the Bible, there is the mention of prophets, including John the Baptist, eating locusts.

(37)It will be interesting to see the eventual uses of these fascinating research results. (38)Perhaps they will be featured in the next book published about taboos and the subconscious. (39)Or, maybe someone was merely trying to figure out what might be the most disgusting new challenges to feature on *Fear Factor*.

1. What change should be made in sentence 3?

   A. Insert a comma after *items*.
   B. Insert a hyphen between *honey* and *based (honey-based)*.
   C. Replace the comma after *toothpaste* with a semicolon.
   D. Insert a comma after *important*.

2. What change, if any, is needed in sentence 9?
   A. Change *prohibition was* to *prohibition is*.
   B. Change *identifying* to identified.
   C. Change *was seen* to *were seen*.
   D. Make no change.

3. To clarify the meaning of sentence 12, replace *They* with—
   A. The prohibitions   C. These misfortunes
   B. He   D. Some people

4. What change, if any, should be made in sentence 14?
   A. Change *seem* to *seems*.   C. Change *existing* to *to exist*.
   B. Change *put forth* to *explained*. D. Make no change.

5. What change is needed in sentence 18?
   A. Change *logical* to *logically*.   C. Change *dangerous* to *dangerously*.
   B. Change *easy* to *easily*.   D. Change *potential* to *potentially*.

6. What is the **most** effective way to revise sentences 21 and 22?
   A. The subjects drank one cup of water and spit into another.
   B. After drinking from a cup of water, subjects were told to spit into it and then take a drink.
   C. Before spitting into a cup of water, subjects had to drink the water first.
   D. Subjects were asked if they ever spit into their water before drinking it.

7. What change, if any, should be made in sentence 22?
   A. Change *told* to *telling.*
   B. Change *drink* to *drinking.*
   C. Change *spit* to *spitting.*
   D. Make no change.

8. In sentence 32, the <u>best</u> Standard English substitute for *grossed out* is—
   A. disgusted.
   B. alarmed.
   C. weirded out.
   D. scared.

9. What is the <u>most</u> effective way to reorganize the ideas in paragraph 7?
   A. Make it a continuation of paragraph 6 (not a new paragraph).
   B. Move sentence 36 before sentence 35.
   C. Start a new paragraph with sentence 35.
   D. Place sentence 34 at the end of the paragraph.

10. Which word in sentence 37 is misspelled?
   A. interesting
   B. eventual
   C. fascinating
   D. no misspelled word

A "Current" Issue

(1)You're enjoying a beautiful day at the beach. (2)But something waits just under the surface of the water. (3)One minute you're bobbing along peacefully in the surf, the next you're being dragged out to sea at top speed! (4)No, it's not Jaws—it's a rip current.

(5)Rip currents cause about 150 deaths every year in the United States. (6)About 80 percent of all beach rescues are related to rip currents. (7)They occur in any kind of weather, they are found on a wide range of beaches, including those on the Gulf of Mexico. (8)A rip current is a narrow, powerful current of water running perpendicular to the beach, out into the ocean. (9)These currents can be 200 to 2,500 feet long, and they are typically less than 30 feet wide. (10)Rip currents can move at a pretty good speed, often five miles per hour or faster. (11)They are terrifying because they catch you off guard.

(12)A rip current occurs when many waves break one after another, and more water collects on the beach than can flow back out. (13)Wanting to equalize it's level, the water begins to flow back in a fast, narrow current. (14)This rip current can sweep you into deep water fast! (15)It also cuts deep holes in seeming shallow water near man-made structures. (16)That's why it is dangerous to swim near rock juts, jetties and piers. (17)Stay at least 100 feet away.

(18)The most common cause of rip currents is a break in a sandbar. (19)Sandbars are long, narrow hills of accumulated sand just off the shore. (20)They are formed by the motion of oceanic waves and tides. (21)When a large sandbar forms, it can produce a sort of basin along the shore. (22)Waves push water over the sandbar, but the water in the basin has a hard time making it back to sea. (23)When it finds a break in the sandbar, the water rushes out, just as water in your bathtub rushes out when you unplug the drain, toward the sea. (24)The resulting rip current sucks water from the basin and spits it out on the other side of the sandbar. (25)This can last a few minutes or a few hours.

(26)Many swimmers don't know about rip currents or how to survive them. (27)Despite how common and lethal rip currents can be. (28)If you encounter one, do not try to swim straight for shore; the strong current can make even the best swimmer tired—and getting tired is dangerous. (29)Instead, swim sideways, parallel to the beach. (30)If the current is too strong to swim in, just wait until it carries you past the sandbar. (31)It will be much calmer there. (32)Keep calm and conserve your energy. (33)If you thrash about, you could drown.

11. How would you revise sentence 7?
    A.   Change the first comma to a semicolon.
    B.   Change the second comma to a semicolon.
    C.   Make *Gulf* lower case.
    D.   Make no revision

12. In sentence 9, what would be a better conjunction to use than *and*?
    A.   nor   B.   so   C.   for   D.   but

13. What is the <u>most</u> effective way to combine sentences 10 and 11?
    A.   Only those rip currents which move fast, five miles per hour or faster, are terrifying.
    B.   Because rip currents move at a pretty good speed, often five miles per hour or faster, they can catch you off guard and really scare you.
    C.   Rip currents move quickly, scare you, and then catch you off guard.
    D.   If you let yourself get caught off guard by a speedy rip current, you will probably be terrified because it's moving at five miles per hour or faster.

14. What change should be made in sentence 13?
    A.   Change *equalize* to *equalise*.   C.   Change *flow back* to *flow-back*.
    B.   Change *it's* to *its*.   D.   Change *narrow* to *narow*.

15. What change, if any, should be made in sentence 15?
    A.   Change *deep* to *deeply*.   C.   Change *near* to *nearly*.
    B.   Change *seeming* to *seemingly*.   D.   Make no change.

16. What is the <u>most</u> effective way to reorganize sentence 23?
    A.   When it finds a break in the sandbar, the water rushes out. Just as water in your bathtub rushes out when you unplug the drain.
    B.   The water in the basin rushes out of a break in the sandbar, just as water in your bathtub rushes out when you unplug the drain, toward the sea.
    C.   When it finds a break in the sandbar, the water in the basin rushes out toward the sea, just as water in your bathtub rushes out when you unplug the drain.
    D.   Just as water in your bathtub rushes out when you unplug the drain, when it finds a break in the sandbar, the water in the basin rushes out toward the sea.

17. What error do you see in sentence 30?
    A. run-on   B. fragment   C. non-parallel   D. no error

18. The meaning of sentence 31 could be clarified if the word **It** were changed to:
    A. The water   B. You   C. The noise   D. Fish

B. In the following draft paragraphs, choose the sentence that should be eliminated because it contains an unrelated idea.

19.   (A) Jenna certainly gave Donna an assist on the first play of the game. (B) She passed the ball to Donna the first chance she had. (C) Donna aimed the shot high and swished the basketball through the hoop. (D) Donna and Jenna went to the same college.
    A.   B.   C.   D.

20.   (A) Calligraphy is one of the most difficult forms of art I know. (B) I hope to open a business selling calligraphy pens and ink supplies. (C) For example, the ink runs if the stroke is too slow and the letters have gaps if the stroke is too fast. (D) Each stroke of the pen has to be perfect.
    A.   B.   C.   D.

21.   (A) A few nonconformists are building dome-style homes because of their stability and energy efficiency. (B) The dome's shape is especially resistant to storms and earthquakes because the foundation supports all portions of the structure. (C) Other people enjoy traditional four-sided brick homes. (D) The lack of walls in a dome-shaped house allows more equal distribution of heating and cooling, making it more energy efficient.
    A.   B.   C.   D.

22.   (A) Nuke-Clean wants to move its operation to Smith County, so it can clean clothe that are contaminated with radiation. (B) This move brings Nuke-Clean closer to one of its big customers—the nuclear plant down the river; it also brings Nuke-Clean closer to my neighborhood. (C) The nuclear plant in Chernobyl was shut down recently. (D) Some people in the neighborhood don't mind, but I think we should take action now.
    A.   B.   C.   D.

C. The paragraphs below may be missing a topic sentence or a concluding sentence. Also, they may contain supporting details that restate the topic or describe unrelated ideas. For each paragraph, choose the answer that best identifies the problem.

23.   Getting the right tennis shoe for school can be an important decision. Getting blue jeans to fit is difficult sometimes. Whenever I try to tie-dye my t-shirts, they always turn out brown! My skin feels better after a long dip in the swimming pool. In summary, comfortable tennis shoes are vital for school survival.

    A.   topic sentence missing
    B.   concluding sentence missing
    C.   a supporting sentence restates the topic sentence
    D.   a supporting sentence contains an unrelated idea

24.   Exercising will improve blood flow to the brain and condition the muscles and bones to support the body under stress. In addition, a proper diet will ensure that the brain and other parts of the body are supplied with the proper nutrients. Third, a proper amount of sleep will keep the receptors in the brain connected for maximum efficiency. These three life activities in proper balance will keep the body and mind in shape for each day.

    A.   topic sentence missing
    B.   concluding sentence missing
    C.   a supporting sentence restates the topic sentence
    D.   a supporting sentence contains an unrelated idea

25.   Misha Patel enjoyed his visit to Disney World in July. The July visit to Disney World was very enjoyable for Misha. Disney World provided Misha with many interesting experiences. In conclusion, Misha was very happy experiencing many of the attractions offered at Disney World.

    A.   topic sentence missing
    B.   concluding sentence missing
    C.   a supporting sentence restates the topic sentence
    D.   a supporting sentence contains an unrelated idea

26.   Global warming is a very real and measurable phenomenon. Over the past century, glaciers near the poles have receded. In addition, the polar ice caps have thinned up to 40% from their previous thickness. Finally, air temperatures have warmed over 1° Celsius.

    A.   topic sentence missing
    B.   concluding sentence missing
    C.   a supporting sentence restates the topic sentence
    D.   a supporting sentence contains an unrelated idea

27.   The world now produces more than enough food to feed every man, woman, and child currently living. However, land useful for farming is not evenly distributed. Another challenge lies in lack of transportation to areas where there is no arable land. Furthermore, many nations lacking the arable land also lack the resources necessary to purchase the food they need. Together, these factors point to a problem in food distribution, not a lack of food.

    A.   topic sentence missing

    B.   concluding sentence missing

    C.   a supporting sentence restates the topic sentence

    D.   a supporting sentence contains an unrelated idea

Chapter 9
Writing the Essay

This chapter addresses the following expectation(s) and their related indicators from **Core Learning Goal 2: Composing in a Variety of Modes**.

Expectation 2.1	The student will compose oral, written, and visual presentations that inform, persuade, and express personal ideas.
Expectation 2.2	The student will compose texts using the prewriting, drafting, revising, and editing strategies of effective writers and speakers
Expectation 2.3	The student will locate, retrieve, and use information from various sources to accomplish a purpose.

THE WRITING PROCESS

Whether you are writing a letter, an in-class essay, or a lengthy homework assignment, your writing does not appear magically. You need to follow a process.

The Writing Process
Think
Make sure you understand the purpose for writing. If you are responding to a writing prompt, read it carefully to make sure you understand what question it is asking, the type of essay you should write, and who your audience is.
Prewrite
Generate ideas by making a list or a map, and focus those ideas to decide which is best for the essay you need to write.
Draft
Get your ideas on paper and develop them into paragraphs, using your prewriting activities.
Revise
Revise your draft for coherence, transitions, and sentence variety and structure. Delete any unnecessary words, phrases, or sentences. Think about any other ways you can improve your essay. Write a final copy and proofread it for punctuation, spelling, capitalization, word choice, and grammar. Correct errors neatly.

PREWRITING

The first step in the writing process is to plan. This is done through **prewriting**.

After reading a writing prompt carefully, or considering your writing assignment, you need to generate ideas. **Brainstorming** and **freewriting** are two methods of getting your ideas out of your head and on paper, where you can work with them.

- **Brainstorming** involves writing down whatever comes to mind regarding the topic and questions provided by the writing prompt. When you brainstorm, you create a list of ideas and details that you can use to develop your essay.

- **Freewriting** also involves writing down your ideas, but rather than generating a list, it produces more of a free-flowing narrative about anything in your thoughts.

Example topic or writing prompt: What makes a person a hero?

Brainstorming		Freewriting
brave	selflessness	What is a hero? a hero is someone who helps others, does things for people and the world. Superman, only real! great scientists like Marie Curie or humanitarians like Mother Theresa. Pioneers like Harriet Tubman. They inspired people.
courage	Mother Theresa	
dedication	helping others	
overcoming fear	serving humanity	
doing what you need to	sense of purpose	
overcoming obstacles	changing things	
Harriet Tubman	noticing what's wrong	

FOCUS IDEAS

Once you have generated ideas using brainstorming or freewriting, you need to **focus** those ideas. First, you need to choose the best topic by determining which ideas can best be utilized. There are many prewriting strategies that can help you do this; use a graphic organizer, like the one shown, and have your teacher suggest others you should use.

In the following graphic organizer, called clustering, the idea from the prompt above is further developed. Start by writing your topic in a central circle: in this example, a hero. Think about how the topic might act, sound, feel, or appear. Think about what it means to be a hero. Think about examples and situations. Cluster these ideas around the center circle. Circle each idea you write and draw a line connecting it to a related idea. Let your mind wander as you are clustering to try to include as many ideas as you can. You want lots of details here, so write everything down. Look at the following example of clustering.

Sample of Clustering

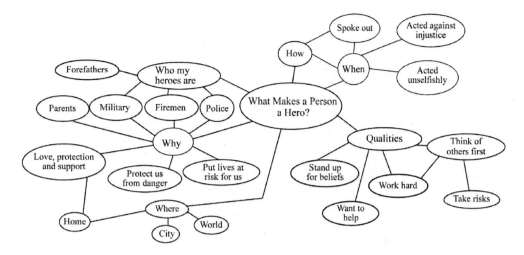

You might notice that this example of clustering has several different examples of heroes. The clustering process can continue many times until you've narrowed your ideas and thought of enough supporting details to write your composition. For example, the student who created this clustering might want to create another cluster about just one of the heroes. Based on the ideas already generated, which hero do you think would be a good choice?

There are many other diagrams and maps you can use to help focus your ideas. Ask your teacher for more resources or refer to American Book Company's *Basics Made Easy: Writing Review*, available at www.americanbookcompany.com.

OUTLINE

An **outline** lays out the plan for your essay in a very structured way. It is the road map you will follow in writing your draft. Here is a sample outline based on the prompt about heroes.

   I.   **Introduction:** General discussion including thesis

   II.   **Body**

       A. Paragraph 1: Topic 1 (from thesis) and supporting details

       B. Paragraph 2: Topic 2 (from thesis) and supporting details

       C. Paragraph 3: Topic 3 (from thesis) and supporting details

  III. **Conclusion:** Summary of discussion

An outline for the paper about heroes might look like the one on the next page.

I. **Introduction:** Heroes dedicate themselves to improving the world. Harriet Tubman and Mother Theresa are heroes.

II. Body

    A. serve humanity

        1. Mother Theresa took risks to help people

    B. fight for beliefs

        1. Harriet Tubman fought for human rights

    C. inspire us

III. **Conclusion:** Following their passion to help others and see justice done, heroes improve the world and inspire us all.

DRAFTING THE ESSAY

The second step in the writing process is **writing**. It may seem like an obvious step, but just as there are many ways to cook foods, there are many ways to go about writing essays. There are also many individual skills involved in writing an essay. The more you practice, the easier writing will be. This is especially important with timed writing, like an in-class writing assignment or writing an essay for a state test.

In the last three chapters, you learned about grammar and usage, controlling language, and sentence and paragraph structure. Now, it is time to write an essay. Writing a draft is a way of getting your ideas on paper so you can work with them. A draft is like the first pancake out of the pan—it can be messy or a little underdone. You will continue to improve a draft in the next stage of the writing process. When you write a draft, you want to focus on capturing the meaning from all of your planning in the prewriting stage. You already have a sense of where you are going; you just need to show it on paper. Let's say that you were given this writing prompt: *Which real-life heroes do you admire the most? Explain why you admire them*. Based on this prompt, here is one method of drafting a basic three-paragraph essay:

Paragraph 1: For the **introduction**, write the topic sentence. Next, write one to two sentences that connect the topic to subtopic(s). Make sure your sentences blend together to form a strong introduction.

Paragraph 2: For the **body**, use the subtopic(s) to form the paragraph, expanding the subtopic(s) with details. Write two to four sentences to explain and provide examples. Make sure that the sentences also support the main topic.

Paragraph 3: For the **conclusion**, reread the essay.
- Choose two to three of the most important ideas.
- Summarize the ideas in three sentences.
- Restate your central idea using different words.

Here is the draft:

[Mother Teresa and Harriet Tubman both <u>served humanity</u>.] Mother Teresa spen her entire life helping the sick and the poor. She founded The Missions of Charity in 1948, ~~who~~ which *worked to treat the sick and dying people, especially children, in India. Harriet Tubman spent ten years leading escaped slaves to freedom. She was* ~~a~~ also served as *nurse during the Civil War. Both women helped make people's lives better.*

[Harriet Tubman and Mother Teresa had to <u>fight for their beliefs</u>.] Harriet Tubman believed that every human deserved freedom. She believed that slavery was wrong, and risked her own life to help ~~free slaves~~*. Bounty hunters were* **Harriett Tubman** *offered a lot of money to capture her for these things, but she kept returning to the slave states anyway. Mother Teresa believed that every human should be able to die in peace and comfort. Mother Teresa founded many organisations and shelters to help people with illnesses such as leprosy and AIDS. These were the people no one wanted to help. She often had to convince governments to let her to set up these shelters. She spent a lot of time raising awareness and money to help those in need.*

[The lives of Mother Teresa and Harriet Tubman have <u>inspired many people</u> around the world to take action for their beliefs.] Mother Teresa was awarded the nobel peace prize in 1979. After hearing of her good words, many people began to offer aid through her organizations around the world. Harriet Tubman was one of many people working the Underground Railroad. She encouraged others to take risks by courageously coming to the aid of escaped slaves.

As you can see in the sample draft essay, there are errors in writing. That is acceptable in a first draft. The format, however, is in good shape. The **central idea** of the essay is clearly stated in the first paragraph, the **introduction**. The **subtopics** *serving humanity* and *fighting for beliefs,* which *inspires people,* are also stated. They are explained more in the **body** paragraph of the essay.

The subtopics in the second paragraph, the **body**, are <u>underlined</u>, and the topic sentence is in brackets [like this]. This sample shows how details support the subtopics. The subtopics now have complete paragraphs which support the central idea. Notice how the paragraph begins with a topic sentence and how the subtopics are supported by explanation and examples.

In paragraph 3, the writer concludes the essay. This **conclusion** reminds readers of the most important ideas. The writer also restates the central idea, which is the kind of qualities heroes possess.

REMEMBER: A well-written essay responds to the writing prompt with:

- a clear topic sentence;
- an engaging introduction, supporting body and conclusion;
- a detailed discussion focused completely on the topic.

WRITING INTRODUCTIONS

You learned how to write a basic introduction in the section before; however, a good writer develops the introduction to do more than just present the topic. A good **introduction** does three things:

- grabs the interest of the reader (remember to keep your audience in mind)
- introduces the topic
- states the central idea

The introductory paragraph is one of the most important parts of an essay; it gives a first impression. The introduction sets up the essay's structure by introducing the topic and sub-topics. After reading an introduction, a reader should be able to name the author's purpose and tone. Use one of the following methods to begin your introductory paragraph. These methods will help get your readers' attention.

There are several ways to develop interesting and effective introductions. These include **asking a question, using a quotation** that is related to the topic, **stating an important fact, giving a description** in vivid detail, or **telling a brief story** that introduces the topic. Following is an example of an introductory paragraph that asks a question to begin the discussion of the topic.

Asking a question at the beginning of an essay immediately forces your reader to start thinking. It sets up a curiosity that encourages the reader to keep reading. Read the following example:

> Can you imagine paying $2,500 for a family pet? Bulldogs are such valued pets that some people don't think twice about paying that much to own a prized puppy. However, a lot of money is wasted if you aren't able to keep the dog. Popularity of a dog is not a good enough reason to bring one into your family's home. Choosing a family pet is a difficult decision —one that should be based on knowledge, not emotion. Just because an animal is cute, does not mean it's the right pet for you. Before you choose a bulldog or any pet, you should consider the advantages and disadvantages of living with pets.

This introduction accomplishes all an introduction should. From the first sentence, the topic is clear. This essay will be discussing pets. The question draws readers in and encourages them to keep reading to find out more. The introduction clearly shows the writer's purpose is to educate the readers. The final sentence of the introduction states the central idea of the essay, the advantages and disadvantages of owning a pet.

Practice 1: Writing Introductions

Write an introduction for two of the writing prompts below. Before you begin writing, be sure to use what you have learned in the previous section to generate and focus ideas.

1. Recall a time when you felt proud of yourself. Write about the experience, what happened, and how it made you feel.
2. What are your feelings about war? Write an essay that explains your position.
3. Describe a favorite childhood pet or toy. What did it look like? How did it act? Why was it your favorite?
4. What is your definition of normal?
5. Many students have a difficult time in high school because of bullying. What advice could you offer a student who has been the victim of a bully?

NOTE: Keep your introductory paragraphs for use in Practices 2 and 3.

ELABORATION AND SUPPORT IN THE BODY PARAGRAPH

Elaboration means to go into detail, explain or say more about a topic. Once you have decided on your focus, written your introduction with a central idea and chosen your sub-topics, you need to fill in the gaps where you lack information. You do this by providing **specific details** that answer questions that readers might have about the topic, including **relevant facts** that support your central idea, and sharing **examples** and **experiences** that illustrate your ideas for readers.

Here is an example of how to develop supporting detail using specific details. A good way to develop specific details is to think of questions a reader might ask about your topic and then write the answers. These answers can then be written into specific details to elaborate on your topic. Here is an example:

Topic: Cats are Better Pets Than Dogs	
Questions	**Responses**
Why are cats better?	Cats are better behaved.
Is their behavior better?	They don't bark or jump.
How do they act?	They don't need to be trained as much.
Is there less responsibility?	They are cleaner creatures.
What kinds of responsibility do cats require?	They don't need as much entertainment.
	They don't need to be walked.
	They don't need as much supervision.

From this list, you can develop multiple paragraphs, including a paragraph like the following:

A cat's behavior makes it a better choice for a pet than a dog. Cats can entertain themselves and spend much of their time on self-grooming. Dogs need lots of attention and entertainment. Cats are content to be left home, especially with a feline friend. Cats don't bark when they are disturbed, in need or happy. Their quiet meows and purrs let you know they are happy. A cat's gentle rubbing against your leg is much more pleasant than a drooling dog jumping in your face. Cats' calm behavior makes them great choices for pets.

Practice 2: Elaboration

Working with the prompts given in Practice 1, write body paragraphs about your topic, using appropriate supporting detail. Save your introductions and body paragraphs for use in Practice 3.

WRITING CONCLUSIONS

The ending of an essay is just as important as the beginning. However, because it is the last part of an essay, it is often the most poorly written. You want your essay to end as strongly as it began. A well-written **conclusion** ties the main ideas in the essay together and leaves readers with a clear understanding of the importance of the topic. A good conclusion does three things:

- restates the central idea
- summarizes the main ideas
- gives readers something to think about or act on

There are many ways to give your readers something to ponder. In the same way you captured the readers' attention in the introduction, you can continue to have their attention in the conclusion. A conclusion can end with a **quotation**, a **call to action** that urges readers to do something or consider a viewpoint, or **makes a prediction** that keeps readers thinking about the topic.

One effective way to end your essay is to urge the reader to **take some action**. Consider the following example that ends the essay on pets:

If you want an animal to become a part of your family be sure to consider the advantages and disadvantages before making a purchase. A dog can be a great friend and protector. However, that same dog requires a great deal of responsibility and time. Spend some time at your local animal shelter or research animal types on the Internet; then you can be sure everyone will be happy.

This conclusion successfully completes the essay by restating the central idea and summarizing the most important advantages and disadvantage to pet ownership. Then it asks the readers to take action for themselves by researching.

Practice 3: Writing Conclusions

Using your ideas from Practices 1 and 2, write conclusions to match the introductions and supporting paragraphs you wrote. Try out different types of conclusions.

USING TRANSITIONAL WORDS

Clear transitions help readers understand the flow of ideas, as you learned in chapter 8 (see page 192). You need to lead the reader through your essay by showing how the ideas are related to each other. **Transitional words** help the reader see the relationship between your ideas. These relationships include **chronological order, order of importance**, **cause and effect**, and **comparison** and **contrast**.

CHRONOLOGICAL ORDER (TIME)

You can use transitional words to show chronological order, as those underlined in the example.

> **Example:** Our family has a daily routine to get us to work and school. <u>Before</u> my father leaves the house, he wakes up my brother and me. I get up <u>first</u> and take a shower. <u>Then,</u> my brother takes a shower <u>while</u> I'm getting dressed. <u>Meanwhile,</u> my mother gets our lunches ready. <u>After</u> breakfast, we jump in the car for the drive to school. <u>Lastly,</u> Mom drops us off on her way to work.

Using transitional words is a simple and effective way to present your ideas and descriptions clearly.

Sample Transitional Words for Chronological Order				
after	currently	immediately	second	third
again	during	in the future	soon	too
and then	eventually	later	subsequently	until
as long as	finally	meanwhile	suddenly	when
as soon as	first	now	then	whenever
at the same time	gradually	presently	thereafter	while
before				

ORDER OF IMPORTANCE

Transitional words help show which idea you want to emphasize when you are arranging ideas by **order of importance**.

> **Example:** You should always be aware of your surroundings in parking lots at night. <u>First,</u> look over the lot carefully for potential danger spots, for example, areas of low visibility and areas that do not have parking attendants. <u>More importantly,</u> be sure you have a defensive weapon, such as pepper spray or a loud noisemaker, in your hand as you walk to your vehicle. <u>Above all,</u> before entering your vehicle, look through the windows to make sure no one is hiding inside.

As you can see, using these transitional words helps to rank the steps required to reduce the potential danger of parking lots at night.

CAUSE AND EFFECT

Linking **causes and effects** is an important aspect of writing a convincing persuasive essay. You can use transitional words to make these connections clear. Read the example below.

Example: Local graffiti "artists" are becoming more brazen. Two weeks ago, they sprayed paint across three community centers. Last week, several businesses found their buildings "decorated" against their wishes. Last night, some graffiti writers took their work inside to the twelfth floor of the Baxton Building. <u>As a result</u>, the city council announced a special hearing for Thursday of next week to discuss possible responses to this problem.

Because the writer used the underlined transitional phrase, the whole paragraph is clear. The phrase "as a result" shows that the city council's announcement is an effect of the graffiti writing.

COMPARISON AND CONTRAST

Transitional words help a writer show **comparisons,** that is, how certain ideas or subjects are similar. Comparison words and phrases include *also, both, likewise, in the same way,* and *neither...nor.* Transitional words also help show contrast, when a writer is pointing out how two things or ideas differ. **Contrast** words and phrases include *although, but, in contrast, instead of, rather than, whereas,* and *while.* Take a look at this example, which compares and contrasts ideas.

Example 8: <u>Neither</u> the United States nor the USSR wanted to enter World War II. <u>Both</u> countries were forced to enter the fighting because of sneak attacks. The Soviets were caught off guard when Hitler broke his non-aggression treaty and invaded the Soviet Union on June 22, 1941. <u>Similarly</u>, the United States suffered a surprise attack when the Japanese struck the US naval base at Pearl Harbor on December 7, 1941. From that time on, the two countries were allies in fighting the Axis powers of Germany, Italy, and Japan.

"Neither" and "nor" may not sound like comparison words, but they point to something in common between two things. The other underlined transitional words make the comparisons between the US and the USSR clearer. Also, note the importance of "from that time on" in the last sentence to show the order of events.

Practice 4: Transitional Words

A. On your own, or in small groups, skim through articles in newspapers, in magazines or on the Internet. Find paragraphs that contain transitional words based on each of the following: chronological order, order of importance, comparison and contrast or cause and effect. Share these paragraphs with your teacher or other students. Do the transitional words improve your understanding of the paragraph? Why or why not?

B. On your own, or in small groups, write four different paragraphs. Each paragraph should include transitional words from the different categories discussed in this chapter: chronological order, order of importance, comparison and contrast or cause and effect. Return to the lists of these words to help you. Then, exchange your collection of paragraphs with your teacher or with another group, and evaluate the paragraphs by noting how well the transitional words are used within each paragraph.

Here are some possible topics for each of your four paragraphs:

Chronological Order: Your first driving lesson, A time you got lost

Order of Importance: Prioritize your duties for today, Who are the three most important people in your life? Why?

Comparison and Contrast: Do you prefer pizza or hamburgers? Why? Which is better on a Friday night — watching television at home or going out to a movie?

Cause and Effect: Why is a high school diploma important? What are the effects of sports programs on high school students?

USING TRANSITIONS BETWEEN PARAGRAPHS

As you red in chapter 8, transitional words link ideas from one sentence to another, but they also link ideas between paragraphs to make the whole essay "stick together." Without these transitional words and phrases, the writing becomes less interesting or even less understandable. Review "Transitions and the Flow of Ideas" in chapter 8, and read the following additional strategy.

REPEATING KEY WORDS AND PHRASES

While you don't want to say the same thing over and over, repeating certain key words and phrases can improve reader understanding. By including key words or ideas from your thesis in the topic sentences of your paragraphs, you make it easier for the reader to follow your train of thought. These repeated words are like landmarks along the road of your essay, reminding the reader where you have been and where you're going. For example, look at the following plan for an essay, in which the topic sentences repeat key words from the thesis:

Thesis: Citizens of the United States could greatly improve the country by obeying the law, protecting the environment, and being kind to other people.

Topic Sentence: The first and most basic step to improving the country is to obey the law.

Topic Sentence: In addition to obeying the law, citizens can make this country even more beautiful by protecting the environment.

Topic Sentence: A third way to make the United States a better place to live is for citizens to reach beyond their own self-interest and be kind to one another.

You can also repeat key words or phrases throughout the essay, not only in topic sentences.

FINDING AND EVALUATING RESEARCH SOURCES

Sometimes when you write an essay, you will be asked to support what you write by citing sources. If so, you will need to do some research in **information resources** that you read about in chapter 4.

Research should not be scary! We all do research: when you compare a college or technical school you may attend, you are conducting research. Using your topic, issue, and research questions, you can list some **key words** that will guide your research efforts. In the case of writing about pets, these key words could include *dogs, cats, pets, behavior, grooming, companion,* and *training.*

Research sources are available from many places, including libraries, book stores, and Internet sites. In some cases, people also do field research, meaning that they make firsthand observations or conduct interviews about their topic. The key words derived from the topic, issue, and research questions are helpful in locating research sources.

Remember that, with so many websites on the Internet, a single key word will often turn up an enormous and jumbled array of possible pages to view. For example, just entering *pets* as a key word could result in millions of possible sites with information about not only cats and dogs but also iguanas, guinea pigs, and turtles! To avoid this, narrow your search by choosing keywords more specific to your topic. For example, entering several keys in a search engine (such as *dogs cats differences pets)* returns results much more closely tied to the topic.

Print out several of the pages from sites you find, so that you have the information when you draft your paper. Note the website names and addresses on each printout, which you will need for your bibliography. Sometimes websites may be difficult to find a second time.

When you conduct your research, remember not to give up after the first few searches. You may need to refine your search to get the results you need. In addition, expand your research to include a variety of sources, rather than relying on just one source for all of your information. Below is a list of some research sources to keep in mind.

- Reference books, such as dictionaries, encyclopedias, and almanacs
- Periodicals, such as journals and magazines
- Audio and video collections
- Internet and the World Wide Web
- Firsthand research and interviews

Next, you need to **analyze and evaluate** all of your sources: the printouts from the Internet, any books you have read, films you have seen, and lessons you remember from class. Decide which ones to use and how they might fit into your essay.

Practice 5: Finding and Evaluating Research Sources

Begin doing research about your topic. On your own paper, write down the sources you find and what information each adds to your topic. Write and test your topic statement.

VALIDATION: CHECKING SOURCES

Why should you bother with validating sources? After all, if you can find material on a website it must be OK, right? No, not always. Many websites are created by students and other citizens, who may believe what they have posted is true, but are mistaken: "Let the searcher beware!" Researchers protect their work by screening the material they find for quality and accuracy.

- Find two or more sources that agree with the information that you wish to use.
- Read material carefully, watching for any bias or particularly strong opinion expressed in it.

- Look at the URL for the source of the material. It should name an organization or individual. If the organization is an educational (.edu), government (.gov), or professional center (.org) the material is probably valid.

- Look for "links" within the text of a Web site; these are an indication of a serious, validated work (they're like footnotes in a book). Go to some of the linked sites to check the accuracy of the source, as well as to find additional material.

- Look at the homepage of the source for other related works by the author of the site. The more the author has published on a topic, the more trustworthy the material.

- Check the date on the material. Obviously if your topic is on a current event, the more recent the date, the better the information. Less urgent, but still valid, is the point that recent data and theories are valuable for any topic.

- If you are using informal sources, such as chat rooms, for clustering or sharing ideas, again, the information needs to be confirmed by two or more other sources before it is validated.

The name of the author or organization and the date when the site was updated (modified) can usually be found on the last page of the material:

> ABOUT // CALENDAR // PLACES // RESOURCES // MARKETPLACE // LINKS //
>
> <http://www.ohiohistory.org/about/index.html> Last modified Friday, 10-Nov-2000 15:43 EST **Ohio Historical Society** - 1982 Velma Ave. - Columbus, OH 43211© 1996–2001 All Rights Reserved

SAFETY

The use of the Internet, without special "safe" servers is basically unregulated and unguarded. This situation brings up concerns over credibility, safety, and privacy issues. The following is an informal listing of ways to make your Internet use as safe and as positive as possible.

- Develop a <u>healthy distrust</u> of much of what you read on the Web. Databases are usually OK, but chat rooms and personal websites are open to all sorts of deceptions and second class information, causing frustrating detours for you.

- Always use a very different name on the Internet and understand that others are doing the same as a safeguard or as a false identity.

- Make sure that you understand and follow the expectations that your school, library, or home has about the way the Internet is to be used.

- Understand that some sites have built-in roadblocks; there is no way for you to exit the site. Should you run into this trap, disconnect from the Internet. Then, sign on again. You will also want to alert your teacher or the webmaster to the problem.

- Watch out for anyone on-line asking you personal questions. This is a flashing red stoplight. Do not respond to those questions and exit that site.

INTEGRATING RESEARCH SOURCES

Working with an outline of your essay, make notes of articles or books in places where you want to use these sources. Once you draft the essay, you will add in-text or parenthetical citation wherever you quote or paraphrase the materials you found, and you will list all of your sources in a works-cited page or bibliography at the end of your essay. There are several different styles in which citations and bibliographies can appear, so be sure to ask your teacher for the style you should use for the assignment.

When you revise your research report to integrate research sources you found, there are guidelines that will help you. First, you need to decide the **amount of research data** to use, including enough of your source material to show the thorough research you did, but not so much that the supporting material overshadows your own writing. Next, you need to use correct **documentation conventions** for integrating source material, through **direct quotation**, **paraphrase**, or **summary.** Whatever format you use, you must always properly cite your sources. Otherwise, you will be **plagiarizing** (taking someone else's words or ideas and passing them off as your own), which is against the law.

BIBLIOGRAPHIES

Each citation in the research report must have a matching entry in the bibliography or works cited page at the end of the paper, in which complete information is provided about how to find the source cited. A citation in the text means nothing without its corresponding reference listing.

Sometimes you will be asked to include a works cited page or a references page, and other time you will need a bibliography. What's the difference between these lists? A **works cited page**, also called a **references page**, lists only works cited in the text. A **bibliography**, also called a **works consulted page**, is a list of all works that were part of the research and are pertinent to the subject, even though some may not be cited in the text. Sometimes, an **annotated bibliography** may be called for, which not only lists the research sources, but also includes a brief summary of each source. Make sure that you are clear about the type of research source list you must include with your research report, and look up the proper conventions and formatting to use in the guide for the style you are using.

CHAPTER 9 SUMMARY

Following the **writing process** helps you compose any writing you need to do.

- **Think** about what the purpose or assignment is for writing. Make sure you understand the writing prompt, if you are responding to one on a test.

- **Prewrite** to generate and focus ideas, using tools like the spider map, and plan your essay using an outline.

- **Draft** your essay, developing your ideas as you have generated and focused them through prewriting.

- **Revise** the draft for coherence and appropriate grammar and usage, sentence structure, and paragraph development. Proofread to catch any errors.

Remember that a good **introduction** grabs the interest of the reader, introduces the topic, and states the central idea of your essay.

Elaborate and support your ideas in the body paragraph(s).

Write a strong **conclusion** that restates the central idea, summarizes main ideas, and gives readers something to think about or act on.

Keep in mind that appropriate **transitions** clarify the relationships of ideas in your essay. These relationships include spatial and time order, order of importance, cause and effect, and comparison/contrast.

For some papers, you will need to **find and evaluate research sources** to use as supporting material for the points you make. Remember to choose **key words** carefully to find appropriate information, include various **information resources** in your search, and **validate** your sources. **Integrate research sources** into your essay, using in-text citations and a list of sources such as a **bibliography**.

CHAPTER 9 REVIEW

Now, based on this chapter's writing activities and what you learned in this chapter, write a draft of an essay for one or more of the following writing prompts.Use the skills you practiced in this chapter. You may also use the English Language Arts Writer's Checklist on page 226.

1.

> Your local community center is creating a youth position for its kindergarten after-school program. The position requires a written application including a descriptive essay that tells about yourself, your experiences with young children, and your educational goals.
>
> Before you begin to write, think about why you would be well suited for this position. What skills do you have? How would the children benefit from your presence? How would this position prepare you for your future?
>
> Now write a multi-paragraph essay for the job at the community center. Be sure to give specific details and to support those details with clear examples.

2.

> Your English teacher has asked you to write an essay that describes your favorite holiday or festival day.
>
> Before you begin to write, think about all the different holidays. Which one do you like best? What do you like about this holiday? Are there specific traditions that make the holiday your favorite?
>
> Now write a multi-paragraph essay describing your favorite holiday. Be sure to give specific details and to support those details with clear examples.

3.

> Your English teacher has asked you to write an essay that compares school now to what school might be like in the future.
>
> Before you begin to write, think about specific ways school may change in the next 50 years. In what ways will school be different? In what ways will school remain the same?
>
> Now write a multi-paragraph essay comparing school now to school in the future. Be sure to give specific details and to support those details with clear examples.

4.

As a class assignment, you need to write an essay that provides instructions about how to do something. Your essay could explain how to cook a favorite food, make something, play a sport, do an activity, or complete a specific job.

Before you begin to write, think about something you know how to do well. What are the main steps a person should follow? Organize your instructions in chronological order so they are easy to follow.

Now write a multi-paragraph explanation giving instructions about how to do something. Be sure to provide all the information needed for a person to complete the action you are describing.

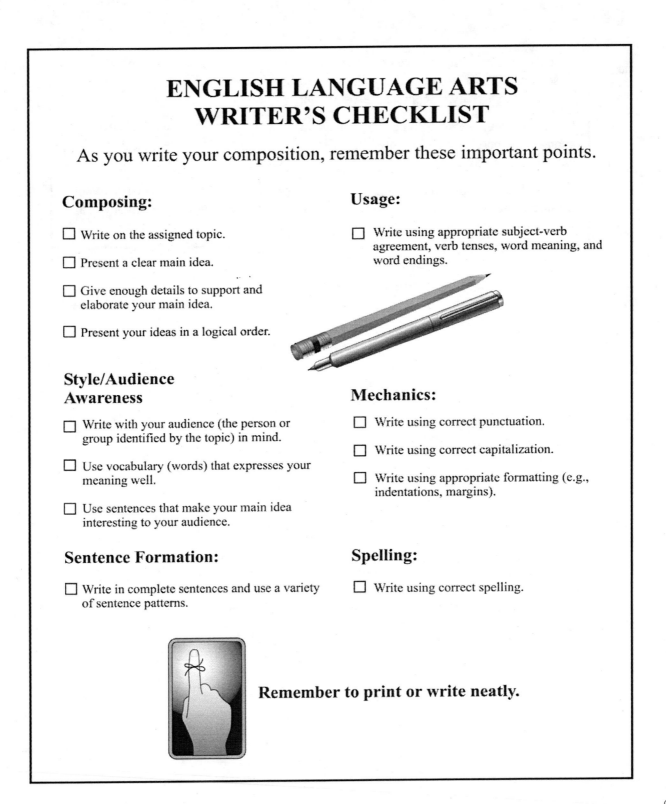

ENGLISH LANGUAGE ARTS WRITER'S CHECKLIST

As you write your composition, remember these important points.

Composing:

☐ Write on the assigned topic.

☐ Present a clear main idea.

☐ Give enough details to support and elaborate your main idea.

☐ Present your ideas in a logical order.

Style/Audience Awareness

☐ Write with your audience (the person or group identified by the topic) in mind.

☐ Use vocabulary (words) that expresses your meaning well.

☐ Use sentences that make your main idea interesting to your audience.

Sentence Formation:

☐ Write in complete sentences and use a variety of sentence patterns.

Usage:

☐ Write using appropriate subject-verb agreement, verb tenses, word meaning, and word endings.

Mechanics:

☐ Write using correct punctuation.

☐ Write using correct capitalization.

☐ Write using appropriate formatting (e.g., indentations, margins).

Spelling:

☐ Write using correct spelling.

Remember to print or write neatly.

Chapter 10
Writing the Constructed Response

This chapter addresses instructional strategies from the current English rubrics for brief and extended constructed responses. The full rubrics are available in Appendix A.

This chapter also addresses the following expectation(s) and their related indicators from **Core Learning Goal 2: Composing in a Variety of Modes**

Expectation 2.1	The student will compose oral, written, and visual presentations that inform, persuade and express personal ideas.

In this chapter, you will learn about writing a constructed response, which is something you will need to do on the Maryland High School Assessment in English. Whether you are writing an essay for class, composing an oral or visual presentation, or writing a brief or extended response to a prompt on a test, you will need to keep in mind what you have learned about writing in the last few chapters and make your response in an appropriate way.

THE BRIEF CONSTRUCTED RESPONSE

On the Maryland HSA in English, the **brief constructed response items** require you to briefly but completely answer questions based on a passage and/or graphic. These can include questions that explore your understanding of how plot, character, setting, and other structures affect meaning in a text or how to apply reading strategies to non-print text.

Read the following passage. Then, study the sample responses, noting why each one would score as it does.

Dream On

For years, psychologists have been fascinated by the human subconscious and how it manifests itself in dreams. There are about as many explanations for dreams as there are dreams themselves, but there are five widely accepted, although contradictory, theories for why people dream.

Sigmund Freud (1856–1939) was one of the first psychologists to explore the world of dreams. His theory is that dreams are a combination of our innermost desires and the previous day's events. He believed that dreams represented conflicts between our conscious and our subconscious.

When our desires are repressed and not met, our minds play them out in dreams. In this way, our dreams protect us from an unhealthy build up of psychological tension.

Whereas Freud felt that only a psychologist could interpret dreams, Carl Jung (1875–1961) believed that everyone could and should interpret their own dreams. Rather than interpreting an isolated dream, Jung suggests examining a dream in relation to other recent dreams as well as recent events in waking life, like chapters in a book, to get the whole story.

Edgar Cayce (1877–1945) believed that dreams are spiritual gifts that tell us how to solve our problems in life, how to improve our health, or how to live up to our full potential. In order to interpret your dreams, you must know yourself: your feelings, fears, goals, interests, longings, dependencies, etc. Only when you know yourself will your dreams carry any meaning for you. Once you have drawn correlations between your dreams and your life, you must choose a course of action based on your interpretation of those relationships. According to Cayce, some dreams can predict your future for you.

Christopher Evans (1951–present) theorizes that dreams are our minds' way of cleaning house and organizing information. He sees the mind functioning much like a computer to store and organize all our data files. The mind disconnects from the body during REM (rapid eye movement) sleep to sort through all the input from the previous day. Dreams are when we reconnect and get a brief glance at the data being sorted through.

Francis Crick (1916–present) argues that dreams do not store data but function to clean out the memory banks of the brain. During our waking hours, we gather so much data that we can easily experience an overload. Dreams are a way to get rid of "cognitive debris," those sometimes useless and sometimes harmful memories.

All these theorists have one common belief: they all believe dreams have an important biological or spiritual function in our lives. When people are deprived of their dreams, they become irritable, nervous and forgetful; their bodies begin to break down like a computer with a virus. So, no matter what you believe, make sure you get plenty of sleep and sweet dreams.

The brief constructed response question on the Maryland HSA might read as follows:

> Using information from the passage, compare two of the dream theories discussed.

Brief constructed items that require short answers are scored using a 3-level scale. Level 3 is the best possible score. Always be sure to read the prompt carefully and answer the question completely to receive the highest number of points possible. As always, zero points are given if there is no response, if the response provided does not address the question adequately, or if it cannot be understood (makes no sense due to errors or illegibility).

Model Student Response – Level 3

Sigmund Freud believed that dreams can help us avoid an unhealthy buildup of tension. Francis Crick seems to have updated Freud's theory to say that dreams help us get rid of "cognitive debris." In both these theories, dreams are serving to reduce the amount of clutter in our brains by disposing of memories or thoughts we don't need.

Discussion – Level 3

The response, which sums up both theories and infers a relationship between the two theories and the time in which they were created, demonstrates an understanding of the complexities of the text.

Model Student Response – Level 2

When we sleep, we dream. Nobody really knows why we dream, but many psychologists have tried to figure out why we dream when we sleep. Two psychologists who study dreams are Freud and Crick. They have similar theories for the purpose of dreams.

Discussion – Level 2

This response demonstrates a partial or literal understanding. While it compares the theories, it uses no examples of each to support its claim.

Model Student Response – Level 1

Freud and Crick are both psychologists who studied dreams. Freud was first, and he is famous. He said dreams show desires. Crick came later. He said dreams were a way to clean out data in our brain.

Discussion – Level 1

This response shows minimal understanding and does not compare the two theories.

Model Student Response – Level 0

I don't get this, I've never had psychology.

Discussion – Level 0

This response is completely irrelevant.

Practice 1: Reviewing the Sample Response

Now that you have read sample brief constructed responses, take a moment to notice which facts and details from the passages were in some way used when writing the responses. Discuss these with your teacher.

Practice 2: Writing Brief Constructed Responses

Read the following passage. Make note of the details, and then answer the questions that follow.

A Soldier's Lesson (*A True Story*)

It was in the sixth week of basic training, and I was getting quite tired during our mock battlefield training exercise. After a six-mile march in full gear, we had to dig our foxholes (underground defensive positions) and settle in for the night. The afternoon sun was beating hard, and we had to dig with a very small shovel known as an entrenching tool.

As we dug, my ranger buddy (person who works with you as a team), Private Nixen, turned to me and said, "Hey! We need branches to camouflage our foxhole! Why don't you go get them?"

"Sure," I said. "As long as you can watch my M16. You know how the enemy unit is always trying to outwit us. They may try to steal it from me as I gather wood."

"No problem," Nixen said.

Private Bryant, who was within earshot of our foxhole, shouted, "Be careful out there—you never know when the enemy is going to strike."

So, off I went to gather branches loaded with leaves. This task took longer than I expected. It took me almost thirty minutes to get back to camp. However, when I returned, I would wish I had stayed away.

My drill sergeant, Oglethorpe, was standing next to Nixen and had a look that would melt mountains. He thundered, "Private, do you know where your M16 is? Do you?"

"Drill Sergeant, I don't know where it is," I stammered. I looked over at my ranger buddy, but Nixen remained silent.

"Well, the enemy unit returned it to me. They said they had found the rifle unattended, and so they took it. Do you have any idea how embarrassing that is to me?" Oglethorpe thundered.

"It is my fault," I said. "I know, ultimately, the rifle is my responsibility."

Once I said this, my drill sergeant shared some unsavory words with me, ordered me to hold my rifle in front of me for thirty minutes, and stomped off. My arms grew very sore during this exercise. The next day, Friday, the platoon returned to the barracks. Everyone was allowed to go off post Friday and Saturday on leave and return Sunday. Unfortunately, I was not permitted to leave the barracks for the weekend. Because of the loss of my rifle, I had to stay behind and clean the latrines of my barracks. However, I suffered through this and just considered it one of life's memorable experiences. I still remember Nixen's look of relief and happiness when he left for his two day leave.

– Dick Regis

1. Write a response that discusses what the narrator of this story learned from this event. In your response, support your conclusion with appropriate details from the text.

2. Write a response that explains how the graphic which accompanies the text does or does not help a reader to understand the story.

THE EXTENDED CONSTRUCTED RESPONSE

The two most common forms of writing that call for specific extended response, **expository writing** and **persuasive writing**, are reviewed in this chapter. When you are asked to write an extended constructed response on the Maryland HSA, you will write an essay either to inform (expository) or to support, modify, or refute a position (persuasive). Assessment of the responses is based on the 4-level rubric you will find in Appendix A.

COMPOSING TO INFORM

When you compose to inform, you are writing an expository essay. The purpose of expository writing is to explain a topic. Essays of this type can include topics like "Learning on the Internet," "How to Sink a Free Throw Every Time," "Why Skateboarding is Popular," and "What to Look For in a Good Movie." From these examples, you can see that expository writing provides information. It helps us learn more about the world around us.

In expository writing, you can explain how something works or why something happened. You may want to present general information by answering questions like "who, what, when, where, why, and how" about a subject. These key questions are sometimes called the **five Ws and H**. Pointing out similarities and differences between two subjects or ideas is also expository. Expository essays can also include **process essays** (explaining a process, or how to do something), **cause/effect essays,** and **comparison/contrast essays**.

You can find expository writing in newspapers, magazines, and on the Internet. Cookbooks, instructional manuals, and school texts include expository writing.

In chapter 9 of this book, you learned about the basic structure of an **essay**. This structure consists of three main parts: an introduction, a body, and a conclusion. A **basic expository essay** also contains these three parts. Its purpose is to inform or to explain a particular topic.

Let's say that a student named Emmi has a writing assignment. She must write an essay about a particular animal. Since she is being asked to explain or inform her audience about this animal, she would be writing a basic expository essay.

Based on chapter 9, the **first step for writing** her essay would be to **brainstorm** about the topic. Emmi's brainstorming list looks like this:

Animals I Could Write About

dog	squirrel
cat	parrot
hamster	lizard
rabbit	monkey

Writing the Constructed Response

The **second step for her essay** is to **choose the animal** that she will discuss. Emmi chose her dog, a purebred Labrador retriever. Once she chose to write about her dog, Emmi moved to **step three, developing the thesis or controlling statement** for her essay. Here is what she wrote for her thesis: **The Labrador retriever is an interesting breed of dog. Learning about this dog can help anyone who wants a Lab for a pet.**

Emmi's Outline

Creating a rough outline, Emmi used the **five Ws and H** to develop the body of her basic expository essay. Here is what she wrote for the outline:

The Labrador Retriever

Who?	Labrador retriever, a type of dog
What?	Size, weight, colors, personality, life span
When?	Feeding times, play time
Where?	Origins
Why?	Benefits of owning a Lab
How?	Treating diseases, puppy care

Emmi's Rough Draft

Now that Emmi has decided on a specific topic, a thesis, and a rough outline, she is ready to write a rough draft of her basic expository essay. As she writes, she will incorporate information from her secondary sources. Read her draft for content, organization, and English language conventions:

The Labrador Retriever

There are many kinds of dogs. Some are big. Some small. They come in many colors too. The Labrador retriever I know best because I own one. The Labrador retriever is an interesting breed of dog. Learning about this dog can help anyone who wants a Lab for a pet.

My veterrinarion, Dorothy Howe, says these dogs came from Newfoundland in Canada. The Labrador retriever stands about 2 feet tall. It weighs 60 pounds sometimes 75. Puppies weigh less of course. Howe says a dog should match your personality. So observe a dog before picking one out. So both of you get along. You can also expect Labs to live 8-12 years or longer. depending on keeping up with shots and illnesses.

Care of the Labrador retriever involves regualr feeding. Usually 2 cups of food each day with plenty of fresh water. A high qwuality dog food should be bought. Snacks are ok, but not too many. Labs will overeat if allowed. So don't overfeed them. labs also love to play fetch. So keep a frisbee or rubber bone handy. A Lab are also a very strong. They'll pull you, train it to walk with you and not chase other dogs.

I also know that these dogs can get diseases like dihrea, blindess, worms, especially heartworm, distempr, and hip disease so they deed regulr checkups. A Lab can also get skin infecsin. So be careful. Puppies can die quick if its too cold. So keep it warm. Pups are nice too because they play a lot. He knows you right from birth.

Lab retrievers are an animal that eevery one likes. They're playful, loyal, and good hunting dogs too. I look into my dog's eyes and see smart and lovable eyes. That's what I know about Labs.

Practice 3: Evaluating a Draft of a Basic Expository Essay

Reread Emmi's rough draft on the Labrador retriever. Then, answer the following questions.

1. How does Emmi's draft fulfill the assignment?

2. List several ideas which are relevant and support her main point.

3. What improvements can Emmi make in the organization and language of her essay?

Emmi's Revision

After feedback from other students and her teacher, Emmi wrote the following revision of her basic expository essay on the Labrador retriever:

The Labrador Retriever

Dogs come in many sizes, shapes, and colors. Some dogs are large while others are small. I own a Labrador retriever which is an interesting breed of dog. Learning about this dog can help anyone who wants a Lab for a pet.

My veterinarian, Dorothy Howe, says Labrador retrievers originally came from Canada. These dogs stand about 2 feet tall and weigh between 60 and 75 pounds. They come in either black, yellow, or chocolate, and they are sometimes used for bird hunting. Howe says the personality of a Lab should match that of the dog's owner, so, before choosing a Lab, a person should observe its personality and behavior. Labrador retrievers can live 8 - 12 years or longer depending on the owner's attention to their health.

Care of the Labrador retriever involves regular feeding, usually two cups of food each day with plenty of fresh water. Dog experts recommend a high quality dog food with a few nutritious snacks now and then. Labs should never be allowed to overeat. Labrador retrievers love to play fetch, so always keep a frisbee or rubber bone handy. Labs are also very strong dogs who will drag you along on their leash unless they are trained to walk with you. They also must learn not to chase other dogs or cars.

I learned that Labrador retrievers can get diarrhea, worms, especially heartworm, and distemper. They also can become blind, get hip disease or a skin infection. They need checkups and shots on a regular basis. As puppies, Labs can die quickly if they become too cold. Both puppies and adult Labs are fun-loving, affectionate, and protective of their owners.

Most people enjoy Labrador retrievers. They're playful, loyal, and good hunting dogs too. When I look into my Lab's eyes, I see a smart and lovable dog. That's what makes him interesting to me.

Emmi's revision shows definite improvement over her rough draft. She adds the dogs' colors and includes more discussion of the benefits of Labs. She has also improved the variety of her sentences and has corrected most of her errors in grammar, punctuation, and spelling.

Your answers from practice 3 should generally match the improvements Emmi has made to her basic expository essay, which now would receive a passing score in her class. You may also find other minor errors which Emmi should correct.

Practice 4: Writing the Expository Essay

Now that you have read about the qualities of expository essays and seen an example of how to draft and revise one, try writing some of your own.

1.

> Think about games that you like to play. These could be board games, video games, or interactive games in which you role play with friends. Write an essay about your favorite game, making sure to explain clearly how it is played.

2.

> Consider interesting places you have visited. These could include nearby attractions, a friend's home, a vacation spot, or a faraway destination. Write an essay about the place in a way that will inspire interest from readers and explain vividly what this place is like.

3.

> Choose from the topics below and write an essay explaining the cause and effects surrounding the topic. For example, if your topic were exercise, you could explain why (causes) people exercise and what (effects) exercise does for a person.
>
> Topics: earthquakes   dirty laundry
>   overspending   volunteering
>   new hairstyles   tattoos
>   success   good grades

For more practice writing expository essays, refer to Appendix B.

COMPOSING TO PERSUADE

In **persuasive writing,** you try to convince readers to agree with your point of view. You can write a letter to persuade an employer to hire you, compose an email to convince someone to attend the prom with you, or create a letter to the editor of a newspaper to express your opinion about a current issue.

As always, it's important to keep in mind the **purpose** and **audience** for which you're writing. Additionally, in a persuasive essay, you need to use **persuasive language** and **build an argument**.

PURPOSE

With persuasive writing, your purpose is fairly clear: you want to convince readers to agree with you. However, the amount of convincing you need to do may depend on your topic. For example, convincing your dad to lend you 100 dollars will be more difficult than convincing him to lend you 20 dollars.

AUDIENCE

Knowing your audience is especially helpful in persuasive writing. Then, you know what points of agreement or disagreement you may have with your readers. You also know which reasons your readers may accept and which reasons they may not. Your audience could be friends, parents, teachers, local citizens, or an employer to name a few. Before you write, carefully consider who your audience is and what you know about your audience.

USING PERSUASIVE LANGUAGE

When you are trying to persuade, you need to present information in a particular way in order to make the reader agree with your position. You must emphasize points of interest to the reader and describe them in language that is attractive to your audience. For example, let's say you worked in a hardware store last year, and you are applying for a new job. When the manager asks what you did at your last job, you could answer with either of the explanations below.

> **Example 1:** *I worked for a while doing odd jobs.*

> **Example 2:** *I mopped floors in the hardware store, and then I took orders at the counter. After proving my abilities in these tasks, I was promoted to sales associate. My grasp of details is as strong as a river's current.*

Both explanations provide the same truthful information. However, the second makes you sound like a responsible and hard-working employee, while the first isn't very impressive. If you want to impress your future employer and convince the manager to hire you, the second explanation would be a better choice. The writer uses vivid description, concrete words, and figurative language.

Tips for Using Persuasive Language

1. **Use vivid description:** Notice how the writer in Example 2 uses phrases like "mopped floors" and "took orders at the counter." Persuasive language should include strong descriptive details. In Example 1, the phrase "I worked for a while" is vague and too general to convey a clear message.

2. **Use concrete language:** In Example 2, the phrase "promoted to sales associate" contains concrete and specific words. In Example 1, the phrase "odd jobs" does not provide a concrete picture of the work this person has done.

3. **Use figurative language:** Figurative language does for words what spice does for food. It livens up your argument. The phrase "my grasp of details is as strong as a river's current" conveys a vivid image that reflects positively on the job applicant.

Practice 5: Persuasive Language

For each of the following situations, write two or three sentences that will influence or persuade the intended reader. The example provided is NOT persuasive.

1. Convince your mother to let your friend sleep over.

    Example: Mom, can Chris please stay tonight?

2. Motivate your team to win.

    Example: It's half-time, and we're down by five points. We can win.

3. You took care of your sick brother last night, so you couldn't finish your homework. Persuade your teacher to give you an extension.

    Example: Is it o.k. if I turn in my homework tomorrow?

4. While mowing your neighbors' lawn, you ran over their flower bed. Convince them to give you another chance.

    Example: I think your flowers will grow back before I mow the lawn next time.

BUILDING AN ARGUMENT

Your ability to persuade depends not just on *how* you say something, but also on *what* you have to say. You must be able to build a strong **argument**. In everyday speaking, an "argument" is a disagreement between family members, friends, or enemies who exchange heated words. However, in the context of persuasive writing, an argument is a carefully reasoned way of presenting a point of view. The three steps to building an argument are to **make a claim**, to **support the claim**, and to **answer objections**. This process may be compared to building a pyramid.

MAKE A CLAIM

The first step in building a good argument is to **make a claim**. A **claim** is the position you take on a particular issue. It can't be just a statement of fact. A **fact** stands alone, cannot be argued, and requires no support. A claim, however, argues for one side of a controversy. Someone may disagree with your claim, so you must support it, just like the pyramid builder needs to support the top of the pyramid. The claim is the "point" you are trying to make, so keep it focused, like the pointed top of a pyramid.

Read the following six statements, and decide which are claims that provide a good starting point for an argument.

1. According to a 1999 Harris poll for the National Consumers League, a majority of Americans believe that water is our second-most-threatened resource, after air.

    – Sarah Milstein

2. Through personal choices, economic reform, and improved schools, we, the citizens of this great democracy, must stop the irreversible destruction of our most precious resources: air, water, and children.

3. We ought to be increasing programs that help the hungry children in our country rather than giving more money to an already well-financed program like the military.

4. Though the Cold War is over, the unpredictable nature of our present national enemies demands that we maintain a strong military through increased funding.

5. The best, indeed the only, method of promoting individual and public health is to teach people the laws of nature and thus teach them how to preserve their health.

– Dr. Herbert Shelton

6. Over the past three decades, there has been increasing public interest in personal self-help books, including the maintenance of health through self-regulated programs of exercise and diet.

Statements 1 and 6 present information in a factual, non-persuasive way. The information presented could be used to support a claim, but neither statement encourages one belief over another. Statements 2, 3, 4, and 5 urge the reader to take a certain action or have a certain belief. In other words, they make a claim. These statements use words like *must, should, ought, demand, only,* and *best.* These key words often indicate that the author is taking a position and encouraging the reader to do the same. You may also notice that the persuasive statements sometimes use the subject *we* in an attempt to involve the reader in the position or idea.

Statement 2 requires a special note. It makes a claim that requires support, but the claim is not focused. Air, water, and children are, indeed, precious resources. However, protecting the environment and improving schools are two topics that would be better addressed by two separate arguments. Try to pick *one* side of *one* issue and take a stand. Make sure your "pyramid" has a focused point.

SUPPORT THE CLAIM

The entire structure of a pyramid comes to a focused point at the top. Each and every block of the pyramid supports this point. In a similar way, you want each and every sentence of your argument to support your claim. You also want to support your argument with "solid blocks," so it will stand. A **strong argument** is supported by good logic, solid evidence, and appropriate reasons or examples. A **weak argument** suffers from poor logic, weak evidence, and **fallacies** (faulty reasons or examples). Like a pyramid, a strong argument will stand the test of time.

Read the following two passages about weight loss and decide whether the arguments are strong or weak.

Rapidly Burn Off Pounds And Inches With SUPER DIET PILL!

You Can Lose 10, 20, 50, Even 100 Pounds!

This is it! This is the diet pill researchers around the world have hailed for its powerful, quick-working ingredients that help people shed stubborn fat—fast!

Super Diet Pill Satisfies Need For Fast Action Without Strenuous Dieting

So fast-working, you can see a dramatic difference in just two days, without complicated calorie counting or suffering from biting hunger pains. Even people with long-time weight problems find they can burn off up to a pound of fat and fluid every five hours.

50% Fat Loss In 14 To 21 Days

The longer you use the super diet pill, the more weight you lose. You don't have to stop until you reach the weight that *you* want. Without making major sacrifices or drastic changes, you can shed as much as 50% of your fat in just 2 or 3 weeks.

Increased Metabolism Means Weight Loss

One-half of the women and one-fourth of the men in the United States are trying to lose weight and become fit. The sad truth is that most of us will regain our original weight in a year or less. What's the real secret for losing weight And keeping it off?

The answer is developing and maintaining a healthy metabolism. Metabolism refers to how the body burns energy. A person with a high metabolism burns more calories than a person with a low metabolism. Consequently, the person who burns more calories has an easier time losing weight. Here are some tips for improving your metabolism and melting away that extra fat:

1. **Drink plenty of water.** Filling up on water decreases the appetite. Three quarts of water each day are ideal.

2. **Don't skip meals, especially breakfast.** Eat small meals every two to three hours. In this way, carbohydrates and protein will not be converted into fat.

3. **Eat fat-burning foods.** Raw vegetables, whole grains, fruits, and legumes are your best choices. Consume fruits between meals for extra energy. This healthy snack won't be converted to fat.

4. **Exercise regularly.** Aerobic exercises like swimming, running, and walking are best. Also try lifting weights–a good muscle builder and fat burner. Exercise before you eat. It will decrease your appetite and increase your metabolism.

Each passage strongly suggests a way to lose weight and provides reasons to support its method of weight reduction. Which one is based on valid reasons, and which one is based on fallacies?

There are two big clues that the diet pill advertisement is based on **fallacies,** false statements: 1) It sounds too good to be true; and 2) It's trying to sell you something. A good rule of thumb is that if it sounds too good to be true, *it is*, and if someone is trying to sell you something, *beware*. Beyond these initial clues, an examination of the evidence shows that the diet pill ad offers very limited information about the diet pill. Little proof is presented to support its dramatic claims. The ad never mentions the names of the diet pill researchers, the people who lost weight, nor where or when the testing was done.

The description of metabolism, however, bases its argument on biological principles that are common knowledge to most people who have taken a biology class. From this basis, it provides logical explanations of how to increase your body's metabolism. The author is not selling anything and is not offering an easy "quick fix." A decision to follow the suggestions for changes in diet would be based on much better information than a choice to try the diet pill.

Three Ways to Build a Strong Argument

1. **Show cause-effect connections** between your position and the reasons you use to support it. Use clear logic and valid facts. Avoid fallacies and use commonly-known, easily proven facts.

2. **Illustrate your point of view** with a personal story. Although each person's experience is different, your reader can understand or empathize with events from your life that illustrate your point of view.

3. **Contrast your choice or position** with another. One way to show the strength of your choice is to show the weakness of another choice.

Practice 6: Analyzing an Argument

Read the following passage about the arts in public schools. Then answer the questions that follow.

Do you like art class? Are you taking music or dance classes? What if these were not part of the curriculum? There are many students who would miss this important aspect of their education. Music and art education are sometimes seen as *extras* on top of the core classes like English, math, science, and social studies. Some people say that students shouldn't be wasting time in public school with anything but the core subjects, but arts classes are just as important and should be supported in the same way.

People who don't support teaching the arts in school point to statistics showing how many students go from grade to grade without knowing basics like how to read well. It's true that the fundamentals need to be taught and tested, and students who are not at the appropriate level need to get extra help. But just because a few people slip through the cracks, all students should not be denied access to art, music, and drama classes. Critics also say that students interested in the arts could go to other, "special" schools instead, but that's not fair. We all deserve a well-rounded education and all have a right to get it in public schools. Still others say there is not enough funding for all programs, and that if a choice needs to be made, physical education is more important than arts to promote a healthy body alongside the sturdy learning of core classes. Well, both are important, and there has to be a better solution than "either/or."

Those who support the arts being taught in public schools make the excellent point that such classes promote expression, creativity, and ways of using core knowledge that open up students' minds. For example, math is applied in music (meter and rhythm) as well as in fine art (geometry of perspective), psychology and historical perspective are applied in drama class, and all of the theory and history learned in arts classes also apply to interpretation of today's world. Studies have found that arts classes promote higher attendance. One study even found that students active in arts curricula did better in core subjects than those who were not. So, where's the waste of time in that?

1. What is the claim?

2. Is the argument strong or weak? Cite examples from the passage to support your viewpoint.

ANSWER OBJECTIONS

Knowing your audience not only helps you choose an appropriate language and tone, but it also helps you anticipate objections to your position that your audience may have. Answering these possible objections is like building a wall around your pyramid to protect it from anyone who may want to tear it down.

Let's say that you wanted to go out dancing on Saturday night until 1:00 a.m. Your parents want you home by midnight. You would have to answer their objection to staying out until 1:00 a.m. Since your audience is your parents, you would have to decide how you could convince them to let you dance for one more hour. Think of three ways you would respond to their objection. Would you use impassioned pleas, logical reasoning, or an objective third person's opinion? What type of language and tone works best with your audience? This is a good question to ask yourself before you begin any persuasive writing.

Read the following passage regarding capital punishment, and decide which objections the author is trying to answer.

No More Executions

I want to applaud the governor of Illinois for his recent decision to stop all executions in his state until further review of the capital punishment system. Contrary to popular belief, capital punishment is not a deterrent to crime. In fact, statistics show that states without capital punishment had a lower rate of violent crime in 1999: 3.6 murders per 100,000 persons. States with capital punishment had a higher rate of violent crime in 1999: 5.5 murders per 100,000 persons. Some people claim that the appeals process takes too long, and that's why the death penalty is not a deterrent. However, the Death Penalty Information Center reports that 21 condemned inmates have been released from death row since 1993. This includes seven from the state of Illinois. We cannot risk the execution of innocent people by speeding up the appeals process. The lengthy appeals process also makes capital punishment very expensive. Anyone who has been in a court case knows how much lawyers cost. Those who do not want tax money wasted on criminals should oppose capital punishment because it is actually more expensive to execute someone than to imprison him or her for life. Overall, the system is terribly flawed. The other 38 states with capital punishment laws should join Illinois in placing a moratorium on all executions.

Writing the Constructed Response

The author of this passage opposes capital punishment and wants to convince others to oppose it as well. In doing so, the writer addresses three popular reasons that others use for supporting the death penalty:

1. capital punishment deters crime;

2. capital punishment would be a deterrent if the appeals process were shorter; and

3. execution is less expensive than life imprisonment.

The author answers these objections to her argument with statistics, authoritative information, and common sense.

Practice 7: Writing Persuasively

A. Choose one or two of the topics below, and write a persuasive letter or essay, paying attention to the elements of persuasion that you have reviewed in this chapter.

Topics

- Should there be Parental Advisory stickers on music CDs?

- Is it safe to make friends on the Internet?

- Are celebrities good role models for teenagers?

- Should people be giving money to the homeless?

For more practice with writing persuasive essays, refer to Appendix B.

B. Analyzing an Argument

Read the following argument for CFLs (compact fluorescent lamps). What is the claim? Is the argument strong or weak? What examples from the passage support your viewpoint?

Light Up Your Life!

The best improvement to our house this year has been the addition of compact fluorescent lamps (CFLs). This, no doubt, sounds like an incredibly boring change. However, if you consider the environment and economic impact of these little gadgets, it can be quite "enlightening." For example, nearly 99% of the energy used by a regular incandescent bulb is turned into heat. I don't know about you, but I don't think light bulbs are a very efficient way to heat a house. I want light bulbs to give off light. That's what fluorescent lamps use 90% of their energy to do. Another great thing about compact fluorescent lamps is that you hardly ever change them. Unlike traditional light bulbs that last a month or two, CFLs last from 5 to 7 years. Yes, that's years, not months! Of course, these long-lasting bulbs are more expensive to buy than the old bulbs. However, when you add up the money that you save in using less electricity, a CFL pays for itself three times over the course of 5 years. So as you can see, a simple change in your life can have a big impact.

CHAPTER 10 SUMMARY

On the Maryland HSA, you will be asked to write **brief** and **extended constructed responses**. The rubrics for these responses are found in Appendix A.

Whether writing a brief or extended response, be sure to **read the prompt carefully** and **respond fully to the question** being asked.

An **extended constructed response** is an essay written to **inform** or to **persuade** in answer to a prompt.

An **expository essay** informs or explains a topic. When writing an expository essay, you can use the **five Ws and H** to guide you in explaining your topic. Additional types of expository essays include the **process essay**, **cause/effect essay**, and **comparison/contrast essay.**

The purpose of writing a **persuasive essay** is to convince readers to agree with your point of view. Use **persuasive language** so that your audience will understand and appreciate your arguments. The three steps to **building an argument** are to make a claim, to support that claim, and to answer objections. Good arguments include logical reasons, solid evidence, and examples.

CHAPTER 10 REVIEW

A. Read the following passage.

Banning Books

Banning a book is a way of depriving students of one of the most important things in life—knowledge. It is the parents' and teachers' responsibility to equip children with that knowledge, since it could be their best defense against immoral material. It is like a flu shot. To prevent ourselves from getting sick from the flu, we must take small, controlled doses of the flu virus. Even Dwight D. Eisenhower understood the value of knowledge, good and bad. In his address to Dartmouth's class of 1953, he said:

Don't join the bookburners. Don't think you are going to conceal faults by concealing evidence that they ever existed. Don't be afraid to go into your library and read every book. [...]And we have got to fight [communism] with something better, not try to conceal the thinking of our own people. They are part of America. And even if they think ideas contrary to ours, their right to say them, their right to record them, and their right to have them at places where they're accessible to others is unquestioned, or it's not America.

1. Write a response that presents your view on this topic. Use appropriate detail to support, modify, or refute the points made by this author.

2. Write a response in which you explain how an adult might rationalize censorship.

B. To practice writing in a variety of modes, compose a response to each of the writing tasks that follow. Read each writing task carefully, and consider the purpose and audience. Refer back to previous chapters for help with planning, drafting, and revising your essay

1. Choose a person in history that you find interesting. Write a well developed expository essay that provides information about this person and why he or she is important.

2. Read the excerpt below, and complete the writing task that follows:

There is still a great deal of controversy about the future of the space program. While some people believe it is a waste of much needed funds, others point to the great scientific and technological advances that have resulted from the exploration of space. Supporters of the program most frequently cite the wide uses of microprocessors as one of the major contributions to space-related research. Opponents believe the billions of dollars dedicated to the space program would be better spent on the needs of education, health care, and job training for the poor and disadvantaged.

Pick one side of the controversy described in the passage about the space program, and write a letter to the editor of a newspaper that aims to persuade readers to your point of view.

3. Make a list of several movies or TV shows you have seen recently. Choose one of them, and write a persuasive essay in which you persuade readers why they should or should not see the film or watch the TV show.

For additional practice, see Appendix B for more writing prompts.

ENGLISH

Maryland High School Assessment in English

Practice Test 1

The purpose of this practice test is to measure your progress in reading comprehension and English Language Arts. This practice test is based on the Maryland Core Learning Goals and Expectations for English Language Arts and adheres to the sample question format provided by the Maryland Department of Education.

General Directions:

1   Read all directions carefully.

2   Read each question or sample. Then choose the best answer.

3   Choose only one answer for each question. If you change an answer, be sure to erase your original answer completely.

GO ON

Session **1**

Directions

For number 1, read the prompt below. Follow the directions in the prompt for writing your essay.

> **1**   **Consider the saying, "Honesty is the best policy." Is it always best to be**   2.1.4
> **completely honest? Think about times when it might not be—or perhaps**
> **you believe that there are no exceptions. Using examples from personal**
> **experiences, current events, literature, and/or any other relevant area, write a**
> **well-organized essay in which you agree or disagree with this saying. Be sure to**
> **fully develop and logically organize your essay, and use clear and descriptive**
> **word choices.**

Use your own paper to plan your response and to write the final draft of your essay.

GO ON

Directions

Read the excerpts from the poems "Sympathy" and "On Another's Sorrow." Then answer numbers 2 through 5.

excerpt from "Sympathy"

I know what the caged bird feels, alas!

When the sun is bright on the upland slopes;

When the wind stirs soft through the springing grass

And the river flows like a stream of glass;

When the first bird sings and the first bud opes*,

And the faint perfume from its chalice steals—

I know what the caged bird feels!

– Paul Laurence Dunbar

*opens

excerpt from "On Another's Sorrow"

Can I see another's woe,
And not be in sorrow too?
Can I see another's grief,
And not seek for kind relief?

Can I see a falling tear,
And not feel my sorrow's share?
Can a father see his child
Weep, nor be with sorrow filled?

Can a mother sit and hear
An infant groan, an infant fear?
No, no! never can it be!
Never, never can it be!

– William Blake

2 In "Sympathy," the author <u>most likely</u> uses the imagery of a bird in a cage to communicate   1.2.3

F that he has a special bond with birds.

G that birds should not be kept confined.

H that he identifies with a caged bird.

J that the bars of a cage cannot keep one from enjoying springtime.

3 Which word best describes the tone of "On Another's Sorrow"?   1.3.3

A furious

B rebellious

C contradictory

D compassionate

Read the last two lines from "On Another's Sorrow."

No, no! never can it be!

Never, never can it be!

4 The poet <u>most likely</u> uses these lines to   4.2.1

F prove that these scenarios are impossible.

G express how strongly he sympathizes with people in pain.

H show his anger about the sorrow in the world.

J play with words to phrase things more poetically.

5 Which idea **best** connects these two poem excerpts?   1.3.5

    A   Sorrow is contagious, but happiness is hard to find.

    B   Both authors seem to see the world as a sad place.

    C   A defining human characteristic is to feel sympathy.

    D   Both are ancient and use old-fashioned wording.

Directions

The short essay below requires revisions and editing. After reading it, answer numbers 6 through 8.

Tanning is a Half-Baked Idea

Are long, lazy hours at the beach or poolside your idea of a great vacation? Do you dream of the perfect summer tan? That dream might turn out to be a nightmare. Studies show that prolonged exposure to the sun can put you at increased risk for malignant melanoma, a serious form of skin cancer. **(5)** Even a bad sunburn, just one, can double your risk for developing melanoma. More teenagers and young adults are being diagnosed with skin cancer than ever before.

Doctors now recommend the use of sunscreen every time you go outside. You should also avoid prolonged sun exposure between the hours of <u>10 am and 2 pm</u> when the sun's rays are the strongest. A little precaution and moderation you can have your summer fun and your health.

6 What is the **best** way to revise the fifth sentence to make it clearer and more effective?   2.2.3

    F   A bad sunburn, even one, can double the risk for developing melanoma.

    G   The developing-melanoma risk can double even with one bad sunburn.

    H   Doubling your risk for developing melanoma, even one sunburn can be bad.

    J   Your risk of developing melanoma can double with even one bad sunburn.

7 What is the correct way to punctuate the underlined parts of the eighth sentence?   3.3.1

    A   10: am and 2: pm

    B   10 a.m. and 2 p.m.

    C   10, a.m., and 2, p.m.

    D   Best as it is.

8 How should the last line be revised to correct an incomplete sentence? 3.1.4

F A little precaution and moderation; you can have your summer fun and your health.

G With a little precaution and moderation, you can have your summer fun and your health.

H You can have your summer fun and your health, a little precaution and moderation.

J You can have a little precaution and moderation, your summer fun and your health.

Directions

Read the essay "Finding My Village," and then answer numbers 9 through 12.

Finding My Village

"Are you crazy?" asked my father. "After all we sacrificed to put you through college, you're going to Africa to work for nothing?"

It was 1965 and I had just told my family that I was becoming a Peace Corps volunteer in the Somali Republic. I assured my father that my college loan would be deferred and now he could get that new truck for his electrical business. I would complete two years of service. Then the Peace Corps would give me a readjustment allowance. This would pave my way into graduate school and jobs.

My mother worried about my health and safety, and I assured my mother that the Peace Corps was not sending volunteers where it wasn't safe. My assurances didn't soothe my Catholic grandmother. She feared for my salvation in a far-off Muslim country. "Will you promise me you will go to Mass every Sunday?"

At 25, I was restless. I longed to see the people and places I had read about in mission magazines as a child. I was in turmoil over the civil rights movement's conflicting methods, which ranged from the Rev. Martin Luther King's advocacy of non-violence to the Black Panthers' urban activism. I wanted distance to gain perspective.

And I did. My two years as a Peace Corps Volunteer helped me find my focus and led me to an exciting, satisfying career as a Foreign Service officer, an ambassador and—completing the circle—the Deputy Director of the Peace Corps.

Nowadays when I urge African-Americans to contribute two years of their energy and abilities, I tell them from firsthand knowledge that they will receive more than they give. Hundreds of the 182,000 Americans who have joined the Peace Corps since 1961 have told me this. They say it no matter where they served, or whether they volunteered in the idealistic 1960s, the cynical 1970s, the materialistic 1980s or the rejuvenated 1990s.

GO ON

9 Which conclusion about the author is **most** supported by information in this essay?   1.1.3

A   International travel is irresistible for him.

B   He was active in the civil rights movement.

C   Making the world a better place is one of his goals.

D   His grandmother fostered his religious beliefs.

10 What strategy does the author use **most** to talk about how rewarding the Peace Corps is?   1.2.3

F   exaggeration

G   repetition

H   analogy

J   details

11 The tone in this essay progresses from   1.3.3

A   yearning to confused to gratified.

B   adventurous to defiant to gloating.

C   brave to fearful to apprehensive.

D   hesitant to disobedient to triumphant.

Read these sentences from the second paragraph of the essay.

I would complete two years of service. Then the Peace Corps would give me a readjustment allowance. This would pave my way into graduate school and jobs.

12 Which of these **most effectively** combines these ideas into one sentence?   3.1.6

F   Paving my way into graduate school and jobs, I would complete two years of service, and then the Peace Corps would give me a readjustment allowance.

G   When I'd completed two years of service, the Peace Corps would give me a readjustment allowance to pave my way into graduate school and jobs.

H   After two years of service, I would pave my way into graduate school and jobs with the readjustment allowance that the Peace Corps would give me.

J   I would complete two years of service, then the Peace Corps would give me a readjustment allowance; then my way into graduate school and jobs would be paved.

250

GO ON

Directions

The paragraph below requires revisions and editing. Read it carefully, and then answer numbers 13 and 14.

Hand Grips

① Hand grips can help give your arms those bulging forearms you're after, but only if they offer enough resistance. ② If you can squeeze them repeatedly for one to two minutes, and your hands don't get tired, they're too weak for you. ③ You can keep buying stronger ones or make something at home that can do the same job. ④ Try tying a 3 pound barbell plate to a rope. ⑤ Then drill a hole through the middle of an old rake handle. ⑥ Standing straight with your feet shoulder-width apart, roll the rake handle horizontally until the weight is lifted up. ⑦ Then slowly unroll letting the weight back down. ⑧ When this gets too easy, just add more weight. ⑨ Doing this exercise three or 4 times each day will work your forearm muscles and help you in any sport where you throw or hit a ball. ⑩ It will also give you an impressive handshake!

13 Both the numbers in Sentence 9 should be spelled out. Choose the correct spelling of the number 4.

3.3.1

A   for   C   four

B   fore   D   foure

14 Which sentence could be deleted without the paragraph losing its flow and meaning?

2.2.2

F   Sentence 1

G   Sentence 4

H   Sentence 7

J   Sentence 10

STOP

Session 2

Directions

Read the essay "The Tao of Rice." Then answer numbers 15 through 21.

The Tao of Rice
by S. A. Snyder

S.A. Snyder was a Peace Corp forestry trainee in Thies, Senegal (1990). Snyder has degrees in Forestry, Wildlife Biology and Journalism from the University of Montana. She lives in Missoula, Montana.

Scott swerved his Honda 350 on the jungle path, narrowly missing a green mamba, one of the most poisonous snakes in Africa. I clutched his waist tighter. The dense, green tangle on both sides of us blurred as we passed, like a cartoon tunnel carrying us from the real world into a dream. Beige cement buildings appeared out of nowhere among the trees and vines, as if we had discovered some lost civilization. This was the sprawling village of Diourou in southern Senegal, near where I would be living for the next two years.

We pulled up to Jean's house where a dozen children and adults milled about. Scott had taught Jean how to plant mango seedlings and start his own orchard. He wanted to show me the orchard to give me a feel for the work ahead.

"Kasumay," they said as we approached. Peace.

"Kasumay keb," we replied. Peace only.

(5) Scott introduced us. I panicked and fell back on sketchy French, hoping they could understand.

Jean walked us through a maze of corridors inside his dark, cool house to the kitchen. His mother, Inay, appeared from a back doorway, clutching a chicken by its legs. It hung motionless, then flapped its wings and squawked when she carelessly tossed it aside. She smiled at us and squawked too.

"Kasumay!"

"Kasumay keb," we replied. Jean and Scott told Inay who I was and what my mission in Senegal was. She smiled and laughed, but threw me suspicious glances. Then Jean quietly conferred with Inay, who listened intently before knitting her brows and screeching an angry reply. Scott looked at me. My eyes begged for translation.

Several minutes of negotiation passed between Inay and Jean. Scott gave me a quick translation.

(10) "He wants to show you the vault," Scott said, motioning to a large box suspended from the ceiling. "It's where they keep the rice." Inay shook her head, pointed to me, and made an angry remark to Jean. "She doesn't want you to see it," Scott said. Jean's

253

GO ON

voice grew more demanding, while Inay held her ground. "She doesn't think you're Diola," Scott said.

"I'm not," I said, wanting to leave.

"You will be soon." Scott ribbed me with his elbow. "Use your Diola name."

Inay turned to me, sighed, and said, "Kasumay."

"Kasumay keb," I said, shrugging my shoulders. Hadn't we already been through this? She looked at Jean, then turned back to me.

(15) "Kares'I bu?" she asked.

Quick, what was my Diola name? "Saly," I said, gaining a bit of confidence. She pressed on.

"Kasaaf'I bu?" I had my Diola surname on my tongue.

"Mane," I said, now rising to the challenge.

"Au bay?" Inay threw her head back, confident I would fail. Should I say, "America," or give her the name of my future Diola village? I hesitated, and she smiled, certain she had me.

(20) "Dana," I replied. Quickly she retorted, "Kata sindo'ay?"

"Kooku bo," I answered. My people are there; they are fine.

Inay squealed and clasped her hands together. She turned to Scott, waving her arms and chattering in Diola I didn't understand. He laughed. Inay grabbed my hand and led me to the ladder that rose into the sacred vault. I suddenly took an interest in rice. We crouched side by side in the blackness of the vault. Jean brought up a lantern. Hessian bags,

enough to sustain a small family through a drought year, were revealed in its glow. Inay stroked one of the plump bags, speaking to me with care now. She plucked a small handful of spilled grains from the floor and displayed them in her palm. She separated one, rubbed it between her thumb and finger, and talked about the rice. I began to see its significance, even though I couldn't understand her words.

"Help me, Scott. I need to understand," I said.

Inay pounded her empty fist on her palm.

(25) "She says they have to beat it," Scott yelled up to me. Inay shook an invisible object in her hands.

"Then they sift out the chaff," Scott continued. Inay pummeled her palm again.

"Then they pound it a second time," Scott said. Inay opened her palm, the rice grains wet from moisture. She flicked a few grains off, and they stuck to one of the bags.

"The girls pick out the rest of the chaff. Then it's pretty much ready," Scott's voice trailed up the ladder.

Inay showed me her worn, wrinkled hands and cradled one inside the other. Her voice was soft now, tired. She took my right hand and turned my palm upward. She scooped up another small handful of rice from the floor and placed the grains in my hand.

(30) "Un cadeau," she said in French. A gift.

Reprinted by permission from *The Great Adventure: Volunteer Stories of Life Overseas* by Peace Corps.

GO ON

15 What would be the <u>best</u> reason to read this essay?   1.1.1

A   to learn about the Diola people

B   for instruction on how to prepare rice

C   as source material for a report about Africa

D   for a glimpse of being a Peace Corp volunteer

16 Which of these ideas is <u>most closely</u> related to the theme of this essay?   1.3.5

F   Everyone fears deadly animals and diseases.

G   A person's outward appearance can be deceiving.

H   Trying to fit in can make your hosts more comfortable.

J   The poorest families must work together in order to survive.

17 How do the sighting of the snake and the mention of a mango orchard contribute to a sense of setting?   1.2.1

A   These details help paint the picture of a hot jungle environment.

B   These descriptions clarify the route that Scott takes on his bike.

C   They signify that the village is both untamed and cultivated.

D   They show that the jungle is encroaching on the village.

18 In the fifth paragraph, the narrator says, "I panicked and fell back on sketchy French, hoping they could understand." The word *sketchy* <u>most nearly</u> means   1.1.2

F   artistic

G   imprecise

H   irregular

J   obscure

Read this sentence from paragraph 9.

Scott gave me a quick translation.

19 What does the pronoun me in this sentence refer to?   3.1.3

A   Jean

B   Scott

C   the narrator

D   the translation

20 In the first paragraph, the narrator describes how "The dense, green tangle on both sides of us blurred as we passed, like a cartoon tunnel carrying us from the real world into a dream." What is the <u>best</u> explanation for why the author uses this imagery?   1.2.2

F   The narrator feels disoriented in a place that's so unlike what she knows.

G   The motorcycle is moving much too fast on the dirt path through the jungle.

H   Thick, humid air and buzzing insects are making the narrator imagine things.

J   Fear of the deadly animals and unknown village is making the narrator dizzy.

GO ON

Directions

Carefully examine the photographs below.

| 21 | Write a response that discusses how these images are related to the essay, "The Tao of Rice." Be sure to support your conclusion with appropriate details from the essay as well as the photographs. | 1.1.4 |

Use your own paper to plan your response and to write a final copy.

Directions

Read "Pledging Allegiance to Their New Nation." Then answer numbers 22 through 24 about both "The Tao of Rice" and "Pledging Allegiance to Their New Nation."

Pledging Allegiance to Their New Nation

There were no doubts or second guesses. Hussain Jalil knew he wanted to be an American. "I had experience in Europe and America and my home, a third world country," said Jalil, a Bangladesh native. "I have seen three sides, and there is no greater country than the USA."

More and more Europeans, Asians, Mexicans and Central Americans have, like Jalil, chosen the United States to be their home. From October 2004 to August 2005, more than 475,000 individuals became United States citizens.

But it takes more than desire. The naturalization process is lengthy—taking as long as two years between the application and the citizenship oath. It includes background checks, fingerprinting, and tests—written or oral—with questions about history and politics. Questions like "Who is the chief justice of the Supreme Court?" a name few Americans could come up with off the top of their heads. To keep up with the pace, the Immigration and Naturalization Service district office has several ceremonies each week to swear in new citizens.

Iryna Federova, a 31-year-old Ukraine native, was among 44 people from 32 countries who took the oath last Monday. This is her first Independence Day as a citizen, but she has long believed her new home is the best place to live. "The U.S. has always been a country of freedom, not England, not Japan or anywhere else," said Federova,, a hairstylist who lives in Norcross. "That's what I thought as I was growing up. I got that from the movies and the books."

When Federova, moved to the United States, she knew of about two dozen Russians in the area. But she's noticed that the population has increased, to almost 30,000. "Now, I hear Russian in the grocery store, and anywhere I go," she said.

Jamil, 41, bought his first restaurant two years after becoming a citizen. He worked as a cook in an Indian restaurant and saved the bulk of his earnings. Then he made an agreement with a soon-to-be-retiring couple that if he successfully ran their Forest Park, GA deli, he could buy it at a bargain.

He now owns a successful sandwich shop in downtown across the street from the INS and can attest to the benefits of a healthy economy.

But it wasn't the lure of wealth that pulled Jalil to America. John Kennedy's Peace Corps gave me respect for the USA," said Jalil. "Then I read about Martin Luther King, and that is why I had to come here. We can eat together and stand together and work together because of him."

Jalil speaks proudly of the franchises he has owned and sold, and the addition of hand-dipped ice cream to his store, where he sells subs and salads.

He becomes passionate and forceful when he talks about the homeless drunk he turned around. Jamil hired the man, sent him to a rehabilitation center, and encouraged him to make contact with his young son whom he hadn't seen in years.

"We must do for the weaker person. All they need is love," he preaches with a clenched fist. "That's my advice to American people. Come to reality and help them. No one here is better than anyone else."

22 Both "The Tao of Rice" and "Pledging Allegiance to Their New Nation" present different settings and topics. Nevertheless, which statement best describes what the characters in both texts have in common? `1.1.3`

F   All of the characters feel disoriented and unsettled in some way.

G   Neither set of characters can adjust to their environment, be it natural or man-made.

H   Like the narrator in "The Tao of Rice," the new citizens in "Pledging Allegiance to Their New Nation" are trying to fit in.

J   The Diola people in "The Tao of Rice" want to come to America like the immigrants in "Pledging Allegiance to Their New Nation."

23 Both of these texts would be useful if you were writing an essay about `1.1.3`

A   traditions in different countries.

B   poverty levels in different nations.

C   learning the language of a new country.

D   making friends after moving to a new place.

Read these sentences related to both texts.

Where one is born cannot be chosen.

The place where you feel best might be very far from there.

You can consider this place your true home.

24 Which of these **most effectively** combines the ideas into one sentence? `3.1.6`

F   Where one is born cannot be chosen, but the place where you feel best is the one you can consider your true home, though it might be very far from there.

G   You can't choose where you were born, but your true home is where you feel best, though it might be very far from there.

H   Even though you were born far from there, you can consider the place you feel best your real home, but you can't choose where you were born.

J   You can't choose where you're born, but you know where you feel best (it might be very far from there); you can consider this place your true home.

258

GO ON

Directions

For Numbers 25 and 26, read the sentence in bold print. Then choose the clearest and <u>most</u> effective revision of the sentence.

25 **The sandwiches Mom made tasted great but we didn't know what was in them...the meat was dark, strangely salty, and the sauce was nothing like our usual mayo.**   2.2.3

   A   We didn't know what was in the sandwiches Mom made; they tasted great, but the meat was strangely salty dark, and the sauce was unlike our usual mayo.

   B   We didn't know what was in the sandwiches Mom made, which tasted great; but they had dark, strangely salty meat and a sauce that was nothing like our usual mayo.

   C   Made with dark, strangely salty meat and sauce that was nothing like our usual mayo, the sandwiches Mom made tasted great but we didn't know what was in them.

   D   The dark, strangely salty meat and the sauce that was nothing like our usual mayo tasted great, but we didn't know what was in those sandwiches Mom made.

26 **Warren has nearly catalogued all the baseball cards he's collected his whole life.**   2.2.3

   F   Warren nearly has catalogued all the baseball cards he's collected his whole life.

   G   Warren has catalogued nearly all the baseball cards he's collected his whole life.

   H   Warren has catalogued all the baseball cards he's nearly collected his whole life

   J   Best as it is.

Directions

Cheryl is writing an essay about the famous magician Harry Houdini. The draft of her essay requires revisions and editing. Read the draft, and then answer numbers 27 through 31.

Harry Houdini

In the summer of 1912, a man was chained and then nailed into a wooden box. Then the box was bound with rope and steel cables and lowered into the East River. Minutes passed as the audience waited to see what would happen. Fearing for the man's life, many gasped for breath themselves. Suddenly, the man emerges from the water, unharmed and freed from his chains. His name was Harry Houdini.

Houdini spent a lifetime performing escapes that left his audiences astonished and clamoring for more. Dangling upside down from a crane he could wrestle himself out of a straightjacket in minutes. He could be handcuffed and lowered into a steel drum secured with padlocks and filled with water. Three minutes later, he would emerge alive and well. Once, he was handcuffed to a post in a police station, with the police vowing to return in an hour. He freed himself before they left the room.

How did Houdini accomplish his feats? Besides being a master of illusion, he also possessed two extraordinary talents. His body was flexible and muscular. He also trained himself to hold his breath under water for up to four minutes. Besides that, he could pick apart any lock or chain in the world. In fact, he often showed people from his audience that he could open locks they brought to him. In this way, he proved that the ones he picked were not fake. All this and more about the famous escape artist is revealed in a book called *The Secret Life of Harry Houdini.*

---

27 Where does the following pair of sentences **best** fit in Cheryl's essay? 2.2.2

In 1903, German police accused him of cheating and encouraging criminals. He escaped in the courtroom and won the case.

- **A** at the end of paragraph 1
- **B** at the beginning of paragraph 2
- **C** at the end of paragraph 2
- **D** at the beginning of paragraph 3

28 What is the correct way to punctuate this sentence from the second paragraph? 3.3.1

Dangling upside down from a crane he could wrestle himself out of a straightjacket in minutes.

- **F** Dangling upside down, from a crane he could wrestle himself out of a straight-jacket in minutes.
- **G** Dangling upside down from a crane, he could wrestle himself out of a straight-jacket in minutes.
- **H** Dangling upside down from a crane, he could wrestle himself out of a straight-jacket, in minutes.
- **J** Dangling upside down from a crane; he could wrestle himself out of a straight-jacket in minutes.

GO ON

29 Which of these <u>most</u> clearly and effectively adds supporting detail to the third sentence in the last paragraph?   3.1.8

   A   His body was flexible and muscular, allowing him to bend, twist and untie knots with his fingers and teeth.

   B   His body was flexible and muscular, so he could maintain the same position for a very long time.

   C   Because his body was flexible and muscular, he could swim very fast.

   D   He performed so much that his body became flexible and muscular.

30 Which of the following items, if any, requires documentation?   2.3.3

   F   the event description in paragraph 1

   G   the list of feats mentioned in paragraph 2

   H   the book mentioned in paragraph 3

   J   none of the above

Read this rule from a language handbook.

Do not switch verb tenses unnecessarily.

31 Keeping this in mind, which sentence from Cheryl's first paragraph should be changed to be consistent in verb tense with the rest?   3.3.2

   A   Then the box was bound with rope and steel cables and lowered into the East River.

   B   Minutes passed as the audience waited to see what would happen.

   C   Fearing for the man's life, many gasped for breath themselves.

   D   Suddenly, the man emerges from the water, unharmed and freed from his chains.

Session 3

Directions

For number 32, read the prompt below. Follow the directions and write your essay.

> **32** Write a well-organized essay about a place in the United States or the world that   2.1.1
> you have studied or read about and would like to visit. Support your choice with
> details about what is interesting or important about the location and why it would be
> significant to visit in person. Your essay should be well-developed, logically
> organized, clear, and descriptive.

Use your own paper to plan your essay and to complete your final draft.

Directions

Read the essay "The Way Geese Fly," which Steve is writing for an assignment. Notice that it requires some revisions and editing. Then answer Numbers 33 through 37.

The Way Geese Fly

(1)The other day, I heard geese honking and looked out the window to see them flying in their distinctive V formation. (2)I decided to research the subject because this is something we all see from the time we're kids, but this time, I stopped to think about why the geese fly this way.

(3)Scientists have long suspected that the V formation which geese use during their long flights migrating north in spring and south in fall has something to do with conserving energy. (4)For a long time, they could not find proof. (5)Ornithologists (scientists who study birds) did studies to get proof. (6)They studied various birds that use the V, also called the squadron formation. (7)By measuring the heart rates of the birds, they found that the V formation does conserve energy. (8)The formation is aerodynamic (lessens wind resistance) so the birds toward the back can glide more often and not beat their wings as much. (9)The birds take turns in various positions in the formation, so all get the benefit of this energy conservation, and the entire group can fly longer before it has to take a breather.

(10)In addition to energy efficiency, scientists found the V formation has other advantages. (11)One is safety. (12)The simple formation provides every bird with a clear line of sight. (13)No bird directly behind another, so they can all see clearly around them, as well as each other. (14)Also, with the single-file lines of the formation, it is easy to tell whether all of the members of the flock are there. (15)Geese, and other birds, perform all this marvelous teamwork by instinct. (16)Humans have wisely adapted these natural systems for the same reasons the birds use them, as when fighter pilots fly in similar formation. (17)It's a great example of what we can learn from nature!

33 **Which of these is the clearest and _most_ effective way to revise sentence 2?** 2.2.3

  A   This is something we all see from the time we're kids, but this time, I decided to think about the subject of why the geese fly this way and I stopped to research.

  B   This time I stopped to think about why the geese fly this way, and I decided to research the subject; this is something we all see from the time we're kids.

  C   This is something we all see from the time we're kids, but this time, I stopped to think about why the geese fly this way, and I decided to research the subject.

  D   I stopped to think about why the geese fly this way, but this time, I decided to research the subject; this is something we all see from the time we're kids.

34 What is the correct way to punctuate   3.3.1
sentence 3?

F Scientists have long suspected, that the V formation which geese use during their long flights migrating, north in spring and south in fall, has something to do with conserving energy.

G Scientists have long suspected that the V formation, which geese use during their long flights migrating north in spring and south in fall, has something to do with conserving energy.

H Scientists have long suspected: that the V formation which geese use during their long flights migrating north in spring and south in fall, has something to do with conserving energy.

J Scientists have long suspected that, the V formation which geese use during their long flights migrating north in spring and south in fall has something to do, with conserving energy.

35 Which of these <u>most effectively</u>   3.1.6
combines sentences 5 and 6 in the second paragraph?

A To get the proof, ornithologists (scientists who study birds) studied various birds that use the V, also called the squadron formation.

B Ornithologists (scientists who study birds) did studies: is it true that various birds that use the V, also called the squadron formation, actually do conserve energy?

C Studying various birds using the V, also called the squadron formation, ornithologists (scientists who study birds) tried to get proof.

D Ornithologists (scientists who study birds) did studies and studied various birds that use the V, also called the squadron formation, to get proof.

Steve found the following information in his English book:

Avoid using trite expressions and clichés.

36 According to this information, which   2.2.5
sentence in the essay should be revised?

F sentence 7
G sentence 8
H sentence 9
J sentence 10

37 Which of these sentences from   3.1.4
paragraph 4 should be revised to correct an incomplete sentence?

A sentence 11
B sentence 12
C sentence 13
D sentence 14

GO ON

Directions

Read the essay, "Circus Acts." Then answer Numbers 38 through 44.

Circus Acts

Opening our front door, I was battered by the volume and bass escaping from my sister's radio. Her voice was blaring into the phone twice as loudly as she paced around the kitchen like a caged animal.

"Yeah, can you believe it? They think we're excited about some third-world circus! Why couldn't our school skip it like yours? The May Day picnic sounds better than that lame show."

I interrupted her, "You know, Moscow, uh, I mean, Russia is not a Third World country!"

Tory stuck out her tongue and kept complaining as I knew she would—even days later on the bus headed for downtown.

(5)In the darkened arena, our class was directed to a front section. Tory wanted to sit in the back. I knew she would go prowling if she got bored, so I mentioned we'd get food first in front.

"Ok, whatever."

Tory's voice was loud as usual, but there was one voice even louder, "Nachos! Peanuts! Popcorn! Get yer drinks right here!" For a moment, I felt smug about picking the right seats, but the show was starting, and Tory turned to watch. The Russian ringmaster introduced the acts: the high wire, clowns, Siberian tigers, and dancing bears. I was beginning to enjoy the show when Tory started to wave a program wildly in the air.

"What's the matter? Cut that out!" I muttered, irritated.

"I can't," Tory hissed back, "there's something after me."

(10)I heard a menacing droning sound as Tory leaped up and began running for the exit. I followed, pausing to look back at the tiger act entering the ring. One of the trainers glared at me over the audience as I stumbled up the stairs. In the restroom, Tory washed up while I fussed at her.

"Thanks to you, I'm missing the best part of the circus!"

"What makes some nasty tiger the best part?"

"Not the tiger, the Russian tiger trainer."

That got Tory's attention. We went back out to see the end of the tiger act, but we were too late. The show had moved on to the dancing bears. Tory held me back.

(15)Let's look for the tigers. I bet they're, like, backstage."

Normally, I would warn Tory that we'd get into trouble, but tonight I was feeling a little reckless, a little over the edge. As we went further and lower into the dark stairwell, we could hear the deep growls of the big cats and the low commands from the trainers. At the last step, the overhead lights blazed white and hot revealing the trainers urging the tigers back into cages. After a moment, we walked slowly towards the bustle and noise as the trainers locked the cages. One of the Russians whirled around summarily.

"Don't ever come quiet upon us!" He spat out in a heavily-accented voice, "We are always careful for escaped cats."

The other trainer walked towards us quickly. He smiled and held out his hand in greeting.

"Please to take no offense. Sasha is good for tigers, but he is like one after shows. I am Oskar."

(20)As we shook hands with Oskar, Sasha sarcastically asked if we had seen rude people running out of the arena during their act. Tory turned her charm his way and said we were very sorry

about that and told them about the savage insect. When Sasha heard Tory imitating the noise of the bug, he began to laugh.

"Such an insect must have come from the bears; they have their own group of Russian bees following them from home!"

As he said the word "home" Sasha's laughter switched off like a blown light bulb: a bright flare, and then darkness. Oskar took up the conversation, telling us about the life of a circus member, offering us Russian coins and Russian cigarettes.

"Quick, look through your pockets," Tory jabbed me with her elbow. "I know you always have gum or money on you." But it was Tory who made a connection with our new friends. She pulled the handout for our town's May Day picnic from her pocket. She showed it to Sasha and Oskar.

"In our home, May Day is most important holiday, a day of freedom!" Sasha exclaimed. "We lose time, always traveling. Thank you for reminding us. Oskar! Do we have any tiger whiskers left?"

(25)"Nyet, Sasha. I think we burned the last ones after Nicholas lost his hand . . ."

We watched horrified while Sasha unlocked the tiger cage and cried out harsh Russian words. One of the four tigers roared, leaping towards Sasha and the open door with its claws extended. The animal dropped just short of his trainer and looked up to be scratched. Sasha ran his hands over the big cat's fur, murmuring to it softly. After a moment, Sasha turned his back to lock the cage again. He walked over to where we stood. He held out his hand. In it were four bright tiger whiskers. "That is part of our act," said Sasha ruefully. "Even with the open door, the tiger would not know what to do with his freedom if he chose to go. Our May Day gifts for you. Memories of cages and freedom."

Read the following sentence from paragraph 17.

One of the Russians whirled around summarily.

38 **The word that most closely means summarily is** 1.1.2

F   at last.   H   neatly.

G   abruptly.   J   uneasily.

39 **Which word best describes Tory in "Circus Acts"?** 1.2.1

A   pathetic

B   sensitive

C   audacious

D   introverted

40 In the second paragraph, Tory says, "The May Day picnic sounds better than that lame show." What does the word lame mean here? 3.2.2

F   crippled or physically disabled

G   impared or defective

H   weak or unsatisfactory

J   unsophisticated or pathetic

41 Which of these __best__ expresses a theme that is explored in this story?　1.3.5

   A Being is cages can affect circus animals in various ways.

   B Sisters can influence one another's behavior considerably.

   C The circus is wonderful entertainment for people of all ages.

   D No matter where you are, home and family remain important.

42 What is the __most effective__ way to combine the ideas in these sentences from the last paragraph of the story?　3.1.6

He walked over to where we stood. He held out his hand. In it were four bright tiger whiskers.

   F Walking over to where we stood, he held out his hand to show us four bright tiger whiskers.

   G He walked over to where we stood, holding out his hand; he showed us that in it were four bright tiger whiskers.

   H He held out his hand to show us four bright tiger whiskers, after he walked over to where we stood.

   J He held out his hand, walking over to where we stood, to show us four bright tiger whiskers.

43 After reading this story, a reader would __most likely__ conclude that　1.2.5

   A going to see the circus is more fun than most teenagers think it will be.

   B even people who lead fascinating lives get homesick and nostalgic.

   C sisters who are close in age seldom seem to agree on anything.

   D being able to work with animals constantly is very rewarding.

44 Which word __best__ describes the tone of this essay?　1.3.3

   F puzzling   **H** useful

   G adventurous   **J** dismal

GO ON

Directions

Read the poem, "The New Colossus," below and answer numbers 45 and 46.

The New Colossus

1   Not like the brazen giant of Greek fame,

2   With conquering limbs astride from land to land;

3   Here at our sea-washed, sunset gates shall stand

4   A mighty woman with a torch whose flame

5   is the imprisoned lightning, and her name

6   Mother of Exiles. From her beacon-hand

7   Glows world-wide welcome; her mild eyes command

8   The air-bridged harbor that twin cities frame

9   "Keep, ancient lands, your storied pomp!" cries she

10 With silent lips."Give me your tired, your poor

11 Your huddled masses yearning to breathe free,

12 The wretched refuse of your teeming shore

13 Send these, the homeless, tempest-tost to me,

14 I lift my lamp beside the golden door!"

– Emma Lazarus, 1883, a poem about the Statue of Liberty

45 In lines 5 and 6, the name "Mother of Exiles" <u>most likely</u> refers to   1.2.2

A   the real name that was actually given to the portal into the United States.

B   how the statue resembles a mother waiting for her children to return.

C   the fact that many refugees come to America from other countries.

D   why people think of the statue as a welcoming, nurturing sight.

46 In line 11, "free" modifies   3.1.3

F   huddled

G   masses

H   yearning

J   breathe

Directions

Read the story, "The Mendoza Family." Then answer numbers 47 and 48.

The Mendoza Family

"Well," Mother said, "if God wills it, we will have a better year next year." Mami was sad, you see, because the fast food Mexican restaurant my father ran was growing, but it still did not pull in enough business to support the family.

"Don't worry," I told her as I ran my fingers through my little brother David's straight hair. "Next year will be better." I approached her and laid my hands on her face worn from many worries and hard labor, saying, "You know, Mami, ever since my quinceñera (15th birthday), I've been thinking. I can make you and Papi so proud by going to college. So I've talked to the counselors at school, and, if it's all right with you, I would like to take the college track courses."

Mami turned around to face me as she spoke. "Hija (daughter in Spanish), you know I always want what's best for you. But you know, it would be difficult because Papi will need you at the restaurant. The business is growing, and you would probably make more money working there than you ever would with a college degree."

"Mami, I know Papi needs me, but I can contribute more to the family by getting a degree. Plus, it would be a great honor to the family name!"

Mami then turned to me, sighed, and said, "Hija, remember what I told you it was like when we first came here, not knowing the language at all. Many people treating us like outsiders. Even today, when I applied for part-time work in customer service, they turn me down because I have an accent! Will a college diploma change all that?"

"Mami, I know you and Papi have gone through a lot here, good and bad, but getting a degree will open doors! Not everyone in this world is closed-minded. Many people, including my teachers at school, have encouraged me to go ahead and pursue my dream and get on the college track with my courses."

I turned and watched as my father, very tired from a long day working at the restaurant, came home. I led him to the kitchen table, and as Mami and I served him dinner, I told him of my plans.

He dropped his fork in shock, looked me straight in the eye, and said, "Hija, you can't be serious. You know how badly I need you at the restaurant. I've built this whole restaurant from the ground up for you and David. Did I do all this for nothing?"

"No, of course not, Papi. You've worked so hard for us, and I will never forget that." I grabbed his hands in mine and told him, "But Papi, I would learn things at school that I could come back and apply at the restaurant when I graduate. Not only that, but if business ever turns bad, I will be able to get a job and help support you and Mami. The degree can bring us better opportunities and resources, Papi." The last words were spoken as a whisper. I watched and waited.

My father looked up. With tears in his eyes and pride in his voice, he said, "All right, Hija. You know Mami and I only want what's best for you. Get on the college track, and when you go to college, make everyone proud of the Mendozas!" I gave Mom and Dad a big hug and went to sleep.

GO ON

47 Which of these phrases is <u>most</u> likely related to the theme of the story?   1.3.5

   A   the value of families eating together
   B   the hardships of starting a business
   C   the importance of education
   D   the trials of immigration

48 Janey is writing an essay about how family relationships vary among people of different cultural backgrounds. She decides to use this story as a resource, and then she looks at other materials. Which of the following would probably have the <u>most</u> relevant information for her research?   2.3.1

   F   an article called "Ethnic Minority Groups in the Workforce"
   G   a book titled *Cultural Traditions*
   H   a magazine feature called "Personal Relationships Across Cultures"
   J   a Web site with information about social and economic impact on family relationships

Directions

Use the poem "The New Colossus" and the story "The Mendoza Family" to answer numbers 49 and 50.

49 Which statement <u>best</u> expresses a main idea of both the poem "The New Colossus" and the story "The Mendoza Family"?   1.1.3

   A   Hard work is the best remedy for poverty.
   B   America is a land of opportunity for all people.
   C   Immigration is not the answer to life's problems.
   D   The grass is always greener on the other side of the fence.

50 Write a response that compares the narrator in the poem "The New Colossus" with the narrator in the story "The Mendoza Family." In your answer, support your conclusion with appropriate details from <u>both</u> the poem and the story.

1.2.1

Use your own paper to plan your response and to write a final copy.

STOP

Maryland High School Assessment in English

Practice Test 2

The purpose of this practice test is to measure your progress in reading comprehension and English Language Arts. This practice test is based on the Maryland Core Learning Goals and Expectations for English Language Arts and adheres to the sample question format provided by the Maryland Department of Education.

General Directions:

1 Read all directions carefully.

2 Read each question or sample. Then choose the best answer.

3 Choose only one answer for each question. If you change an answer, be sure to erase your original answer completely.

Session 1

Directions

Read the essay "The Making of a Marine." Then answer numbers 1 through 7.

The Making of a Marine

(1) The large, bulky bus slowed down as it turned onto a long, narrow bridge. The bridge led to an obscure island in the distance and was lined with dimly lit street lamps. The vibration, caused by the bus rolling over the planks of the bridge, startled me out of my listless sleep. I cupped my hands around my eyes and peered out of the dust-covered window. All that was visible, as far as I could see, was the somber water leisurely moving below the bridge. Little did I realize that this bridge was the beginning of my passage from boyhood to manhood in the Marines.

(2) Suddenly the interior bus lights flashed on. I had to blink several times to adjust my eyes to the unexpected flow of brightness. A husky, darkly tanned man stood up and faced the group of boys on the bus. He was immaculately dressed in a sharply pressed uniform, with rows of ribbons and badges over his left pocket. The bus jerked to a stop, and the man who stood up introduced himself as the drill instructor. Then I and the rest of the boys on the bus were issued the first of many commands: "Recruits, get off the bus, NOW! Move, move, move!"

(3) I joined the ranks of many other boys coming off the bus, and they all moved through the small door leading to the receiving barracks. Glancing at the sign above the door, I silently read to myself, "THROUGH THIS PORTAL PASS PROSPECTS FOR THE WORLD'S FINEST FIGHTING FORCE: THE UNITED STATES MARINE CORPS." This was it. The process of becoming a Marine was beginning for me, and I couldn't turn back now.

(4) The first few weeks were the toughest. The drill instructors concentrated on breaking down the morale and hard-fast habits of all the recruits in our group. I had to learn how to start living all over; I had to learn how to dress, eat, even go to the bathroom. I learned that every action of the day was limited to a certain time period. When it was time for chow, all of us recruits marched to the chow hall together. Inside the chow hall all of the trays, plates and utensils were carried the same way, by every recruit. We were taught how to fold our clothes, brush our teeth, and make a bed (known as a rack). There was even a specific form of vocabulary we were instructed to use. We were also introduced to the basics of military life which included marching, shining boots, and the use of a rifle (never called a gun).

GO ON

(5) The first phase of training examined the recruits' mental processes and was the hardest emotionally. The second phase began to test our physical abilities. Day after day was spent running in the scorching heat, with a ten-pound backpack on my back. I quickly learned that the purpose of running is more than just exercise: it is for the sake of staying alive. I and my group learned how to repel off seventy-five foot towers, crawl through live mine fields, run through obstacle courses and tread water.

(6) Boot camp became progressively harder as I moved from the second phase of training to the third phase of actually performing certain procedures. All of the recruits in my group had to fire their rifles and pistols, throw live grenades and successfully complete their individual combat training courses. Many recruits began to drop out in the third phase due to the stress and difficulty of this stage. I began to see changes occurring in my life. I was becoming physically fit, more confident, and proficient in a leadership role.

(7) The ultimate phase of training was graduation. As graduation approached, I found it difficult to sleep due to all the excitement. I quickly learned how to control my anxiety because there was still a great deal of work to prepare for in the final drill. Graduation day was the finale of all of our hard work. The sun sparkled off of the neatly polished shoes of the recruits as we marched onto the parade deck. The feeling of pride in ourselves, our country and our sense of accomplishment radiated from all the Marines in the group. I made a sharp right turn into the sunlight to face the crowd of onlookers. A smile turned up the corners of my mouth as I straightened my back to stand just a little taller.

(8) I had made it through the process of becoming a Marine, an accomplishment not many can claim. I had also achieved a personal goal that changed me from a boy to an independent man. I had become a Marine!

---

1 Doing research in which of the following materials would best prepare a reader to understand what the author describes in the essay?   2.3.1

A   the manuscript of the Congressional Act of 1798, "Establishing and Organizing a Marine Corps"

B   the official Web site of the United States Marine Corps

C   the novel *Marine Sniper* by Charles W. Henderson

D   poetry in the book *The Marines, and Other War Verse*

2 Which of these ideas most closely relates to the theme of the essay?   1.3.5

F   male bonding

G   testing physical ability

H   coming of age

J   learning business skills

3 In paragraph 4, the narrator says the "instructors concentrated on breaking down the morale and hard-fast habits" of the recruits. What does "breaking down" mean here?   3.2.2

A   dividing into parts

B   losing control

C   analyzing

D   weakening

GO ON

Read this sentence from paragraph 7 of the essay.

The ultimate phase of training was graduation.

4 **As it is used here, the word *ultimate* most nearly means**   1.1.2

   F   extreme.   **H**   vital.

   G   awesome.   **J**   final.

Read this sentence from the first paragraph of the essay.

The large, bulky bus slowed down as it turned onto a long, narrow bridge.

5 **The pronoun *it* stands for what noun?**   3.1.3

   A   large   **C**   bus

   B   bulky   **D**   bridge

Read this sentence from paragraph 5 of the essay.

I quickly learned that the purpose of running is more than just exercise: it is for the sake of staying alive.

6 **Which of these statements best explains what the narrator is referring to here?**   1.2.2

   F   The point of the training is to prepare the Marines for battle, and running well might save their lives then.

   G   Because of the tough drill instructors, the boys had to run well or they would not get their regular meals.

   H   There were live mines in the road, and only running quickly around them could the Marines stay alive.

   J   If the boys did not finish each run in a timely manner, their life in the Marines would be at an end.

Examine the photograph below.

7 **Write a response that explains whether the photograph communicates ideas similar to those found in the essay. In your response, support your conclusion with appropriate details from both the essay and the photograph.**   1.1.4

Use your own paper to plan your response and to write a final copy.

Directions

Read the essay "My Bar Mitzvah." Then answer numbers 8 through 10 about both "The Making of a Marine" and "My Bar Mitzvah."

My Bar Mitzvah

"Mike, is your homework done yet? I hope you've been practicing your Hebrew assignment, because you are getting closer to your big day." I heard this phrase over and over again during the three months before my thirteenth birthday. Classes held at the synagogue after school were demanding. I was learning Hebrew as a language and was preparing for what I would say at my Bar Mitzvah. At the same time, I was taking an additional class in Jewish history.

I needed to prepare for my Jewish rite of passage into the adult community, the Bar Mitzvah. During the ceremony, I was required to be close to the podium for the reading of the Torah, the five books of Moses. I was also planning to chant the reading of the Haftarah, the book of the prophets, in Hebrew.

In addition to the religious ceremony, I had a party to plan. Friends and family were coming from as far away as Chicago to be there that day. I planned to be with them for part of the day, and then leave with my friends to play some high-tech interactive games involving the firing of lasers. It was a fast three months, and I was eagerly awaiting the final days.

My birthday fell on a Tuesday, we had cake and ice cream, but the real party was saved for Saturday—the day I would go to the synagogue and become a man in many respects. My father was beaming with pride as we drove to the synagogue. He turned to me and said, "Son, I'm really proud of you today. I know you'll do a good job." This was good to hear, because I was really afraid I was going to mess up.

Everything happened so quickly once we got there. I was rushed into the center of the synagogue. I donned my yarmulke[1] and tallis[2], and awaited my turn to speak. My knees bobbed up and down with nervous energy as our rabbi sang the opening prayers. After what seemed like an eternity, I approached the podium and stood while the cantor[3] sang the blessing over the reading of the Torah. I sat down and waited as the Torah was read to the congregation. Once again, Rabbi Samuel motioned me forward. This time, I approached the podium, unrolled the scroll, and sang the reading of the Haftarah. I took a moment to look out at the congregation. There were my mother, father, and two sisters. In addition, three of my grandparents, two aunts, and four cousins were there. With a smile, I sang loudly.

After the service ended, we left and headed to the reception. Talking with all of my relatives, who were normally scattered across the United States, was exciting. I really liked all the food, gifts, and congratulatory speeches people gave me. When I thought my head could not get any bigger, my friends burst into the reception hall, picked me up, and walked me out of the building so we could be driven to a high-tech venue of fast-action entertainment. Lasers flared, and we had a good time.

As I came home, I thought back on what had just happened. In many important respects, I had become a man. I was now personally responsible for keeping the commandments, observing my faith and honoring the traditions of my forefathers. In addition, I would now have a voice in the congregation by being able to read from the scriptures and give blessings. Through this experience, I felt like I was a real part of the adult Jewish community.

[1] **yarmulke:** skullcap

[2] **tallis:** prayer shawl

[3] **cantor:** religious official of a synagogue who sings or chants prayers

GO ON

Read these sentences conveying the narrator's thoughts in paragraph 7 of "The Making of a Marine."

I quickly learned how to control my anxiety because there was still a great deal of work to prepare for in the final drill. Graduation day was the finale of all of our hard work.

8 Which paragraph from the essay "My Bar Mitzvah" **best** expresses similar thoughts by its narrator?   1.2.1

F   Paragraph 1

G   Paragraph 2

H   Paragraph 3

J   Paragraph 4

9 Reading these two essays would **most likely** encourage a reader to   1.2.5

A   seek out situations in which skills are tested.

B   develop a plan for things to accomplish in life.

C   realize that learning any new skill takes practice.

D   recognize the importance of teamwork.

Read these sentences about growing up.

Growing up isn't always easy.

Sometimes all you want to do is have fun with your friends.

It's challenging to get good grades and show respect to parents.

10 Which of these **most effectively** combines the ideas into one sentence?   3.1.6

F   Growing up isn't always easy—sometimes all you want to do is have fun with your friends, but then it's challenging to get good grades and show respects to parents.

G   It's challenging to get good grades and show respect to parents when sometimes all you want to do is have fun with your friends; so, growing up isn't always easy because of these things.

H   Growing up isn't always easy because it's challenging to get good grades and show respect to parents, when all you want to do sometimes is have fun with your friends.

J   Sometimes all you want to do is have fun with your friends, so it's challenging to get good grades and show respect to parents all the time, and that means growing up isn't always easy.

GO ON

Directions

For Numbers 11 and 12, read the sentence in bold print. Then choose the clearest and <u>most</u> effective revision of the sentence.

11 **While Mom baked an apple pie, my sister and I set the table, but before that we got a baked chicken and potatoes ready for the main course.**   2.2.3

A   After we got a baked chicken and potatoes ready for the main course, my sister and I set the table while Mom baked an apple pie.

B   My sister and I set the table after we got a baked chicken and potatoes ready for the main course and while Mom baked an apple pie.

C   Mom baked an apple pie after we got a baked chicken and potatoes ready for the main course, before which my sister and I set the table.

D   We got a baked chicken and potatoes ready for the main course before we set the table, my sister and I, and after that Mom baked an apple pie.

12 **The truck carrying the load of dynamite just missed hitting the gasoline tanker, making us hold our breath as we watched the movie!**   2.2.3

F   We held our breath watching the movie as the truck carrying the load of dynamite just missed hitting the gasoline tanker!

G   Watching the movie, we held our breath as the truck carrying the load of dynamite just missed hitting the gasoline tanker!

H   The truck carrying the load of dynamite just missed hitting the gasoline tanker as we held our breath while we watched the movie!

J   We held our breath, the truck carrying the load of dynamite just missed hitting the gasoline tanker, and we continued watching the movie!

Directions

Marc is interested in space and decides to write an essay about the moon. The draft of Marc's essay requires revisions and editing. Read the draft, and then answer Numbers 13 through 17.

Moon

Through space exploration, scientists have constructed a history of the moon dating back to its infancy. Rocks collected from the lunar highlands date about 4 to 4.3 billion years old. It's believed the solar system formed about 4.6 billion years ago.

The first few million years of the moon's existence were violent. As a molten outer layer gradually cooled and solidified into different kinds of rock the moon was bombarded by huge asteroids and smaller objects. Some of the asteroids were the size of small states like Rhode Island or Delaware.

Still, it measures 30 miles wide by 100 miles long, which makes a big asteroid! Their collisions with the moon created huge basins hundreds of kilometers across.

The catastrophic bombardment died away about 4 billion years ago. It left many craters. Heat produced by the decay of radioactive elements began to melt the inside of the moon at depths of about 200 kilometers (124 miles) below its surface.

Then, from about 3.8 to 3.1 billion years ago, great floods of lava rose from inside the moon. They poured over its surface, filling in the large

GO ON

impact basins to form the dark parts of the moon called maria or seas. Explorations show that there has been no significant volcanic activity on the moon for more than 3 billion years. That's fortunate, allowing missions like the NASA Lunar Prospector to fulfill its mission of "answering outstanding questions of lunar science."

13 Where does the sentence below <u>best</u> fit 2.2.2
in Marc's essay?

There were so many upheavals that few traces of this period remain.

A   in the first paragraph
B   in the second paragraph
C   in the third paragraph
D   in the last paragraph

Read the following sentences from paragraph 2 of Marc's essay.

As a molten outer layer gradually cooled and solidified into different kinds of rock the moon was bombarded by huge asteroids and smaller objects.

14 What is the <u>best</u> way to punctuate this 3.3.1
sentence?

F   As a molten outer layer gradually cooled, and solidified into different kinds of rock, the moon was bombarded by huge asteroids, and smaller objects.

G   As a molten outer layer gradually cooled, and solidified into different kinds of rock, the moon was bombarded by huge asteroids and smaller objects.

H   As a molten outer layer gradually cooled and solidified into different kinds of rock, the moon was bombarded by huge asteroids and smaller objects.

J   As a molten outer layer gradually cooled and solidified into different kinds of rock the moon was bombarded, by huge asteroids and smaller objects.

Read the third paragraph of the essay.

The catastrophic bombardment died away about 4 billion years ago. It left many craters. Heat produced by the decay of radioactive elements began to melt the inside of the moon at depths of about 200 kilometers (124 miles) below its surface.

15 Which of these sentences <u>most</u> clearly and effectively adds supporting detail to the second sentences in this paragraph?　3.1.8

   A   It left the lunar highlands covered with huge overlapping craters and a deep layer of broken rock.

   B   The catastrophic bombardment left the lunar highlands covered with huge overlapping craters.

   C   Big craters and lots of broken rock then covered the surface of the lunar highlands.

   D   It left broken rock and many craters

16 The majority of information in this essay is published in a vast number of publications and ranks as general knowledge. However, which of the following would <u>most</u> need to be documented on a works-cited page?　2.3.3

   F   Then, from about 3.8 to 3.1 billion years ago, great floods of lava rose from inside the moon.

   G   They poured over its surface, filling in the large impact basins to form the dark parts of the moon called maria or seas.

   H   Explorations show that there has been no significant volcanic activity on the moon for more than 3 billion years.

   J   That's fortunate, allowing missions like the NASA Lunar Prospector to fulfill its mission of "answering outstanding questions of lunar science."

17 Marc read in a language handbook, "A pronoun should have only one possible antecedent." With this advice in mind, which of the following sentences should be revised?　3.3.2

   A   It's believed the solar system formed about 4.6 billion years ago.

   B   Still, it measures 30 miles wide by 100 miles long, which makes a big asteroid!

   C   It left many craters.

   D   They poured over its surface, filling in the large impact basins to form the dark parts of the moon called maria or seas.

Directions

For Number 18, read the prompt below. Follow the directions in the prompt for writing your essay.

| 18 | Write a well-organized essay about a talent or skill that you would like to develop. Organize your ideas with appropriate details about how you would use this attribute and whether you have a special flair for it or simply want to learn it. Be sure that your essay is fully developed and logically organized. Describe your thoughts clearly though appropriate choice of words. | 2.1.1 |

Use your own paper to plan your essay and to complete your final draft.

Directions

Sue is writing an essay for her English class. Her draft requires revisions and editing. Read the essay "The Boat Trip." Then answer numbers 19 through 23.

The Boat Trip

I should have known there would be a problem when I saw the oil bubbles rising near the engine of the motor boat. We just thought it would be fun to try out the boat. Freddie, the recreational director, gave us such a good deal on it. $5.00 per hour plus fuel costs! Me and my best friend, Shelly, had our older sisters with us—just us girls having some summer fun, we thought.

We suited up and jumped in the boat. With a little tug, we were off. My sister, Mary, screamed as we crashed through the waves others had made. Soon, we were in an alcove on a deserted island in the middle of the river. Freddie told us that this was as far as we could go before needing to turn back because we would have used half our fuel.

After walking the island a couple times, Shelly's sister, Amy, glanced at the fuel gauge and almost fainted. She screamed, "It's on empty! It's on empty!" While we had looked around the island, an oil slick as big as a Mack truck surrounded our boat. We all screamed, No! We rushed back in the boat and decided we would paddle back using our hands if we had to. Suddenly, instead of enjoying where we were, we were consumed with the need to get back to our everyday lives. We cupped our hands and paddled to get the boat going. I shuddered as I felt the slimy mouths of fish attacking my fingers as if they were a mound of worms.

Getting to the island took a half hour, while getting back to the dock took over six hours! My arms were killing me, I was sunburned and my fingers had been nibbled so much they felt like strips of raw hamburger! We marched into Freddie's office and gave him a piece of our minds. He squirmed as we told him how his bad attention caused us lots of problems. Hours later, I remembered the saying, "If something seems too good to be true, it probably is." I finally understood that.

19 Which of these is the <u>best</u> way to revise the last sentence in the first paragraph?   2.2.3

  A   My best friend, Shelly, and I had our older sisters with us—just we girls having some summer fun, we thought.

  B   Me and my best friend, Shelly, had her and mine older sisters with us—just us girls having some summer fun, we thought.

  C   I and my best friend, Shelly, had our older sisters with me and her—just us girls having some summer fun, we thought.

  D   Me and my best friend, Shelly, had our older sisters with us—just us girls having some summer fun, us thought.

Read the following sentence from Sue's draft.

We all screamed, No!

20 What is the correct way to edit this sentence?   3.3.1

  F   We all screamed No!

  G   We all screamed, "No"!

  H   We all screamed, "No!"

  J   We all screamed: No!

21 Which of these <u>most</u> effectively combines the ideas in the first two sentences of the second paragraph?   3.1.6

  A   We suited up, jumped in the boat, and with a little tug, we were off.

  B   We suited up, jumped in the boat, and were off with a little tug.

  C   Suiting up, we jumped in the boat and were off, after a little tug.

  D   With a little tug, we were off, after we suited up and jumped in the boat.

Sue found the information below in a language handbook.

Avoid vague words and phrases; use specific details instead.

22 According to this information, which sentence from the last paragraph should be revised?   2.2.5

  F   My arms were killing me, I was sunburned and my fingers had been nibbled so much they felt like strips of raw hamburger!

  G   We marched into Freddie's office and gave him a piece of our minds.

  H   He squirmed as we told him how his bad attention caused us lots of problems.

  J   Hours later, I remembered the saying, "If something seems too good to be true, it probably is."

23 Which of these should be revised to correct an incomplete sentence?   3.1.4

  A   I should have known there would be a problem when I saw the oil bubbles rising near the engine of the motor boat.

  B   We just thought it would be fun to try out the.

  C   Freddie, the recreational director, gave us such a good deal on it.

  D $5.00 per hour plus fuel costs!

GO ON

Directions

Read the following excerpt from Jack London's *The Call of the Wild*. Then answer numbers 24 through 30.

excerpt from Jack London's
The Call of the Wild

Buck, a domesticated ranch dog, has been stolen and then sold as a sled dog in Alaska. He is now owned and being trained by Francois and Perrault, two French-Canadian traders. This excerpt is from the beginning of chapter 2, which chronicles Buck's education, changing him into a "working" dog instead of a "pet" which he has been in the past.

Buck's first day on the Dyea beach was like a nightmare. Every hour was filled with shock and surprise. He had been suddenly jerked from the heart of civilization and flung into the heart of things primordial. No lazy, sun-kissed life was this, with nothing to do but loaf and be bored. Here was neither peace, nor rest, nor a moment's safety. All was confusion and action, and every moment life and limb were in peril. There was imperative need to be constantly alert; for these dogs and men were not town dogs and men. They were savages, all of them, who knew no law but the law of club and fang.

Section Deleted

Before he had recovered from the shock caused by the tragic passing of Curly [a dog], he received another shock. Francois fastened upon him an arrangement of straps and buckles. It was a harness, such as he had seen the grooms put on the horses at home. And as he had seen horses work, so he was set to work, hauling Francois on a sled to the forest that fringed the valley, and returning with a load of firewood. Though his dignity was sorely hurt by thus being made a draught animal, he was too wise to rebel. He buckled down with a will and did his best, though it was all new and strange. Francois was stern, demanding instant obedience, and by virtue of his whip receiving instant obedience; while

Dave, who was an experienced wheeler, nipped Buck's hind quarters whenever he was in error. Spitz was the leader, likewise experienced, and while he could not always get at Buck, he growled sharp reproof now and again, or cunningly threw his weight in the traces to jerk Buck into the way he should go. Buck learned easily, and under the combined tuition of his two mates and Francois made remarkable progress. Ere they returned to camp he knew enough to stop at "ho," to go ahead at "mush," to swing wide on the bends, and to keep clear of the wheeler when the loaded sled shot downhill at their heels.

Section Deleted

By evening Perrault secured another dog, an old husky, long and lean and gaunt, with a battle-scarred face and a single eye which flashed a warning of prowess that commanded respect. He was called Sol-leks, which means the Angry One. Like Dave, he asked nothing, gave nothing, expected nothing; and when he marched slowly and deliberately into their midst, even Spitz left him alone. He had one peculiarity which Buck was unlucky enough to discover. He did not like to be approached on his blind side. Of this offence Buck was unwittingly guilty, and the first knowledge he had of his indiscretion was when Sol-leks whirled upon him and slashed his shoulder to the bone for three inches up and down. Forever after Buck avoided his blind side, and to the last of their comradeship had no more trouble. His only apparent ambition, like Dave's, was to be left alone; though, as Buck was afterward to learn, each of them possessed one other and even more vital ambition.

Section Deleted

Dave was wheeler or sled dog, pulling in front of him was Buck, then came Sol-leks; the rest of the team was strung out ahead, single file, to the leader, which position was filled by Spitz.

Buck had been purposely placed between Dave and Sol-leks so that he might receive instruction. Apt scholar that he was, they were equally apt teachers, never allowing him to linger long in error, and enforcing their teaching with their sharp teeth. Dave was fair and very wise. He never nipped Buck without cause, and he never failed to nip him when he stood in need of it. As Francois's whip backed him up, Buck found it to be cheaper to mend his ways than to retaliate. Once, during a brief halt, when he got tangled in the traces and delayed the start, both Dave and Sol-leks flew at him and administered a sound trouncing. The resulting tangle was even worse, but Buck took good care to keep the traces clear thereafter; and ere the day was done, so well had he mastered his work, his mates about ceased nagging him. Francois's whip snapped less frequently, and Perrault even honored Buck by lifting up his feet and carefully examining them.

Section Deleted

And not only did he learn by experience, but instincts long dead became alive again. The domesticated generations fell from him. In vague ways he remembered back to the youth of the breed, to the time the wild dogs ranged in packs through the primeval forest and killed their meat as they ran it down. It was no task for him to learn to fight with cut and slash and the quick wolf snap. In this manner had fought forgotten ancestors. They quickened the old life within him, and the old tricks which they had stamped into the heredity of the breed were his tricks. They came to him without effort or discovery, as though they had been his always. And when, on the still cold nights, he pointed his nose at a star and howled long and wolf-like, it was his ancestors, dead and dust, pointing nose at star and howling down through the centuries and through him. And his cadences were their cadences, the cadences which voiced their woe and what to them was the meaning of the stiffness, and the cold, and dark.

---

24 After reading this story, a reader would most likely conclude that   1.1.3

- **F** sled dogs learn from each other.
- **G** Buck is actually part wolf.
- **H** the people in this story don't talk.
- **J** dogs don't like working.

25 What word best describes the tone of this story?   1.3.3

- **A** alarming   **C** adventurous
- **B** comical   **D** mysterious

Read this sentence from the last paragraph.

> They quickened the old life within him, and the old tricks which they had stamped into the heredity of the breed were his tricks.

26 In this sentence, *quickened* means   1.1.2

- **F** spoke to
- **G** speeded up
- **H** brought alive
- **J** made complete

27 Reading this excerpt would most likely   1.2.5
encourage a reader to

   A learn more about sled dogs and how they were, and still are, used.

   B look into a trip to Alaska on a cruise ship to watch whales.

   C think how different people have animals for different reasons.

   D consider whether dogs have a special language in which they communicate with each other.

28 In which phrase does the author use   1.2.3
simile to describe Buck's new life?

   F Buck's first day on the Dyea beach was like a nightmare.

   G He had been suddenly jerked from the heart of civilization and flung into the heart of things primordial.

   H No lazy, sun-kissed life was this, with nothing to do but loaf and be bored.

   J Here was neither peace, nor rest, nor a moment's safety.

29 Though this story is told from the   1.3.5
point of view of a dog, the author gives Buck human qualities. Which of these statements <u>best</u> expresses the theme a reader can discern from these qualities?

   A If people would find their animal nature, they would be able to work harder.

   B Learning quickly and doing well means lessons don't have to be repeated.

   C If you work hard and keep to yourself, you can get used to anything.

   D It's always best not to socialize too much with your coworkers.

Read these sentences from a student's summary of the story.

Buck went from being a pet to being a sled dog.

He didn't like it much at first, but he grew to take pride in his work.

The other dogs barked and nipped at him when he did anything wrong.

30 Which pair of sentences most   3.1.6
effectively combines the ideas of the sentences above?

   F The other dogs barked and nipped at him when he did anything wrong as Buck went from being a pet to being a sled dog, and he didn't like it much at first. However, he grew to take pride in his work.

   G Buck he grew to take pride in his work when went from being a pet to being a sled dog. At first, though, didn't like it much because the other dogs barked and nipped at him when he did anything wrong.

   H Buck went from being a pet to being a sled dog. He didn't like it much at first: the other dogs barked and nipped at him when he did anything wrong, but he grew to take pride in his work.

   J Buck went from being a pet to being a sled dog, and he didn't like it much at first. The other dogs barked and nipped at him when he did anything wrong, but he grew to take pride in his work.

GO ON

Directions

Read "A Trip to Remember" and answer numbers 31 and 32.

A Trip to Remember

My mother has crazy ideas sometimes. One year, after having moved to Baltimore, she decided it was time to visit Portland, Maine, again. We couldn't get a plane ticket to Portland for the weekend, but that didn't stop her. She just bought tickets to New York instead. "We'll wing it from there," she said. "Winging it" meant landing in New York, taking a cab, and waiting in the Amtrak station for several hours for a train. Then, for 7 hours, the sleek, silver train took us north. But from the time we had left home, we were not able to get in touch with anyone! We didn't have cell phones in those days, nobody did. The station had no phone, there was no time at the airport, and the train never stopped long enough, not even when we changed trains in Boston, to give us time to find a phone booth, call home, and dash back to the train before it departed. My dad didn't know where we were for a whole day. But I knew. I remember sleeping in the passenger car and buying soup in the restaurant car. I vividly recall watching the rising sun outside the window, the passing mountains, and glimpses of the ocean. And I especially remember the feeling of secret adventure, of being aware that no one knew where I was. It was the best trip I've ever had.

---

31 The author <u>most likely</u> tells readers that no one had cell phones at the time this event happened to   1.2.2

  A   convey that the family had little money at the time.

  B   point out that the story took place a very long time ago.

  C   emphasize that the family was out of touch the whole trip.

  D   express how lonely and frightened the narrator was on this trip.

Read this sentence from the story.

> I vividly recall watching the rising sun outside the window, the passing mountains and glimpses of the ocean.

32 In this sentence, the word *outside* modifies   3.1.3

  F   watching

  G   rising

  H   sun

  J   window

 GO ON

Directions

Read the essay "My First (and Last) Horseback Ride." Then answer numbers 33 and 34.

My First (and Last) Horseback Ride

The sun rose brightly over the clear blue skies of Yellowstone National Park. The surrounding mountains reflected the glow of a new morning. Barely 15 years old, I was on a two week vacation out West with my family. We were spending our last day horseback riding in the mountains and valleys near this magnificent park. The night before, I dreamed that my horse was almost flying along the ridges and mountain tops in huge leaps that took us into the clouds and back to earth again. Little did I realize what an incredible day I was about to experience.

Early that morning, my older brother Jes and I jumped out of bed, dressed and ate breakfast in the huge lodge's dining room. First, we had to drive to the stables, so Mom and Dad hurried us along for the short drive there. Before we arrived at the horse stables, I noticed a majestic bald eagle gliding overhead, his screeches sounding an alarm throughout the valley. After we reached the stables, we picked out our horses. I chose a lively brown mare that I nicknamed Hyper. Jes rode a big white stallion named Snowball, and Mom and Dad settled for two gentle older horses called Dolly and Sam.

In a matter of minutes, we were starting to climb the well-worn path along the ridge above the stables. Ahead of us was another higher ridge that led us on to the steeper, more challenging trails above. Eventually, we would be able to reach the top of the mountain where we could view the entire valley and the surrounding mountains.

As we climbed higher, I felt light-headed and dizzy. Meanwhile, Hyper forged ahead, suddenly turning and galloping far off the trail to reach the wild grasses that grew along a gully.

With my family out of sight, Hyper started neighing loudly. I could sense something was wrong, and it was. Ahead of us on a rock ledge was a snarling mountain lion with a menacing look in his eyes. Suddenly, Hyper reared on her hind legs as I hung on her back with all my might. Eyeing those dangerous hooves, the mountain lion howled and screamed but backed away from an attack. At that moment, Hyper quickly pivoted and headed straight down the mountain. Scared and angry, I continued to hang on despite the falling rocks and clouds of dust caused by our quick descent. Hyper was amazing as she bounded over rocks, leapt over gullies and tore through the underbrush. I could tell that her intent was to get back to those stables, and in a short time, we were there. Then, I thought about my dream the night before and how different my ride turned out to be.

About an hour later, Mom, Dad and Jes returned to the stables. "I guess you took the short cut," said Jes. Shaking my head, I told them about the mountain lion.

"We're glad you're safe," Mom said, relieved.

"Well, we went looking for you, Ben, and never got to the top of the mountain," remarked Dad. "Would you like to try again?"

"No, thanks, Dad," I stated firmly. "How about a helicopter ride instead?"

So on that last day, we finally saw the top of that mountain and many other mountains besides and valleys too. And, from now on, I'll stick to horseback riding in my dreams.

GO ON

33 What word would the narrator <u>most</u> <u>likely</u> use to describe his horse's reaction to the mountain lion?   1.2.1

    A   terrified   **C**   inspired

    B   furious   **D**   jaded

34 Which of these words is <u>most</u> closely related to the theme of the story?   1.3.5

    F   daring

    G   pressure

    H   misadventure

    J   enlightenment

Directions

Use the story "A Trip to Remember" and the essay "My First (and Last) Horseback Ride" to answer Numbers 35 and 36.

35 Which statement <u>best</u> expresses the main idea of both "A Trip to Remember" and the essay "My First (and Last) Horseback Ride"?   1.1.3

    A   Taking risks is only for the brave, and not those who frighten easily.

    B   When you begin an adventure, you never know how it might turn out.

    C   The most memorable things happen when you are very far from home.

    D   When you set out on a journey, always make sure you are in control.

36 Write a response that compares and/or contrasts the narrator in the story "A Trip to Remember" and the narrator in the essay "My First (and Last) Horseback Ride." In your response, support your conclusion with appropriate details from <u>both</u> the story and the essay.   1.2.1

Use your own paper to plan your response and to write a final copy.

Session 3

Directions

For Number 37, read the prompt below. Follow the directions and write your essay.

Once a man was walking along a beach. Off in the distance, he could see a person going back and forth between the surf's edge and the beach. As the man approached, he could see that there were hundreds of starfish stranded on the sand by the ebb of the tide. The person was throwing the starfish back into the sea. The man was stuck by the apparent futility of the task. There were far too many starfish. Many of them were sure to perish. As he approached, the person continued picking up starfish one by one and throwing them into the surf. As he came up to the person he said, "You must be crazy. There are thousands of miles of beach covered with starfish. You can't possibly make a difference." The person looked at the man, then stooped down to pick up one more starfish and threw it back into the ocean. The person turned back to the man and said, "It sure made a difference to that one!"

> **37** Write a well-developed essay in which you agree or disagree with the idea 2.1.4 that the action of one person can make a difference in large and overwhelming issues. Support your position with examples from your own experiences, from current events, from what you have read, and so on. Be sure that your essay is logically organized and that your choice of words clearly expresses your ideas.

Use your own paper to plan your essay and to complete your final draft.

Directions

Read the poems "If I Can Stop One Heart from Breaking" and "A Bird Came Down the Walk." Then answer numbers 38 through 41.

If I Can Stop One Heart from Breaking

If I can stop one Heart from breaking
I shall not live in vain.

If I can ease one Life the Aching
Or cool one Pain
Or help one fainting Robin
Unto his Nest again
I shall not live in Vain.

– Emily Dickinson

A Bird Came Down the Walk

A bird came down the walk:
He did not know I saw;
He bit an angle-worm in halves
And ate the fellow, raw.

And then he drank a dew
From a convenient grass,
And then hopped sidewise to the wall
To let a beetle pass.

He glanced with rapid eyes
That hurried all abroad,—
They looked like frightened beads, I thought;
He stirred his velvet head

Like one in danger; cautious,
I offered him a crumb,
And he unrolled his feathers
And rowed him softer home

Than oars divide the ocean,
Too silver for a seam,
Or butterflies, off banks of noon,
Leap, splashless, as they swim

–Emily Dickinson

38 In "A Bird Came Down the Walk," the poet compares the flight of birds to   1.2.3

F   fabric swaying in the wind

G   boats rowing on the water

H   wheels rolling on the ground

J   insects buzzing in the air

39 Which word **best** describes the tone of the poem "If I can stop one heart from breaking"?   1.3.3

A   delighted   C   aggressive

B   wistful   D   hopeful

Read these lines from "A bird came down the walk."

I offered him a crumb,
And he unrolled his feathers
And rowed him softer home

40 The poet **most likely** includes these lines to   4.2.1

F   say that it's interesting to watch nature, but interacting with it may not work.

G   describe the disappointment of having a gift rejected by the bird.

H   depict the incredible grace that a bird displays when preparing to take flight.

J   advise readers about ways to approach shy and cautious wildlife.

GO ON

41 Which of these <u>best</u> states the main idea of both "If I can stop one heart from breaking" and "A bird came down the walk"?   1.1.3

A   Birds are fascinating creatures.

B   Observation is the key to making a difference.

C   Life is precious in all its forms.

D   Living a fulfilled life requires self-sacrifice.

Directions

Read the paragraph below and notice that it requires revisions and editing. Answer numbers 42 through 44 about changes that will make it a better-written paragraph.

Big Bad Wolves and Little Lambs

(1)Ranchers in Montana Idaho and Wyoming have lived as farmers for generations. (2)Americans are fond of images of these cowboys and cowgirls rustling cattle and sheep through vast tracts of ranch land. (3)Many Americans rely on the meat produced by these ranchers for nutritious and delicious meals. (4)Yet, they are facing a threat, these symbols of the American West who also provide food for the country. (5)For decades, there were no wolves in these states. (6)But some people missed having wolves in the wild. (7)In the 1990s, they transported sixty-six grey wolves from Alberta, Canada.

(8)These wolves were released in Idaho. (9)Now grown to over three hundred in population. (10)Now, wolves can't help themselves—they naturally live by hunting. (11)A pasture full of sheep or grasslands full of cattle is attractive to them. (12)When farmers lose livestock, they lose money. (13)When farmers lose livestock, the price of those steak dinners that Americans enjoy goes up.

295

42 Which of these is the <u>best</u> way to revise   2.2.3
sentence 4 to make it a clear and
effective sentence?

F   They are facing a threat, these symbols
of the American West, yet they also
provide food for the country.

G   Yet, these symbols of the American
West and providers of food for the
country are facing a threat.

H   Yet, providing food for the country and
being symbols of the American West,
they face a threat.

J   These symbols of the American West
who also provide food for the country,
however, are facing a threat.

43 What is the correct way to punctuate   3.3.1
sentence 1?

A   Ranchers in Montana, Idaho, and
Wyoming have lived as farmers for
generations.

B   Ranchers, in Montana Idaho and Wyoming, have lived as farmers for generations.

C   Ranchers in Montana, Idaho, and Wyoming, have lived as farmers for generations.

D   Ranchers in Montana; Idaho; and Wyoming have lived as farmers for generations.

44 Which of these should be revised to   1.2.1
correct an incomplete sentence?

F   sentence 6   **H**   sentence 8

G   sentence 7   **J**   sentence 9

Directions

Read the speech below, and then answer numbers 45 through 48.

*President Ronald Reagan leads the nation in mourning for the
seven astronauts killed in the Space Shuttle Challenger
Explosion, Washington, D.C., January 28, 1986*

Ladies and gentlemen:

I'd planned to speak to you tonight to report on
the state of the Union, but the events of earlier today
have led me to change those plans. Today is a day
for mourning and remembering. Nancy and I are
pained to the core by the tragedy of the shuttle
Challenger. We know we share this pain with all of
the people of our country. This is truly a national
loss.

Nineteen years ago, almost to the day, we lost
three astronauts in a terrible accident on the ground.
But we've never lost an astronaut in flight; we've
never had a tragedy like this. And perhaps we've
forgotten the courage it took for the crew of the
shuttle. But they, the *Challenger* Seven, were aware
of the dangers, but overcame them and did their jobs
brilliantly. We mourn seven heroes: Michael Smith,
Dick Scobee, Judith Resnik, Ronald McNair,
Ellison Onizuka, Gregory Jarvis, and Christa
McAuliffe. We mourn their loss as a nation together.

For the families of the seven, we cannot bear, as
you do, the full impact of this tragedy. But we feel
the loss, and we're thinking about you so very much.
Your loved ones were daring and brave, and they
had that special grace, that special spirit that says,
"Give me a challenge, and I'll meet it with joy."
They had a hunger to explore the universe and
discover its truths. They wished to serve, and they
did. They served all of us.

GO ON

We've grown used to wonders in this century. It's hard to dazzle us. But for 25 years the United States space program has been doing just that. We've grown used to the idea of space, and perhaps we forget that we've only just begun. We're still pioneers. They, the members of the *Challenger* crew, were pioneers.

And I want to say something to the schoolchildren of America who were watching the live coverage of the shuttle's takeoff. I know it is hard to understand, but sometimes painful things like this happen. It's all part of the process of exploration and discovery. It's all part of taking a chance and expanding man's horizons. The future doesn't belong to the fainthearted; it belongs to the brave. The *Challenger* crew was pulling us into the future, and we'll continue to follow them.

I've always had great faith in and respect for our space program, and what happened today does nothing to diminish it. We don't hide our space program. We don't keep secrets and cover things up. We do it all up front and in public. That's the way freedom is, and we wouldn't change it for a minute. We'll continue our quest in space. There will be more shuttle flights and more shuttle crews and, yes, more volunteers, more civilians, more teachers in

space. Nothing ends here; our hopes and our journeys continue. I want to add that I wish I could talk to every man and woman who works for NASA or who worked on this mission and tell them: Your dedication and professionalism have moved and impressed us for decades. And we know of your anguish. We share it.

There's a coincidence today. On this day 390 years ago, the great explorer Sir Francis Drake died aboard a ship off the coast of Panama. In his lifetime, the great frontiers were the oceans, and an historian later said, "He lived by the sea, died on it, and was buried in it." Well, today we can say of the *Challenger* crew: Their dedication was, like Drake's, complete.

The crew of the space shuttle *Challenger* honored us by the manner in which they lived their lives. We will never forget them, nor the last time we saw them, this morning, as they prepared for their journey and waved goodbye, and "slipped the surly bonds of earth" to "touch the face of God."

---

45 Which conclusion about the president is __most__ supported by information in the speech?   1.1.3

A He opposes space exploration, considering it not worth the loss of human life.

B He is objective about the positive and negative aspects of space exploration.

C He is in favor of space exploration, believing it is a brave and worthy cause.

D He is neutral and really does not have an opinion about space exploration.

46 Will is writing an essay about the   2.3.1 effects of the space shuttle disaster on America, and he will use this speech as one of his resources. Which of the following Web sites would have the __most__ relevant additional information for his paper?

F Remembering Challenger

E Myths About the Challenger Disaster

H Space Today Online

J Challenger Memorial at Arlington National Cemetary

GO ON

Read these sentences from the third paragraph of the speech.

> Your loved ones were daring and brave, and they had that special grace, that special spirit that says, "Give me a challenge, and I'll meet it with joy." They had a hunger to explore the universe and discover its truths. They wished to serve, and they did. They served all of us.

47 Which word <u>best</u> describes the tone of the president's words in these sentences?   1.3.3

    A   proud

    B   troubled

    C   jovial

    D   soothing

Read these sentences related to the essay.

> The space shuttle *Challenger* had a tragic and deadly accident in 1986.

> It was an event that shocked and concerned Americans.

> The space program is still going strong today.

48 Which of these <u>most</u> effectively combines these ideas into one sentence?   3.1.6

    F   Americans were shocked and concerned in 1986, when the space shuttle *Challenger* had a tragic and deadly accident, but the event didn't stop the space program from going strong until today.

    G   Despite the space shuttle *Challenger's* tragic and deadly accident in 1986, which shocked and concerned Americans, the space program is still going strong today.

    H   The space program is still going strong today, even though, in 1986, the space shuttle *Challenger* had a tragic and deadly accident, and it was an event that shocked and concerned Americans.

    J   The space shuttle *Challenger* had a tragic and deadly accident in 1986; it was an event that shocked and concerned Americans, but the space program is still going strong today.

GO ON

Directions

The paragraphs below require revisions and editing. Read them carefully, and then answer numbers 49 and 50.

Uncommon Soldiers

Every year, hundreds of young Americans go into training for the U.S. military. And every year, over 300 of these "troops" are dogs: German shepherds and Dobermans. Dogs have been part of the military for decades._____

It takes about 100 days to train the dogs to work in the military. The location for training these special soldiers is the lackland air force base in san antonio, texas. After graduation, the dogs serve in all areas of the military: Army, Navy, Marines, and Special Forces. They serve at home and at war. Some are scout dogs. They sniff out explosives, booby-traps, and dangerous chemicals. Others are sentry dogs. They walk the battle line with their handlers to watch for enemies. Dogs are a definite part of national security.

49 What is the correct way to edit the following sentence?   3.3.1

> *The location for training these special soldiers is the lackland air force base in san antonio, texas.*

A   The location for training these special soldiers is the Lackland air force base in san antonio, Texas.

B   The location for training these special soldiers is the Lackland air force base in San Antonio, Texas.

C   The location for training these special soldiers is the Lackland Air Force Base in San Antonio, Texas.

D   The location for training these Special Soldiers is the Lackland Air Force Base in San Antonio, Texas.

50 Which sentence **best** fills the blank line ending the first paragraph?   2.2.2

F   Training dogs to fetch is hard, so just image how tough this is!

G   Would some of these dogs be good pets, too, I wonder?

H   Some human soldiers fear dogs, so they can't work with them.

J   They have played important roles in most American wars.

299

MARYLAND HIGH SCHOOL ASSESSMENT IN ENGLISH
APPENDIX A

The rubric for ECRs was last edited and approved July 2004. The rubric for BCRs was last edited and approved July 2004.

ENGLISH RUBRIC: BRIEF CONSTRUCTED RESPONSE

Level 3

The response demonstrates an understanding of the complexities of the text.

- Addresses the demands of the question
- Uses expressed and implied information from the text
- Clarifies and extends understanding beyond the literal

Level 2

The response demonstrates a partial or literal understanding of the text.

- Addresses the demands of the question, although may not develop all parts equally
- Uses some expressed or implied information from the text to demonstrate understanding
- May not fully connect the support to a conclusion or assertion made about the text(s)

Level 1

The response shows evidence of a minimal understanding of the text.

- May show evidence that some meaning has been derived from the text
- May indicate a misreading of the text or the question
- May lack information or explanation to support an understanding of the text in relation to the question

---

Level 0

The response is completely irrelevant or incorrect.

ENGLISH RUBRIC: EXTENDED CONSTRUCTED RESPONSE

Level 4

The response is a well-developed essay that fulfills the writing purpose.

- Develops ideas using relevant and complete support and elaboration
- Uses an effective organizational structure
- Uses purposeful word choice
- Demonstrates attention to audience's understanding and interest
- Has no errors in usage or conventions that interfere with meaning

---

Level 3

The response is a complete essay that addresses the writing purpose.

- Develops ideas using adequate support and elaboration
- Uses an organizational structure that supports the writing purpose
- Uses clear word choice
- Demonstrates an awareness of audience's understanding and interest
- Has few, if any, errors in usage and conventions that interfere with meaning

---

Level 2

The response is a an incomplete or oversimplified attempt to address the writing purpose.

- Has incomplete or unclear support and elaboration
- Attempts to use an organizational structure
- Demonstrates little awareness of audience's understanding and interest
- May have errors in usage and conventions that interfere with meaning

---

Level 1

The response provides evidence of an attempt to address the prompt.

- Has minimal or no support or elaboration
- May be too brief to demonstrate an organizational structure
- Demonstrates little or no awareness of audience
- May have errors in usage and conventions that interfere with meaning

---

Level 0

The response is completely irrelevant or incorrect.

MARYLAND HIGH SCHOOL ASSESSMENT IN ENGLISH
APPENDIX B

ADDITIONAL WRITING PROMPTS

WRITING TO INFORM (EXPOSITORY WRITING)

1. Imagine your ideal vacation. What would you do on this vacation?

2. A **biography** is a narrative about someone's life written by another person. Read several short biographies of famous scientists, inventors, athletes, entertainers, or world leaders in an encyclopedia or almanac. Using these articles as models, write a short biography of a friend, family member, neighbor, or someone you admire. Before you develop your biography, interview the person you will write about if this is possible. Take notes during your interview.

3. Look at the pictures below. Think about what is happening. Choose one of the pictures, and make a list of actions in that picture. Put the actions in a logical order. Then write a story about that picture.

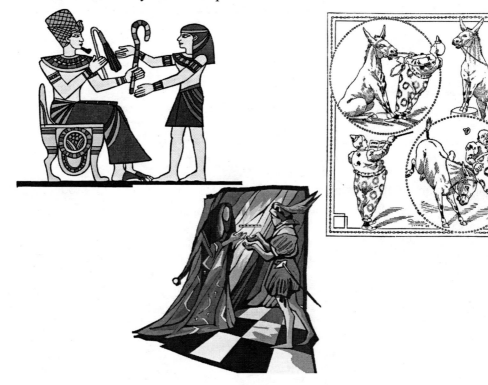

4. Our clothes and hairstyles send a message to others. Why are clothes and hairstyles important in today's society?

5. Deciding on a career is an important step in life's journey. If you could choose any career, what would it be? Why would you choose this career?

6. Your personality often affects others more than you know. Reflect on your own personality. In what ways does it affect those around you?

7. Television's impact on our lives is well-known. Explain why you like or do not like to watch television.

8. When there is money to spend, shopping sprees can be exciting. You have one hour to spend $200 at the mall. What items would you buy, and in what order would you buy them?

9. An old proverb says: "Happiness is a habit to be cultivated." Create a simple recipe for happiness. Explain your recipe step by step.

10. Many people continue debating the issue of crime and violence in our society. Explain the steps you would take to reduce crime and violence.

WRITING TO PERSUADE (PERSUASIVE WRITING)

1. You are entering a contest in which you must write an essay on this topic: **if you were granted one wish to change the world, what would you change and how would you change it?** The writer with the best entry will win $1,000,000. Based on this question, write a convincing essay for the judges. Include reasons and evidence in your proposal.

2. We find out about many issues and topics through newspapers, television, and the Internet. Which recent issue in the news has affected you the most? Give reasons for your opinion.

3. Confucius once said: "Choose a job you love, and you will never have to work a day in your life." Agree or disagree with this statement. Provide reasons for your point of view.

4. Agree or disagree with this statement: "Cars are more dangerous than guns." Support your viewpoint with reasons and examples.

5. Shopping on the Internet increases by 300% each year. Purchasing products is quick, easy, and usually tax-free. Should Internet shoppers be required to pay federal and state taxes like people who shop at malls and stores? Why? Why not?

6. Skim through the editorial section of your local newspaper. Find a controversial issue in the news, and take a position on that issue. Write a letter to the editor explaining your viewpoint.

7. Should the personal life of the President of the United States reflect the high moral standards on

> **Level 1**
>
> **The response provides evidence of an attempt to address the prompt .**

which this nation was founded? Or is the personal life of the President of the United States irrelevant to his/her public contributions? Take a position on this issue, and argue for your point of view.

8. Should separate schools be established for students who frequently disrupt classes? Why? Why not? Provide reasons for your opinion.

9. Do you think athletes should be dismissed from a team for breaking the law? Why? Why not? Support your opinion from your observations or experiences.

10. Are parents or their children more responsible for school success? Explain your viewpoint clearly.